a Word from others

John Hound Brown has taken an epic journey into the heart and soul of his childhood experience and emerged as a hero for generations of folks. He has had the courage to tell the truth, "the whole truth and nothing but the truth" and to find his way, through the mire and muck, toils and snares, to healing and a clear view to higher ground. Great storytelling through the eyes of the child in the fire and the adult coming back for the rescue takes the reader on this journey of reality and redemption. Thank you Hound - the world is blessed deeply and many of us will be inspired in our own epic journeys.

Bedford M. Combs, Family Therapist, Franklin, TN.
Easter 2017

a Word from others (cont)

Nine weeks ago today was my daughter's last day alive. Of course, we didn't do it right. We didn't know at the time.

So when the next day dawned, we realized with an awful brutality that the rest of our lives would have a ragged gaping hole where our daughter used to be.

The pain is indescribable, so I won't make an attempt. But I do want to describe the literally hundreds of people who have come forward to help us bear that pain, each in their own way.

Of course there were flowers and food. There were also the hugs of hundreds, which lasted for two and a half hours straight. Arms of old friends, coworkers, and strangers held me. I cried into many a beer belly. Snot and tears were exchanged. There were cards and letters. There were pictures and posts. There was the presence of a grieving multitude and a hundred honorary pallbearers.

And in the few weeks since, many acts of remembrance and kindness have been committed in our daughter's name: Underprivileged kids learned to swim. College softball players dedicated their seasons and retired jerseys. Mission funds were established. Addresses to the Chamber of Commerce were made. Editorials were written. A song was composed. Numerous tattoos gotten. Jewelry designed and created.

A tribute day held and a memorial garden planned. A YouTube tribute video produced, shared, and viewed 4,000 times. T-shirts ordered. Get-togethers held. Baptisms dedicated. And a Dungeons and Dragons' online marathon held. All in my daughter's name--All in an attempt to help us bear our pain.

These acts run the gamut from Baptist missions to Dungeons and Dragons, and the actors reflect the beautiful diversity of this world. The common denominator? The hope of alleviating the hurt of others.

Many things separate us in this world, and in comparison a relative few bring us together. But I believe in the over-riding power of the few. Pain is one of the few. It is powerful, and it is universal. But in its presence a more powerful force exists, that of compassion.

Yes, pain is universal, but compassion is transcendent.

Compassion rises above our differences, settles our scores, and allows us to face the Enemy--together.

In this book and in your life, may you find the compassion, for yourself and for others, that will shed light in this dark world.

Amen.

April 15, 2017, Holley S. Todd

ABOUT THE AUTHOR

Born into the chaos of the late '60s; the unyielding philosophies of the Bible Belt, the spirituality of the Civil Rights movement, and the idealism of the hippie culture, John "Hound" Brown is a veteran Nashville-based musician/singer-songwriter/producer/satirist/author and homegrown philosopher. He has toured, written, and recorded with national country acts since 1993, including John Berry, Martina McBride, Susie Bogguss, Billy Dean, and the Zac Brown Band.

With many album credits as a musician and songwriter; including a Grammy winner, highlights include: co-writer on the hit musical The Bell Witch Ballet, releasing the indie projects, Next of Kin in 2003, Plowology:Stompin'Grounds in 2008, and 2016's, Rolling Smoke: in the American South, all available on iTunes. Brown co-penned the Joe Nichols Universal Records album title-track, Real Things in '07. His literary work was featured in the ZBB folk art/cookbook Southern Grounds in 2010.

Hound is a frequent guest on the syndicated radio show the BIG SHOW with JOHN BOY and BILLY --- and continues to write, perform, and spread what he calls, "the Gospel of BBQ." Influences include a list of diverse artists, tv shows and supernatural entities like: Jackson Browne and Jesus, the Allman Brothers and Andy Griffith, Darrell Scott and Paul Thorn. Guy Clark and Good Times, Lyle Lovett and Little Feat, Mac McAnally, Mark Twain and the musical magic of Muscle Shoals. Rumi, Rodney Crowell and Randy Newman. Morgan Freeman and Billy-Bob-Thornton, and the original Fat Albert cartoon series. Along with authors

Rick Bragg, Pat Conroy, Faulkner, Hemingway, and of course, the Lord, God-Almighty, and His bestselling work of all-time, The Holy Bible.

This whole mess got started because of a song Hound wrote about the drive-up window at a funeral home in his hometown of Goldsboro, North Carolina. Because of a... Funeral in the South.

visit   facebook.com/plowology
facebook.com/rollingsmokenation
plowology or twitter or houndbrown.com
facebook.com/johnhoundbrown
gofundme.com/houndbrown
patreon.com/plowology

an authentic southern tale:

FUNERAL IN THE SOUTH

by john "hound" brown

a Journey of Family, Faith, Friends and Food
for the SOUL

Inaugural Printing

The Wayne-County Version, long-form

April 2017

edited by Holley S. Todd

additional editing assistance

Andrew Fadyen Ketchum

Kim Herring Langlois

FUNERAL IN THE SOUTH

Cover Design-Creation by **BEAR ROBERTS** @ *thebearroberts.com*
Cover Photo of Edmundson Family Cemetery
Edmundson's Crossroads, North Carolina

For Brother, Daddy, Mama and me.
And the child in all of us.

Claims & Collections

A s you get older, one accepts there is an ending and acknowledges there is a destination, a home for the soul, if you will, at the dead-end road of this life. For it is clear, not a one of us will survive living. Unless you happen to witness the Second Coming of the Christ. Until then, this journey is all there is. Right here. Right now. You think, blink, love or don't, the moment's gone and here's the next one. As Johnny Cash once sang, "It's a mighty world we live in, but the truth is, we're only passin' thru."*

Before we even pull out of the yard and head for the service and cemetery, I feel the need for us to have a quiet, personal, private moment. Just you and me. So you know my heart. They'll wait, over at the Church. This ain't going nowhere, without us. As the organ softly plays, the congregation and the choir whisper and share mints and kleenex, gossip and the Gospel. As our Amen Corner fills and the Family is being seated, I say before I even turn the keys on this hearse, understand this. I offer this disclaimer.

I disclaim nothing. The life of a writer; as well as a son, a brother, and the Journey of a Soul, I'm learning, is full of potholes. I simply aim to be a good driver. I'll do my best to keep us out of the ditches, till we lay this thing to rest. Living this life is anything but a silent, easy ride from the cradle to the grave and beyond. Buckle up.

- *Passin' Thru. written by Johnny Cash and Randy Scruggs.
  Songs of Cash, Warner Brothers Tamberlane BMI

Claims:

I claim everything I tell is the truth or if it is an exaggeration, the whole truth and nothing but the truth, demands it. I speak with a voice, an amalgamation of myself, my family and my people. The voice of heart, mind, and soul. A "trinity" so to speak. And this is how we talk, how we live, and how we die. How we head for Home.

Here, at this funeral in the south, only the Gospel Truth shall set us free. For I believe even one word less, regardless of what that word may be, is an insult to you, me and Almighty God. A lie. So before you get offended understand my honorable intentions. I am a writer. My use of anything and everything deemed "negative, taboo and sinful," as well as politically incorrect, is done solely for the purpose of telling this supernatural story of life, honestly and authentically. I am learning there is a difference between sin and suffering. Love and laughter, sadness and sorrow, grace and hope; as well cussing, insults, irony and injury; these are the vivid colors demanded of the portrait I attempt to paint. And when it comes to the truth, at the very least my truth, I don't give a decent damn about politics. I'm an honest sinner saved by grace alone. There's no room for politics in sin or salvation. Not in mine.

I come from good people, honest folks, I believe author Rick Bragg calls 'em, "flawed people." Sometimes the salt of the earth can be a little salty. The deliberate use of our Lord's name in vain is done solely for one reason. That's exactly how it happened. And if joyful as well as caustic, searing sarcasm offends you, I'd sign the family visitation book and head for the door now.

To my critics. The literary ones will "have at it" as we say, and should. That's what they do. Come on in and fill up. The eating's good! It will be what it will be. I will go on and on at times but this is a soul cleansing for me and me alone. It's the only way for me to lay this to rest, respectfully, reverently. I need some space and by God, I am claiming it. I am marking off, measuring this unmarked grave with each and every syllable. Plus I'm a genuine southerner, that's what we do down here. Use forty-four words when four would do and talk in circles. Least this is about the Unbroken One.

To my people, I love and cherish you above all things in this life. You taught us growing up to "work out our own salvation" through scripture, prayer and discernment. Well, I'm a workin' on it. Hard as I can. Me and Jesus are still workin' on it. Leave room for some grace for me too. 'Cause I sure need it. I'm on His clock, not ours. I may make some of you proud, I guarantee I'll piss someone off, but pull up a chair, at least we'll have a good time. Some stories need telling.

To everyone else. There comes a time, hopefully, in our lives where we become aware, enlightened, as to what we are carrying through this life. And the cost. I have toted the best I can. I have carried many things too long, truth and lies. I've paid too much and not enough. There's what looks like an empty grave between my Mama and Daddy back home in our family cemetery. Trust me, it's anything but empty. I have laid down what I can there. The rest lies in my heart and soul.

Oh hell, lighten up. I'm trying to. Drama gets old, downright expensive, after a while. Funerals ain't free. Neither is living. Sooner or later it's gonna cost you your life and somebody a chunk of change. Spend both wisely

Collections:

This "book" has been welling up, collecting inside of me, since I was a small child playing in the ancient coastal sands of Carolina. With each passing year, celebration and crisis, the message of the scriptures in my heart have become increasingly clearer. Just write them. It is both my rock of responsibility and labor of love. This is my Journey.

It's now years later though it doesn't feel that way. On a hot June day, over a decade ago, already broken myself, I found out all of my immediate family was, for sure, dying. I heard a Voice, I sat down and began writing. Though my point of view would change over the course of this experience, as they began passing on, my first words still ring true and sum up the heart of this matter. As you read, I ask for nothing except this. Come Heaven, hell and high water, and they're all coming, I claim the following collection comes straight from the heart. Savor it.

"*I came home to collect some things. Myself, my past. My life. Inner peace. I came home to find the Rock of my Soul. To find my way, Home. Because along the way I began to lose something sacred. Me. Both of my parents as well as my only brother are dying. We are collecting all we can while we can. I am holding on and letting go, trying to envision my world without them. Everyone goes through the fire. The Good News is, we live on this side of grace. And if it's truly grace, and I know it is, it's always amazing.*"

June 06, 2006 john 'hound" brown

FUNERAL IN THE SOUTH

an authentic southern tale.

by john "hound" brown

ORDER OF SERVICE

xix

PART 3
COMMITTAL AND INTERNMENT

PART 4
BENEDICTION AND DISMISSAL

PRELUDE AND PROCESSIONAL

Broken:
a proper introduction.

I f anyone is going to spin a southern tale, they ought to be a southerner. A real one. Born, bred and raised, with the rights to a family grave. It's the only way to get to the bottom of it and get it right. Such a tale should be sweet as tea, funny as hell, dirty as dog-shit on a flip-flop, and above all else; full of heart and the Gospel Truth. I am the south. I am a storyteller.

I am...

Black and white, sugar and spice; Heaven and Hell. "I'll be damned," and "Bless your heart!" Magnolia streets & cheap perfume, Azalea festivals and Daffodil Queens. Funeral homes with drive up windows and rumor mills….spinning. I am Good Ole Boys and Soul Brothers. Christians. Fine folks, hippies and hypocrites! Church affairs that stink to high Heaven; an odd mix of politics and the Gospel. I am the Light of the Almighty streaming through stained glass windows spreading a little sunshine on centuries of guilt. I am the cross, the blood of Christ and shadows of shame casting doubt and insecurity across innocent children's minds and small southern towns. I am that slow, slow search for grace.

Both myth and reality, "Southology," I am saved and backslidden'. The Boogeyman, and Wampus Cats, haints, hussies & headless horsemen. Both Mayberry and Selma. I am that swift sword of sarcasm sent to cut you to your knees lest you forget, there's only so much shit I'll take but an endless supply I can dish out. A tranquil farm pond, a bucket of whitetail shot through the gut; a mother's screams, a father's insecurities. Divorce and denial, the pain and struggle of irony. I'm a good ole fashioned, "Go to Hell" and "Fine, and You?" The tip of a fine hat, a nod of approval, the wave of my hand across a steering wheel to a complete stranger, the silence of a good friend's ear. I am Spanish moss, repentance, a grove of live oak trees; the sunrise of a swamp. I am the power of a simple faith in a simple people.

A Sunday homecoming with deviled eggs, I am full of gossip and the Holy Spirit. I am the old South; an angry bulldog chained to a metal stake with no water, behind a mobile home, a dinner boiling into a quiet rage. I am hate. Hate, I said. Chicken bones, mildew, beer cans, & old tires; a broken toy that could no longer hold a child's attention and never really did.

I'm a summer storm answering prayers. Tobacco farms, gravel roads and the sweat of a poor man who knows nothing but a slow, steady, silent scream of poverty and a beautiful, dark, black woman teaching a white child the color of love. I am the truth, and the truth doesn't hurt. She aches. Rhythm and blues, a stone country song, the echo of an old hound chasing a deer. I am that last glimmer of sun, set across emerald pines, hope in constant resurrection, born again and again.

Vinegar, salt, red pepper, and pig-pickings, I'm a firm handshake and the eyes of an old man who's seen… enough. I am cancer and cirrhosis tugging at the body, poisoning the spirit, battling the soul. Bruises on my aunt's arms, a childhood of precious memories. One you can't drink away and wouldn't even if you could. Falling leaves, a bed of pine straw, a mourning dove alone atop a lonesome power line. The deafening roar of the silent solitude of the soul.

Long hair and cocaine, summertime, copperheads and copper tans; I am The Allman Brothers, that foolish boy sitting on the dock of the bay, "shooting the breeze," daydreaming about pirates and shooting Yankees. I am unbearable heat, an older girl in a two piece bikini bathed in baby oil, sun rays and salt water, the "baby" hair and sweaty curve of her back. I am the passion of the "first time," the love of my life, fast cars and false freedom. Speaking in tongues, laying it on the altar, I am laying it on the line. I am the bloom of a dogwood, "barbequed" chicken and double first cousins. Guilt trips and vacation bible school, pawn shops and car washes. I am Hiphop and Haggard. Children's castles made of beach sand out of the imagination of love. Gone with the Wind, salt water marshes & low tides.

I am the weight of a little boy's memories.

I am many things, yet in the end, I'm simply a cotton-headed white boy, afraid of the back of my Daddy's hand, the fires of hell and Mama's disapproval. I am Granny's angel, a good lil' boy and a sneaky little buzzard. I'm a dreamer, a seeker. I still wanna build a log cabin in the woods with Jimmy and play baseball forever. Quietly, I hold my sadness, collecting it like fragile seashells at low tide, gently placing them in the center of my heart. Once I was lost but now I'm found, I was blind but now I see. Inside every ounce of sadness I see a pound, at least a pound of pure joy, real joy. Not the kind you jump up and down about, rather the kind that gives and takes, sits with you in that front porch swing at dusk and whispers "you have lived."

I live in my soul, wear flip flops and favor high dollar straw hats, once they're broken in. A few years ago, this journey of mine, forced me to step off the planet and take a seat at the Table of Life and Love. And here we sit; me & my angels, my ghosts & demons; my sin and Savior, salvation, sanity, or something in between, on the line. This is a family reunion of sorts, a face to face conversation & headcount of the spooks; the saints and haints in my closet; complete with truth, hypocrisy, lies and love.

We're taking out the trash, looking for treasures, not answers. At a crossroads in the Deep South lies the heart of this matter and the wind whispers a story. Pen and paper, guitar and soul food in hand, no blessing is invoked. Grace needs no invitation. Me and my people, we live and die in eastern North Carolina and I have been forever coming home. I am all these things, no more, no less, except now I am a man. I am broken.

When I was a kid, soft drinks came in glass bottles stacked in wooden crates. They had a deposit on them, thus they were worth something. Redeemable. All of them. On a nice day, folks would walk the county highways, gravel roads, and edges of fields to search for empty bottles tossed out of cars and trucks. There was always broken glass out on the highway and a sharp kid kept his eyes peeled for present dangers riding his bike. I remember stopping in the middle of the road many times at the crossroads, straddling my bike, sweat pouring down my face staring at a busted Coca-Cola bottle or what was left of a beer, the blacktop dripping-wet with their memory. Crystal clear, lime green & muddy brown, baking in a brutal sun. Broken.

I always thought it was beautiful. But I was careful, not to get cut.

Opening Prayer.

This is no tale of sentimental family portraits, faded photo albums and memories the way we wish they were. It is raw and real. A family's love and loss. A tale of chaos and quiet moments. Wreckage and Redemption. Waters that are holy.

I wish they were still here for without them I feel lost. A wanderer, searching for Home, stumbling, wondering how to get there and when he will. I'm afraid of what tomorrow might bring and have let the clanging sounds of sorrow drown out the Joy of this Life. I don't know life without them and though they live inside my heart, they are indeed gone.

I had to lose all three of them for me to understand I am far more than that little boy they so adored and found endearing. That they sheltered, nurtured and protected. That they leaned on and trusted with their very soul. And I had to go find, that little boy. I held my Brother's heart and hand until his spirit quit running and his race was won. I pulled Daddy close, with my arms around him as he lay there, giving up his ghost into the arms of his Heavenly Father. I stood in the doorway and saw Mama smiling from ear to ear, slipping out the back door of life. I knew, she was going Home.

It is the closest we can get to Heaven, so I thought, to be there for those we love when they die. The highest honor. You can hear the gates swing open, if you listen. You can feel the breeze of the Holiest of Ghosts when his presence takes their Soul. The sheer love will baptize you in those moments, if you open your heart and allow it. An entire lifetime passes by, in silence, as you sit there in awe of the power of Divine Creation. You experience nothing else but love.

Often, I walk down to the shoreline of the river Jordan in my mind but all I can see are the ripples their souls left as they crossed over into New Jerusalem. I can hear the quiet I imagine Heaven holds for the weariest of souls. I've grown weary of looking over my shoulder at yesterday and I need to know that they, that we, are okay. That our greatest wounds and scars, these stripes, are healed. That they are finally Home and free. I need to lay this to rest.

There is never a day that passes, that I don't sense their absence or feel their presence, but I am realizing with each passing day I must get back to the business of living. Come home to life and love. I want to experience it in its fullest manifestation of my spirit. As a grown man, I want that little boy to know, it is all, finally, okay.

I have experienced the amazing grace of the Mystery of Love on this Journey at every step. On this slow reverent ride to the cemetery. It is all enduring and giving. It gives us strength and life, keeps no record of right or wrong, is never jealous or self--serving. Love is sacrificial. Love suffers well and bears the burdens of the flesh and soul. It rejoices in the truth, the whole truth and nothing but the truth. Only, in the truth. If I could tell you a tale, of genuine authentic Love, I would. And it would go something like this.

"Once upon a time there was the cutest, little, cotton-headed white boy and his family loved him to death..."

Funeral in the South

an authentic southern tale

PART ONE

VISITATION WITH THE FAMILY

Spring of '33

In between the flat pine plantations and gentle rolling hills of the swamp land of eastern North Carolina lies a quiet intersection, Edmundson's Crossroads. One can stand beneath the ancient oaks among dilapidated tobacco barns being swallowed up by time, scrub trees, and briars and listen to the wind. You can walk the old paths filled with the sand of the sea from eons ago searching for arrowheads or prehistoric seashells. If you're lucky, like me, you can remember when, and still ache for it.

There, just beyond that curve lies our farm. If you look back up in the field, past the shop, you'll see the pecan grove. That's where Daddy was born. My cousin Steve had to tear the old house down over a decade ago, an inconvenience to modern farming, I suppose. When I came home and saw it gone, I stood in the path, alone, and felt like crying.

That small creek feeding into the finger of hardwoods spilling out into the corner near the grove is called, Buck Meadow Branch. Daddy is the last one left that recalls the names of all the old creeks and crossings, knows where the original roads and paths lie hidden in the woods, and can tell you a story, a good one, with each piece of land you pass. It is here that I grew up with my brother Glenn. This farm, the crossroads, the old country store, they lay quiet now. When I go there these days, it feels like a family member coming to the funeral home in the early morning, to view and approve the body and come to some sort of understanding that life has changed forever, but not having enough time to digest it before the nightly viewing and public wake. Just as my father and ancestors before me, I am bound to this place. At the soul level. It is my home.

FUNERAL IN THE SOUTH

My childhood, well, most of the first decade, was a sort of Wonder Years set on the busy tobacco roads of North Carolina. To think of it now, in this angry, pissed-off world, it seems incredulous that I can be as young as I think I am but know I'm not, and have lived a youth of ice cold Pepsi's, Nehi Grapes, Baby Ruth Bars and Double Bubble-bubble gum. But I did and man was it ever sweet. Life smelled like honeysuckles, tasted like chocolate pies, and the sun was always shining. Summer storms were answered prayers and, of course, proof positive God must favor white tobacco farmers. Cigarettes even smelled good and were good for you back then. Back before our secret was out King Tobacco died and this country went to hell in a hand basket.

My days were filled with the abandonment of a happy child. My Daddy, a proud farmer, would come by the house and pick me up on the big red and black International tractor letting me drive as I sat in his lap. On lucky days, he would take me out to the field and drop me off in a path full of coastal sand where I would be content for hours with nothing but my favorite action figure, Geronimo, his plastic horse and a few toy tractors as Daddy went about the daily family business.

Mama was a full--time homemaker as well as a professional woman, least for those times. She spent her days ten miles away in the county seat of Goldsboro, working as an accountant for Weil's department store, as Daddy continued the beloved, time-honored tradition of raising tobacco. At the age of twenty-one, he also became a tobacco auctioneer, and would go on to sell the sacred leaves all over the Carolinas, Georgia, the Virginias, Tennessee, Ohio and Missouri for some forty-seven years until as Brother would say, "The Merchants of Death hath ceased."

For my pre-school years and most of my childhood, a young, sweet, compassionate black woman named Magalene kept our home front going. Mama would rise, get us stirring and fix breakfast, then as my parents headed out for the field and office, an immense presence of love would enter the house each morning. Magalene would furiously clean, cook a huge lunch, prepare our supper, as well as somehow find the time to teach and entertain me with the basics of life. Most especially unadulterated, unconditional love. She raised me. Each day she set up the ironing board in the den and I would sit quietly but intently, watching her as she watched Dark Shadows, thankfully in the full light of day. To this day, I love her just as she has loved me. I am her boy. We are family.

The highlight of my little rural movie was Uncle Burrell's country store, just past the crossroads. On any given day you might catch a serious checkers showdown, hear the merits of a local Walker deer hound, or catch a retelling of the latest sighting of the legendary Wampus Cat. On a brutally hot Carolina summer day, the dirty concrete floor would drag beneath your boots and the drink box to the left held the coldest Coca-Colas I ever had the chilling pleasure of drinking. Uncle George would give me a quarter to go outside and piss on a different man's hubcap each visit. About the time I would start giggling, always aiming a little higher, the front door would bust open and he would yell, "Damn Walter, some man's out here pissing on your truck!" And Uncle George would howl!

Movie--like characters surrounded me except they were real people. Folks like Harris Hall, four hundred pounds of over-all wearing, chocolate milk-drinking farmer, and black folks with names like Booger, Boots, and Franklin Delano Roosevelt Ward. They may have been poor, uneducated and rough around the edges, but they were rich with life, common sense and possessed a refinement that comes only from the struggle of fighting the good fight. Surviving. I miss them. They were the real deal. They were authentic.

To say we lived on a "family" farm is a bit of a historical understatement. The past, our past, was a living, breathing, sacred ground dripping with tradition and real, genuine, American history, an alternative reality still alive that walked hand in hand with us, daily, from the cradle to the grave. We heard the stories everywhere we went, at home, at church, riding in the back seat listening to our parents. Our entire community, every field and stream, each simple house and old store had a real live tale to tell. A true story with a moral to it. Wisdom. You learned the art of listening as well as storytelling as this was part of your very birthright. You owed it to your ancestors as well as yourself and future generations to pass these stories down the line. Word for word.

My paternal grandparents, Marvin Patrick Brown and Eva Cornegay Edmundson married on September 29th, 1923, and quickly began a simple life here at Buck Meadow Branch. The land has been in our family longer than we've been a country, part of a plantation willed to my sixth great-grandfather, Joseph Edmundson, on August 4, 1743. His first-born son, 2nd Lt. James Edmundson Jr., my fifth great-grandfather, and his 2nd Battalion were sent by the House of North Carolina, to aid South Carolina, in the War of Independence. In return for his loyal service, Lt. Edmundson received an additional land grant of another 1500 acres, making their colonial farm in excess of 8,000 acres, surely one of significance in these brand new, United States of America.

In 1989, his old home-place, the "Bullhead" Farm, was designated a Bicentennial Farm. The name comes from a family legend involving British General Cornwallis, passing nearby Peacock Bridge on his way to Yorktown. Our family turned loose the gift of one large bull, who saw nothing but red.

Red troops. The tall tale ended with that bull's head pegged to the ash tree in the yard with pegs from their now burned down family barn, courtesy of the King of England and his boys. Evidently, it didn't shake us. They went home with their tails tucked between their legs and we stayed here and built a new barn and country. The Lieutenant's grave lies over at Bullhead, some six miles from our place. The current tombstone is not, however, period.

My great, great granddaddy, James Brown of County Kerry, Ireland, arrived in New York sailing aboard the British *"Bark Duncan Ritchie"* on July 21st, 1852, at the age of twenty--two. Fleeing the Great Potato Famine that obliterated much of the Irish, James soon met the fine daughter of another poor Irish farmer, and in 1856, James Brown wed Elizabeth Kelly. They set up home in Richmond just in time for the great Civil War. Family legend says they headed south in Virginia, where their second home was destroyed sometime during the great siege of Petersburg. Timing is everything.

Their fourth child, my great granddaddy, Patrick, was born March 17th, 1867, St. Patrick's Day. As soon as he could, James grabbed one mule and the family and headed for "higher" ground down in Goldsboro, North Carolina, with wife Elizabeth cradling Patrick in swaddling clothes.

Though the Brown clan arrived later than the Edmundsons, they too got busy at the work of life. So, I suppose it goes without saying, me and my people are bound to this land like that bull's head pegged to that tree. Anyhow, in the fall of 1923 Daddy's folks started their life here at Buck Meadow Branch, a part of the old original Edmundson tract of earth.

Back then everyone was poor by today's selfish standards. But for the late 1920s and early 30s Daddy's folks were doing fine, some could even say "in high cotton" for what would lie ahead. They say Eva loved Granddaddy, and he adored her. They had a home place, and I'm sure like all naïve newlyweds they thought the future surely held nothing but the fulfillment of their highest dreams. They set about the simple life of farming and raising a family of their own. There would be nothing so simple about it.

Daddy had a rough-raising although it never seemed that way, least to hear him tell it. His mama, Eva, died at the age of thirty in 1934 after previously losing two of four children. Cruelly, on her very deathbed, just six weeks after giving birth to her fourth and final child, Henry, Grandma Eva had to ask her sister, Mama Ellen, to raise him. A pulled tooth. Of all the things to die of, blood poisoning from an extracted tooth seems almost comically cruel. His Mama had still been alive up at her brother Burrell's house when Daddy went to bed that night. The next morning, bless his heart, no one told him and he went running into that dark bedroom to kiss his Mama only to find her dead and already laid out. I still have Grandma Eva's ponytail that Aunt Molly cut and tied for Daddy. That lil' something the scared lil' fellow could cling to.

Family history was more than important to Daddy, it was sacred. I suppose losing two siblings to death and one live one with your Mama's passing, at the ripe old age of six, would make memories valuable for any of us. Daddy said when the funeral was over and every one left, Granddaddy was never the same. He had always drank but the real drinking, hard and bitter with intent and purpose, started that night. Being half Edmundson and half Brown, Daddy's rural psychosis got started early. By morning, his Mama was cold dead and they found Granddaddy down at the swamp hole in his red trunks, Aunt Marie said, mad drunk in grief and hard liquor. When the sun rose that morning, Daddy was on his own whether he knew it or not. Funny thing about little boys. They do pick up quick.

As Daddy's version goes, after the somber festivities, he was taken from one house to another. His Mama had come from a family of ten, so there were plenty of hands to handle him. Daddy's post funeral adventure started at Uncle Burrell's, then to Jett and Lilly Edwards down in the field, and finally he wound up at his Uncle Les's home. There was an issue over raising him in exchange for Eva's tobacco allotment, which did not sit well with Leslie Edmundson. He took Daddy in 'cause he loved him, "to hell with the tobacco." To say Daddy loved Uncle Les is an understatement. My own memories of the old timer are a sepia-toned reel-to-reel of the classic southern farmer, late enough in life to have acquired the wisdom of patience but young enough to still jerk the young bucks around with a good joke on the backside of a barn. He was tall, always in khaki pants, silver pocket watch dangling from his thin leather belt, simple plaid shirt, and the fedora. Hats are vital to the southern male species. Ball cap, farmer's hat, go-to-hell Gatsby, or fedora, it doesn't matter. They frame more than our face. They introduce us and announce our intent the moment we walk through any given door.

Uncle Les' felt fedora made him look like a well-loved sheriff and when he entered the room, a soft stability and order, a kind of fondness for all things southern, seemed to settle in the air. He adored children and Daddy adored Uncle Les, quite simply because Uncle Les had first loved him. Biblical to say the least. Years later, as I witnessed my first funeral as well as Les' last one, I learned two critical things. They hurt like hell, and the food down here, is out of this world.

That year Daddy had planted extra turnips. Uncle Les dropped by to grab a handful for home, walked in Uncle Burrell's store, removed his hat, took a swig from a small Coca-Cola, threw his head back with a southern sigh of simple satisfaction, smiled and died. During this time of bereavement Daddy recalled countless memories with his Uncle who had legally adopted him. It is one of my fondest and earliest memories of Daddy's words pouring off his tongue with the affection of a polished storyteller.

With my fingernails dug into the back of the front seat we rambled to the home, the funeral parlor, back to the house for vittles and grief, then to the church and graveyard, and finally back to the house for more food. I listened and memorized the verbal video Daddy gave me of his Uncle, his childhood. The importance of it dripped from every syllable like Tupelo honey off his tongue.

My Granddaddy had lost more than his wife, children, and himself to Death and the liquor bottle. By the time the spring of '33 rolled around, he had lost his heart of hearts. Though he lived to be sixty-eight, Granddaddy was a broken man and Uncle Les knew it. So he had stepped in, not replacing a son's love for his father, but simply showering Daddy with the things Granddaddy couldn't. When Uncle Les' died, I vividly remember sensing not only the deepest sadness in my Daddy's spirit for the first time, but recognized the beauty and value of it. Dressed in my little black suit and sitting up proper on that old oak pew at the funeral, I kept staring at my older cousin Timmy's watch and Uncle Les' nose. Uncle Les was leaving for good but his imprint in the absence of a proper Grandfather had made a huge impact on me. Timmy consoled me as I cried, reaching inside his suit, handing me my very first white funeral handkerchief.

Straining to see all I could of Uncle Les for as long as I could, I vowed to always remember the exact moment his nose disappeared beneath that cold dark coffin lid. It was 1:52 pm EST on his nose, literally. As Miss Lottie played that organ like only a white Baptist woman can--semi-fluid, and a little on the square side--two strange men dressed in real suits, high dollar ones, suddenly walked down the aisle towards our altar, removed the funeral spray from the top of the casket, folded the white lace inside the box, and without saying a damn thing to me, shut the lid on my Uncle Les. I was appalled!

At that moment, I'll always believe I told Death to go straight to hell. Then, staring at a stained glassed Jesus in the Garden of Gethsemane, I cried like little boys do when they lose their best'est buddy. I can still smell his chewing tobacco, hear the ticking of the grandfather clock, and feel myself running up to his legs for a good hug and a quarter. By the time I had eaten my third piece of chocolate pie back at the house, I was incensed with the spirit of family. I suddenly had an endless host of cousins, uncles and aunts, and I had witnessed firsthand the surreal, southern spread that a funeral brings to a home here in Dixie. Fried chicken, deviled eggs, honey ham and homemade biscuits; one table endlessly running into another, spilling onto a nearby countertop, filling up every empty space with banana pudding, pineapple cake, congealed salads and fried pies, gallons of sweet tea and strong black coffee for the old folks. Having attended my first funeral and high off of the high-octane attention and sugar, I learned there's nothing like a funeral in the South. I was unaware of the role such occasions would come to play in my life. For in that moment, it was more than enough to be loved and love back. To be family. Come to think of it, it still is. Least it oughta be.

After the burial, Uncle Les's home quickly filled with laughter and love, tears and tales, as it had been when he was there. I recall the first, lonesome chiming of his clock and glancing towards his empty chair, experiencing for my first time that void only death brings to your life and your heart. Running my hands over the cracked leather, I could still hear his voice, see his smile and feel his imprint. Every time I don my straw Colonel Littleton panama and khaki pants, I think of him, smile and walk a little gentler. Uncle Les was kindness incarnate.

The stories Daddy shared with us about his childhood were a poor man's poetry, from the mundane to the magical, the horrific to the heavenly. After fostering with Uncle Les, at the age of eleven he returned home, to the family farm, to live with Granddaddy. To become a man. He and Granddaddy lived alone in a small, simple, four--room, white farmhouse. Everything they ate was either grown, raised, or killed on the farm. Picked and plucked, sheared or shucked. Their running water consisted of a bucket, a well with a pump, and two legs running outside to retrieve it. There was no radio or television back then, and the outdoor outhouse would still be around in the late 1960s for me to enjoy the experience of wiping with our local newspaper. Paper cuts do hurt on a hinny.

Back in those days country folks swept the yard each day with a hand-made yard broom, removing weeds and anything that might take root. One spring before her death, Grandma had planted four pecan trees and daffodils around the base of each one in her hand-swept yard. I've always imagined her out there in a cheap, seed-cloth, cotton dress, her hair pulled back, a loose strand of it blowing in the wind, dreaming of babies strong and healthy and of growing old with her love as she cleaned her yard and planted those trees and flowers, sowed her dreams and hopes. The hurricanes have only claimed one tree over the years, and the three that remain, with their roots planted firmly in this sacred southern ground, still boast the simple beauty of spring each year, as well as the enormous love this family has been blessed and cursed enough to share.

Daddy looked over Granddaddy until he died in his arms on the side of the road at Stoney Creek in June of 1967. Gasping for air, his lungs filling up with fluid, and heart beginning to fail, the EMT, Billy Hood reared back to strike his breastbone, breaking it in one final, futile attempt to save Granddaddy. Daddy knelt down by the roadside and held his daddy in his arms. And then Granddaddy was gone. I always wondered, deeply, how that must have felt. Holding your own Daddy when his body gives up his ghost. Daddy spoke of it with great reverence and honor.

The new house my parents were building out on the blacktop was not completed in time for that funeral. It would be decades later, and I a man when I would realize why Daddy had built the house where he did, placing his recliner in the den looking out a pair of French Windows. There, down the sandy path, up in the field, sat the old home place. The silent pecan grove and scattered daffodils would whisper to his soul the testament of a mother's love, the encumbered duty of family, and remain his window to the Spring of '33. And he would long for that all his days. Any child would.

Each November

Mama was born Sallie Mae Stallings, on April 6th, 1928, just four days after Daddy. Her family of sharecroppers hailed from the red clay country of Franklin County, North Carolina. At the age of fifteen, her mother, my Granny, Mamie Pearl Champion, married John Ernest Stallings Sr. He was thirty-six. Sharecroppers didn't play when it came to having big litters. There was no such thing as a tractor back then, not here in Carolina. Girl or boy, every child was another set of hands and pair of legs to milk a cow, tote a bucket, handle a hoe or crop tobacco. Granny's first two children died within mere days of birth and were laid to rest in boring, unassuming, shallow graves in the family cemetery. The headstones simply state, "Baby Stallings 1 and 2," with their respective brief lives etched in the cold granite. The Stallings would go on to have ten more children. Mama being one of the middle ones, was destined to possess a double dose of piss and vinegar.

To this day Mama still hates her Daddy. If she's said it once, she's said it a thousand times. "If you'll take me to his grave, I'll squat and piss on it. I hate what he did to my Mama." Having been raised in another generation, I can safely say, Mama would likely have killed him had she had access to the proper handgun. John Ernest, otherwise widely known as "Dent," was tough, rugged, prone to liquor, quick to temper with little patience for just about anything. Granny was a saint. She had to be in order to deal with him, ten kids, the beatings and Depression-era life.

Mama's childhood was spent doing exactly the same thing every child of that era's was in this part of the country. Working. They raised tobacco as well, but cotton was a bigger deal in that neck of the woods, and with ten kids to work the fields, Dent raised every hill of cotton the good Lord and the Devil would let him. They say Uncle Bob was often found laying down in the field between two rows of thick white cotton, sleeping. How he got away with it, no-one seems to know. He won't spill a word but his eyes do twinkle when the subject is discussed. And so does Aunt Inez's. Aunt Marie's do not. So, they must know something.

It's strange the way family works on and in us. Though I was raised in my father's community, surrounded by his kin folks, my Mama's huge clan gave me an even deeper sense of family, made me feel connected, and constantly gave us another late breaking news bulletin or family crisis. Daddy's heritage and extended family deeply grounded me with a sense of family history, tradition and deep southern roots, but Mama's was the one that held the yearly Champion reunion up in Louisburg.

I don't recall the first one I attended, but I do recall being amazed at how many people one could be kin to, and again, like a proper funeral, reunion food is always top shelf. Pig picking cake, homegrown BBQ and slaw with our famous North Carolina vinegar based sauce, casseroles, cupcakes, cornbread, the list was endless. As a young boy, I craved hearing Great Uncle Joe's old stories and memorizing vaguely familiar aging faces of wisdom, and while I did play with the children outside, I continually made an excuse to go back in so I could grab another piece of sweet potato pie, a glass of tea or a hug and a kiss from Granny. Each trip in I would hear another tale of hard times and happiness, and as a young boy I instinctively understood that time was fleeting and family was important. I learned early that life gets the best of all of us, having its way when we least expect it, and like any good hurricane worthy of its name, leaves a lot of trash and a little treasure. It's as though life separates us, sifting out the chaff, then death draws us nigh.

Every year I could see Mama's joy as she returned to her roots and sense her sadness, like a captured animal being torn away from its nursing mother, knowing it cannot come back, when it came time to leave. Mama and I would make the ride up past Raleigh, watching the terrain slowly become unfamiliar, changing from sandy, loamy soil to more intense hills, greener grass and that damn red clay. Mama's eyes would light up as she told me wonderful stories and I asked silly questions with a sincere heart.

We would attend that reunion together until we buried enough folks that we had to start our very own. Now we gather the first Saturday in each November to celebrate Granny, her life, love and legacy, as we partake of the annual Stallings reunion.

Mama was always excited to see her favorite aunt, Aunt Clara each year. She was sassy, full of life, and even well into her eighties could cut you down to size with her tyrannical tongue or make you well up with tears as she recalled her most precious memories. I wish my first thought of Mama's favorite aunt was as fond as hers. Aunt Clara was simply one of a kind, and tough as hell. I loved her because my Mama did and that was reason enough for me. Although every time her name comes up, I immediately recall her down at the beach. As I walked in the room, chubby and sunburned early one rainy Sunday morning she proclaimed, "Gracious boy, you need a bra and you got a case of the Gone-Ass!" I was not happy. It has affected my deep insecurities about the shape of my own ass for my entire life. If it looked flat to Aunt Clara, in her eighties, and me ten, how could it possibly ever appeal to a sexy, sweaty older girl in a bikini at Emerald Isle?

Aunt Clara lived alone, and though legally blind, frequently drove her truck wherever or whenever she desired. With or without sheriff escorts. She could walk out her door, down the path, cross the road and walk the final half mile to the pond. Upon catching her catfish, she would return the way she came, dress them fish, fry'em up, and maybe, just maybe she'd save you a piece. Like most homes in the rural south, there was usually a leftover piece of cornbread lying on the table, least up through the eighties. Come to think of it, maybe that's what's wrong with this world. Not enough cornbread lying around anymore. When there was leftover-cornbread, folded up in a napkin cloth, patiently waiting for a griping stomach, hungry child or searching soul, we all had a lot more time for each other. We actually gave a damn about something besides ourselves, back when Sunday afternoon was, Sunday afternoon.

Aunt Clara's home was from another bygone era, the '30s, as worn out, fragile and strong as she was. It was simple and old. It worked, even the broken parts. Smelled like a retired farm house is supposed to smell, like real life, sweetly weathered, drawing you in from one room to the next. Her living room was her inner sanctum, part confessional part backroom bar. I bet ole Aunt Clara even had a nip every now and then. After every reunion, Mama would always quietly slip back to that old house and talk with her for hours, serious, sincere talk that a grown child shares with a parent or priest. When those times came, me and a cousin or three might grab a cane pole and head for the pond or play in the yard until one of us got our pride hurt or we found a snake. Aunt Clara was a good listener because she revered the truth. And her age had led her years ago to the simple fact that most of the time all of us already know the answers to the questions we're about to ask. The one we need validation from is ourselves. And just asking the question often frees the soul. She refused to pull punches on anything, and if you didn't want her opinion, meaning the truth and the whole truth, then damnit, why'd you ask? Like a homemade quilt made of leftover dress patches and seed cloth bags, Mama would be cut from the same soft yet rugged piece of fabric. Aunt Clara would live to the age of ninety-six and see all five of her children buried in the Carolina soil. And her memory would remain encased in every fiber of Mama's spirit and character her whole life.

Now back to Mama's clan. Ten kids, minus the two baby Stallings. And each with their own nickname. There was Louise or TomTit, John Ernest Jr. or Uncle Doc, Elsie otherwise known as Puss, Marie who could be summoned with Sacket and of course Mama or Hannah. Rounding out the bottom half of the litter, Edmund Harrel or Uncle Cap, the one I look the most like, Bobby or Bob, lot of thought into that one, and Inez. Aunt Inez. Oohhh. We gotta pause for the cause on this one.

I informed Aunt Inez before she suddenly, unexpectedly passed last year, I was nearing completion of this book and she said, "You will NOT use my nickname." I respectively shrugged my shoulders and said, "Aunt Inez, I have to." A very petite woman, those eyes lit up with hellfire AND brimstone and she replied, "You do and I'll tear your lil'... your lil'... I'll tear your lil' ass up!" For the record she whispered the hind-end part. I'm fifty-two y'all. And even at fifty-two, my Aunt Inez is still "my" Aunt Inez. I'm gonna buck tradition here and keep her last request. Although I will tell you it has something to do with the hind end of a wild bunny rabbit.

For whatever reason, Aunt Inez never did like it. Finally, rounding out Grannie's litter, there were the two youngest, Lola, known as Fat, and Billy, or Buck, as well as Charming Billy from the old song. The man could eat more BBQ in one sitting, then turn around and do it again a few hours later, and live to tell about it than anyone I've ever known.

With such large families and difficult times, children were raised knowing the necessity and value of hard work, I mean hard work this world wouldn't recognize if it walked up and "hit 'em in the ass." Back-breaking labor, merely for surviving. Attention was something you stole when and if you could-and were sure it wouldn't piss off your Daddy. Mama and her siblings told us story after story of their youth, like, being mad cause today was your turn to wash the "shitty-hippins," the babies' dirty cloth diapers. Or Aunt Lola's "Chicken and Biscuits" tale, still one of my favorites. After sweeping the yard one day, the chickens turned right around and crapped everywhere. Aunt Lola thought, "I'll fix you," and retrieved Granny's left-over biscuits. She sliced 'em open and filled them with chicken shit and fresh tomatoes. Chickens will eat anything, including their own squat. To this day, Aunt Lola don't eat chicken, period.

Being ten years older, Aunt Clara's daughter Susie showered Mama with affection. She made her clothes, primped and curled her hair, and in Mama's own words, "Taught me how to be a little girl." Unfortunately, being a child in the depression era never did last for long. At the age of sixteen, Susie suddenly died at home of a burst appendix. At six years old, Mama had just started school and would lose not only her beloved cousin but part of her innocence as well. Back then funeral directors dressed the dead out and placed them in the casket at home, if they had one, casket that is. Often times the dearly departed were simply laid out on a bed with a thin veil draped over the bedposts gently tracing their outline until it rested at the foot. Susie was inside her coffin as the older ladies continued to jest and joke with Mama, telling her to come on in and touch her, thinking "once you've touched the dead and they don't bite you," all fear subsides. Mama was scared shitless, or so she says. I doubt that. I can honestly say, I never saw Sallie Mae Brown truly scared.

My Mama was substance & backbone in action. A chip off the old Aunt Clara block, even when she was eighty-one, lying in the rest home, she spoke her mind freely, and would often sign off with, "And I don't care if it hair lips the whole Stallings clan." She loved quoting scripture, correctly, according to her, and would remind you and anyone else that repentance of your sins IS required and salvation is yours, and you best take it. Mama was a Baptist, and a damn good one. A southern one. In other words, down here, Mama is always right. I said, Mama is always right. In fact, perhaps the most original, ingenious quote from my Mama is, "Hell, I wouldn't argue with you if I thought I was wrong!"

Mama's childhood stories were usually told around the holidays, for two reasons. Daddy was too busy telling his the rest of the year, and every holiday we found ourselves surrounded by mostly Mama's family at our farm. Although we lived and loved, went to church, the field, Heaven or Hell with Daddy's folks, somehow Mama's were the ones with us more often than not on the weekends and special days.

Mama's family goes back equally as long, from the 1620s family of Nicholas Stallings of Scotland, to the Franklin County, North Carolina clan of Josiah Stallings, circa 1755. Among others, her great, great, Great Uncle George Washington Stallings served in the North Carolina Confederate State Troops, 24th Infantry Regiment, Company-K, along with younger brother Samuel and a first-cousin-Sergeant. Unfortunately, the pneumonia got the best of Sam in late 1861. Uncle George made it long enough to leave a knee joint somewhere near Drewry's Bluff, Virginia, that September. Based on the look on his face in a period photo frame, he was a pretty serious fellow. The colors run so dark on his sack coat you might mistake him for a Yankee, if you are one, until you see his Rebel kepi cap and the lack of twinkle in his eyes. North Carolina was reluctant to secede so the story goes, and ole George was probably not excited about freeing his slaves, which he did on his own before he joined up to fight in 1861. Another family legend says they "all stayed right here at home and lived till they died."

Where the hell else were they gonna go? Montgomery? Ole Uncle George rests in recumbent slumber, "Asleep in Jesus," in nearby Oakwood

Cemetery in Raleigh, proper-like with the rest of his indignant Confederate comrades.

Mama was born in Franklin County at home with a midwife like all the rest. She got her schooling in nearby Bunn and like Daddy, graduated in the spring of 1945. Dent wouldn't come off any money for college, so she farmed that summer. Then in the fall her and her sister Marie headed to Henderson where Aunt Marie landed a job with the postwar burgeoning Carolina Telephone Company and Mama took on at JC Penney's. Based on some of Mama's old photos, she also apparently had a thing for a young man, one E.C. Long. Virginia Beach shows up a lot as well, but Mama just blushes and coos, "Edward C Long, from Henderson," like they starred in Grease together or something. There's more to that story, but Sallie Mae ain't spilling them beans, not in this lifetime. But those old fading black and whites with Mama in her swimsuit, leaning against a storm-bent palm tree, or seductively looking up from the splashing water, tell me much more than I care to know.

All Mama's brothers and sisters, except Aunt Louise, say their Daddy was mean to them, even more so to their own Mama. In fact to this day, if his name is brought up, his ghost never lasts very long, appearing as a vague apparition of near evil, dissolving into at least one good story, then fading slowly and surely back into the silence of death. For some reason I picture him as a broken man knowing he will never heal, not in this world. The previously presented Aunt Clara, my Granny's sister had married Dent's brother, Jack. While Dent may have beat on Granny, he threatened to hit Aunt Clara only once. Jack heard about it and told his brother, well, let's just say whatever he told him it got through to him.

My Daddy instilled in us a deep sense of what a so-called man that ever "lays a hand" on a woman should get. It was and is our righteous responsibility to deliver at least one serious ass-whipping if not something worse, dependent on the situation. I asked Mama what her parents taught her once. She said, "Mama taught us to do the right thing and believe in Jesus. And Daddy? He didn't teach us nothing. Yeah he did! To work my ass off and not take shit off of nobody!" Fortunately for Mama, ole Dent would die in 1956 so Mama had a designated place to pee whenever she got mad for the next fifty-five years.

As far as I'm concerned my Mama hung the moon, well Granny hung it but Mama decorated it with the joys of life. As I recall all the major events or holidays--Christmas, Easter, Thanksgiving--it is perhaps the funerals that I treasure most. For it seems it is with death, when we are faced with the only certain thing in this life, that we all get honest, with each other and ourselves. My Mama never needed a funeral to be honest. If she passed down anything to my brother and me, it was a disdain for anything except the uncomfortable brutal honesty that we all would rather let lay in an unmarked grave or hide amongst a display of cut funeral flowers. Not that we can always even accept it, but at the very least a reverent understanding that the truth, the real truth that aches in us, is the pathway to freedom and with freedom comes real joy. Mama also instilled in us the simple yet profound and dare I say necessary understanding of the immense power of a simple faith, unending hope and the good stuff, unconditional love. I don't have to like you, or respect you, but I am bound by spiritual law to love you. It is through Mama that I learned to turn around every once in a while, when you're troubled and afraid of what might lie ahead, and look back over your shoulder. To rediscover over and over again the proof and beauty of grace in your life, and find the strength to continue to fight your own good fight until they begin to make the funeral wreaths and pot the plants, bake the casseroles and cook the pig, for your very own homecoming. In other words don't dwell on the past, but for God's sake, yours, and everyone else's don't deny it either.

Although there were two distinct sides to my parents families, there was one central figure and family that bound us together in my early years. Preacher Ennis and the Antioch Original Free-Will Baptist Church. Daddy was not very keen on churchgoing; he preferred to commune with God in the outdoors, on a tractor watching the sunset, or walking a pine forest and flushing a covey of quail. Mama, on the other hand, lived for church, She loved worship and adored choir practice. Our church was filled with Daddy's people, and Mama was loved and fully accepted as one of them, and became another of the strong spiritual stones laid in our congregation.

My Daddy's first cousin and best friend, Harold Brown attended church there with us along with his wife Helen and my cousins, Greg and Kim as well. On November 16th, 1977, Uncle Harold would suddenly and tragically pass away, highlighting the crossroads of my childhood. Things would never quite be the same afterwards.

Back then, in a rural environment such as ours, respect still mattered. As children not only were we taught, Yes Sir, and No Ma'am, but every adult who lived nearby and you interacted with either carried the title of Mr. or Mrs. or were referred to as Uncle and Aunt so and so. And they had the permission and righteous right and responsibility to tear your ass up if you got out of line. Antioch was a weekly celebration of the meaning of family. Something living and soul soothing that held us all together.

Daddy would rather tell you his best story or an outright grand white lie, than to allow you to fully enter into the softest part of his heart, uninvited and unannounced. He learned to guard it early in life to simply survive the youth fate had dealt him. Daddy lived with his sadness, burying it in a deep, loamy sandy grave behind a sentimental soul and tender heart. Mama, on the other hand was an open book, with a nice sturdy hard cover and soft supple pages. She could forgive you and/or forget you in the same moment. Whatever the truth demanded at the time. But she always returned to the sanctuary love provides.

Even as I pen these thoughts, I recall Daddy telling the best stories and Mama being the best listener. Whether it was fourteen and facing a beating from her Daddy, forty-seven and looking at starting another life, or eighty and dragging her tired body across the floor with her walker, Mama was proud. Real pride, not puffed up, arrogant and self-sufficient, but faithful, steady as she goes. A seafaring clipper, sailing on the assurance that her sails were always being filled by a wind her God and Savior created and provided, with her name on it.

From my earliest memory up until my parents split in 1977, life made sense, everything was explainable. My most vivid memories are of a home filled with family, huge feasts, and Mama's mashed potatoes, the ones that make clogged arteries wickedly worthwhile. We raised Cain and pulled corn, harvested tobacco, put up pear preserves and canned homegrown tomatoes. We interacted with each other. We were alive, and did not yet have the burden of unending electronic digital devices that are supposed to connect us, but actually prevent us from connecting. I recall playing the drums and performing concerts for my cousins, Aunts and Uncles and always having to do a one on one final performance for Granny of "Put your Hand in the Hand." As I entered school I traveled with my parents on the tobacco market to exotic places like Adel, Georgia with huge rattle-snakes and peanut fields, to Johnson City, Tennessee and mountain roads filled with fresh apples, bee honey, and something that must have been spectacular to see cause they called it "Moonshine." At some point, how-ever, I picked up on the tension. We all can surely agree that children are the most honest souls we know. Somehow, I knew a change was coming. We always feel it deep down don't we congregation?

When I began this journey I share now, I knew in my heart it was to be a life-altering one. There was a clever, experienced, scared little boy deep inside constantly reminding me. My brother Glenn was deathly ill but managing and Mama and Daddy were pushing eighty.

The highlight of Daddy's remaining days, "a good day," would be a visit from one of us children, an old friend, or a cousin and the squirrels that ran rampant outside his window devouring the fresh corn we'd take turns dumping into an old ceramic planter. "A real good day" was the doorbell ringing and Uncle Walter standing there, smiling, himself in his late eight-ies, yet timeless, holding a pair of fresh crappie, "Tell Ed I brought him some dinner!"

Though it would seem to take forever, it wouldn't be long before my Brother was gone from here. Not long after he passed on December 17th, 2007, I wrote these now prophetic words…

"Mama for the time being is back at home. We nursed her back to some sort of "health" with Aunt Louise's Boiled Custard, at least enough that she could go back to her place with her things one last time and become comfort-able with yet another life changing experience. The resthome. I can't spend enough time with them, even if it's all day, for I know time is fleeting and at this point not on our side.

Each November the family reunion and my birthday come, along with the anniversary of Granny and Uncle Harold's death. This Christmas will be my very first one without at least, my Brother, if Mama and Daddy even make it. I have that sinking feeling in the pit of my stomach, this is gonna be another rough family journey. Our final one. Every step counts. Our family reunion is getting thinner and thinner, and every year someone doesn't make it back, but all of them are there, inside our hearts and the spirit of this family. As certain as I write these truths, it won't be long before we have another funeral here in the South. But right now, in this moment, my people, they are all with me. They always are, what else could explain our unbroken circle and what more can one ask for than to be loved and love back, regardless of any cost. For me November is not a month but a state of mind.

One of Mama's favorite songs, and best I can tell based on the one line she knows, the title is "I Love You," she sings or whispers it in my ear whenever she knows I'm down but refuse to admit it.

" a bushel and a peck and a hug around the neck,

I … love… you."

I've heard it a lot this past year so, she knows, Mama always knows something we don't want her to. I soak in every moment we have left, bored to death in a doctor's office, pinching pennies to make it work, sitting in a silent room with the dying. Whether at home or on the road, in church or a lonesome hotel room, alive and dead, I carry them all with me. The anger and regret, lonesomeness and solitude, this mystery of my life, is evolving into some sort of organic gratitude. It is real and alive, living and breathing, searching and finding a grace it is dying to share. I've quit trying to figure it out or at least forgiving myself when I forget and attempt to. Grace needs no invitation. It's always there, readily available in every moment. Watching over us, walking with us. This, I accept, as amazing. Yet each November, just to be sure, I still, look around the room and see everything that counts."

KENNEDYS, CONUNDRUMS
& COLD CO-COLAS

Mama and Daddy met by accident in a Wilson, North Carolina shoe store where Daddy was working as a salesman. Two years later they accidentally saw each other again for the first time since. They dated ten days and got married on Thanksgiving Day, 1950, as all wise "love at first sight" newlyweds should do. Just in time for Daddy to ship off to the Army. The budding military career of Private M.E. Brown was cut short by a fifty-five gallon barrel full of oil falling off the back of a transport truck and nearly breaking his back while he was smoking a cigarette with the boys.

Once he returned home, it wasn't long before they departed the mecca/world capital of tobacco, Wilson and headed back to the farm. Back full circle once again, to care for an aging Granddaddy and for Daddy to take up the family tradition of farming the back forty. They had cleared extra land a few years before, so the farm now offered extra fields for growing cotton and corn in addition to their tobacco allotment. Mama and Daddy moved back into the old farm house where Daddy was born, complete with chickens in the front yard and hogs in the back. The old black and white photographs tell it all. They were tough, resilient and determined to make better with whatever they had earned, were given or blessed with. They were dreaming of babies, strong and healthy, of giving them all they had not received as children.

The next timely death was Ole Dent, Mama's Daddy. My brother Glenn was born January 2, 1955 and the following year "Oh Death" even came for the mean Old Man. Once again, the only thing I ever heard my mother say about him was, "Take me to his grave and I'll squat and piss on it." Mama said it so many times, with a certain "don"t ask-don't tell" conviction, I often wonder if she didn't actually lift that skirt a time or two and make water. The fading pictures taken at the revolving Stallings home place, post Dent-burial, show Mama and her nine siblings all smiling, not a grieving face anywhere in sight, as my brother Glenn, a waddling baby, prances around in one of those ridiculous 1950's outfits they far too often made children of the day wear. Lil blue shorts, mini jacket and some sort of tie-on cap that looks more like a bonnet than a hat any little feller should be wearing. And boy was he a fat baby!

So Mama's Daddy was dead, that was that and it was back to our fam-ily farm after what I'm sure was a classic Carolina funeral spread. Granny would move in with different children for a while until she finally wound up in Goldsboro with Aunt Louise, where she would stay until the age of eighty-two, when she entered a smelly rest home, ticked off because her Peach-Snuff was taken away but just in time for the great "Praise The Lord" scandal featuring Jim and Tammie Faye Baker. When that story broke Granny said from the bed, "I tole you young'uns that man was up to no good. Air conditioned doghouse!" Maybe that's why she'd finally ceased sending him her Social Security money a few years earlier. She always was a Billy Graham woman.

The Brown clan got stir-crazy evidently in the old small farm house because before long they moved into a larger house at the crossroads owned by Uncle Les. There would be enough room for another child and for Granddaddy to pretty much stay drunk and in the way. Daddy got his Social Security check arranged at sixty-five and started taking them to the bank and cashing them for him. After cashing the first few checks, Daddy brazenly informed the old man, "I'll get your checks cashed but Daddy, the drinking is over." It had taken a toll on everyone's nerves and my parents had had enough. Grandaddy put the liquor down cold turkey.

John F Kennedy was elected and, like many young folks was my brother's hero. Glenn was equally enamored with anything to do with the Navy or Coast Guard because of Uncle Henry being a navigator stationed at Governor's Island off Manhattan, and Brother quickly evolved into a brilliant student. Our Aunt Mary Vail and Aunt Helen Edmundson, both school teachers, didn't believe Glenn could read and write and had yet to start school. Once they saw it with their own eyes and spent some time questioning him, the genius of my Brother was born. He was started in school early and raised an additional grade by Christmas. They even tried to raise him another grade at Christmas but Mama said "No."

I recall his school story of being told about the assassination and being sent home early. I'm sure it truly was a terrifying time, especially given the Cold War, the bomb drills at school, and the fact that anybody would actually even think of murdering the President of the United States as he sat beside his beautiful, elegant wife. And someone else would have the audacity to murder his accused on live national television while they buried him! As if to ease my brother's pain a little, exactly one year to the day, on the first anniversary of Kennedy's death, you guessed it, I was born, November 22, 1964, and named John Christopher Brown, after my Great-Granddaddy on Mama's side. Thus began my life as "Chris." That is with the exception of being Daddy's "Rooster." Oh, and "Crisco" to Uncle Ross.

There were two significant things I heard over and over growing up regarding my birth from Mama. "The Immaculate Conception of Edmundson's Crossroads" facts concerning me would be saved for another dramatic southern day far in the future. Mama said the day she brought me home from the hospital, Glenn ran in the door from school, walked up to my crib, and looked down upon my cooing face. Maybe it was what big brothers do, or should do. Or maybe it was coincidence. Perhaps some ass whipping's had already started.

Mama soon walked into the nursery, and Glenn wheeled around, looking over his shoulder, deep into Mama's eyes, and announced, "He's mine," and then walked out. And I was. I would be until he drew his last breath. I am still, my Brother's son. We belonged to each other. Brother wasn't just a title for us. It was our sacred, non-negotiable never-ending bond.

By the time I was born, Mama had been married to Daddy for over a decade, my brother Glenn was already ten, Granddaddy was getting sober. By the time I reached the age of remembrance, I had one Grandparent left living. And she would become another of the salvation saints in my young life. Mama's mother, my Granny was firmly established as our matriarchal saint. I am not being facetious. Granny was a saint long before she left this sorry-ass, beautiful world. And a young kind beautiful black woman named Magalene had shown up to be my sanctuary from a not so distant grumbling of a storm, a' coming up. I was but five months of age and Magalene, maybe eighteen years old when she first took me in her arms. My earliest memories as a child are almost all of being with her and being smothered with kindness, love and the best chocolate pies that ever graced any table.

I don't remember our first house, the one at the crossroads that belonged to Uncle Les. Brother lived most of his childhood there and I loved seeing the twinkle in Glenn's eyes when Granddaddy's name came up. Invariably the story came up how Glenn would be sent to Uncle Burrell's store on his bike each month when Granddaddy's Social Security check came in to fetch him some "cold Coca-Colas." Glenn was always awarded one. I cherish the vivid memories from that period for life seemed so stable, authentic, and innocent. I mean we hadn't even landed on the moon yet! I guess the past always does looking through someone else's eyes and looking back we seem to always find a way to forgive. The past is always the safest place and requires little courage, till you start digging up unmarked graves and letting family skeletons slip out of the closet.

Like the tide of the sea, it is only family that draws us back home, to ourselves, time and time again. For better and worse, till death do us part. July of 1967 came and it was time to move into our new house. Everything seemed promising, least from the outside, we were "moving on up" into *"Good Times,"* and though the possibility is always with us, another death was surely not on our minds. That's when they usually come.

"Well, Shoog, you know we're never ready."

God I hate a cliché. Apparently death don't pay 'em no mind either.

Buck Meadow Branch
March 1968

"**G**od Dammitt! Say it. Say 'Yes Sir!'"
I saw it with my own two eyes. I wasn't scared until my brothers' met mine. I suppose in some way Glenn took it for the both of us. Perhaps that's why the ass whippings got worse over the years. Being ten years younger, let's just say a lot can go over a little fellow's head at three or four. All I know is this. You don't piss Daddy off unless you have a burning desire to get the living shit beat out of you. I did not have that desire, not that particular one. Thus, an Angel was born. Even involved that Immaculate Conception, I mentioned earlier, so says Mama. Let's put that "piece of pie" up for later. I promise we'll get back to it.

I never forgot it. Not that first beating, hand delivered to my Brother. I never thought about forgiving Daddy either. I don't need to. A survivor doesn't seek forgiveness and a son always knows his place. For I now know the baggage he's carried was simply passed down to him with a mule strap. Guilt is one thing; shame is another. Guilt will wear you down, but shame smothers a man one day at a time, slowly killing him, without regard for dignity. When you dig for the truth, the whole truth, be mighty careful. No telling what you'll find. And by the way, in case you've slipped of into stupid or self-righteousness and got the wrong idea already, my Daddy was a good man.

A damn good man.

MAGALENE, MUSIC AND MAYHEM

I was three and half when we built our ranch style paradise on the family farm. When I saw Daddy whip Glenn's ass as we say 'round home, for a "fair ye well," the first time. When I learned, being an Angel might serve my own "flat ass" well in the long run. Grandaddy had died the previous July, yet Buck Meadow Branch was alive with the sights, sounds and success of winning two world wars and getting out of a mired-up and muddy mess in Korea. The fragrance and friendship of a southern farm evolving from the era of mule and plow into the smell of gasoline, diesel, and kerosene fueled this little boy's thrilling fascination with huge new red tractors and a growing work force that felt much more like family than laborers.

Our yearly garden grew large enough to account for Mama's siblings' families, so each year we came together for several days to a week to can tomatoes and put-up corn. To provide fresh vegetables for all of us through the coming year. And us children would sit and listen to the grownups tell magnificent stories about their shitty childhoods and how spoiled we all were. How the only toys Daddy ever had were "a tricycle with two wheels and a corn cob doll." And a good Christmas for Mama's clan meant extra sugar and maybe even a piece or two of hard rock candy for the little ones.

Our personal little family unit, my parents, my brother and I, seemed tight as a tick to this clueless little fellow. Daddy and Mama seemed intent on working their ever loving butts off to provide "a better life than they had" for us and remind of us it nearly daily. To keep us from getting "above our raising." The southern guilt trip was thrown in for free. For tradition and effect. And we *were* blessed. Daddy was content to raise bird dogs on the side and quail and deer hunt with his first cousin/best friend Uncle

Harold as often as possible. Mama was delighted in our local church, Antioch Original Free-Will Baptist, singing in the choir and sneaking in as much bridge as she could, far away from the frowning of her country congregation and the sins of cards. Sallie Mae was a master bridge player. And she would be for the next four-plus decades, right up till the afternoon she died. Seriously. Last thing my Mama did in this world was play bridge, thank the nurses, tell a joke and die.

Magalene was all mine and I all hers. She was the one that taught me each day about life and love. Who dressed my skint knees, saved me from the mighty fire-breathing dragon known as the "Evil Older Brother." Whose skirt I ran to for shelter as well as confessions. She protected me like I was her first born. I could not know then that she was already watching over me for the growing storm forming on the horizon. Magalene loved me, completely, without agenda, simply because I was there for her to love.

As far back as I can remember, Glenn and Daddy were at odds. Daddy loved Glenn the way a southern man loves his first born son. It is a special bond: that child that will carry a man's Christian name on into the future, as well as his faults. He loves him "to death." I don't know the why of the first ass-whippings. I only know they scared my little brain into "being good." I do know now, by the time Glenn was fourteen or so, he was starting to experiment with drugs. He also would go out of his way to antagonize and piss Ed Brown off at any and every opportunity, and it would be a lifetime thrill and weapon of choice for him. It was like he just couldn't help himself. Or maybe he could but he simply chose not to in later years. Most likely some of both.

As I said, I was around three-and-a-half when I witnessed Glenn take that first beating. I doubt somehow it was his first. Playing in the den, I kept hearing sounds coming from the back of the house. My curiosity, sufficiently aroused at some point, I began to ease down the dark corridor of our hallway, hanging as close to the wall as possible. I could hear funny sounds I'd never heard before, punchy, slapping sounds and an occasional short groan at the very end of some of them. Whatever had happened, once resolved, Glenn forgot to say, "Yes Sir," as Daddy left the room. Then like a proper angry protester he simply refused. Unforgivable in Ed Brown's book. There existed no such response as a "Yeah" from a child at any age. It was an extreme non-negotiable respect issue. Both of self and others and would remain that way for his lifetime. One that was encased in his spirit.

Apparently Daddy decided he would force Glenn to say, "Yes sir," and Glenn decided, "The hell you will. Make me!" So the fight they were well into was reaching a climax by the time the sounds fell across my ears in that den down the hall. I remember crystal-clear still, easing my way down the hall like I was the Cowardly Lion without Dorothy and gang in tow. Finally getting to my brother's bedroom I froze. By then I could not only hear but experience our Daddy's anger. Reaching the corner of the doorframe of his room, scared to death to peek around the corner, I finally got the nerve and did. Just as Daddy said, "Goddamnit! Say it! Say "Yes Sir!'"

My brother's eyes met mine, and somehow he got across to me instantly, "Get the hell out of here before he sees you." It was the very first time I felt my brother's guardian spirit. From that moment on, I played the part of the angel as best I could. Perhaps unconsciously, out of fear, I don't know. But I played it well and purposefully as time passed. And for the record, my Brother never did say "Yes sir," even though Daddy punched, slapped and beat his face into some sort of left-over, spoiled southern casserole. Spoil the rod, or fist that is, and by God, you might spoil the child. Won't no room for spoiled children round here. I can still hear Daddy say, "Hush that crying for I give you something to cry about."

Our Daddy was raised with a leather mule strap by his Daddy, without a mother from age six onward. He could be a hard case back then but he was also intensely sweet, especially to small children. He was loyal and deeply dedicated to providing for his family. He was merely a victim himself of the time honored, sacred, southern, bullshit "Christian" duty of tearing up any child's ass that does get "out of line," far beyond all reasonable limits. Anyway, by the time I was approaching ten I was already exhibiting these signs of a frightened child holding his act together for everyone. Holding it together because you have to and frankly you know no other way. Because that hurts less than letting anything else but "love" live inside.

When Glenn and Daddy would go at it, it was as if Glenn held a power over Daddy on the soul level. As if he was saying, "Come on, tear my ass up! But you cannot touch the heart or spirit of who I am." And Daddy would whip the same way, because I imagine as a child, that's exactly how he was whipped too and was probably thinking the very, same, damn thing as a youngun' with his Daddy. I will always wish that it were true, for both of them. That no damage was done. But as they say about even a dog, one that's beat that one time to many, it's bound to show.

There's a reason, a "good one," why I know Daddy was beat with a mule strap. Besides hearing endless first hand accounts from aging family folks that were around back then, I also learned from the horse's mouth. When I was around eight or nine, Daddy decided to move our family garden to the back yard of that old farmhouse he was born in, up in the field. I was with him when he first started plowing, turning the land, to see if it was even possible with the deep roots of those pecan trees, his Mama planted back in '33, already spread like the family tree. I was all about some "Cowboys and Indians." Especially the Indian part. At some point Daddy finally messed around and broke one of the outside disc blades. I began my duties as "Raider of the Lost Country Crap" and starting walking over the freshly churned, dark earth, moist with life, picking up huge earthworms and anything else that moved, stuck up or out. At some point I found part of an old lil box disintegrating back into the earth, with its broken corner sticking up out of the ground. I began to dig like a beaver on a beech tree, until I got inside to what was left of it and felt something rough, and soft. Something old and brown. It was leather so it MUST have been left by some very cool Indians just for me to find that fine day. I began shouting, " Daddy look what I found! This is Indian Stuff. Look Daddy!"

Daddy finally walked up to my left side to appease me, saying out loud, "Yeah son. I know. Show Daddy what ya found," but his mind was immersed in that broken blade and tractor. Losing time was losing money. You were either making it or spending it. Down on my hands and knees, thrilled with excitement, fingernails black from digging, I looked up to see Daddy standing there with his hands on his hips, thinking hard.

"Show Daddy what cha got, Rooster."

I began pulling on the leather about an inch or so wide and it seemed to just keep coming.

"Look Daddy. This is Indian Stuff!"

I'll never, ever forget. Daddy replied, in a new darker but protective tone, "Leave that be son. It ain't Indian Treasure."

"Yes it is!"

"No, it ain't. Leave it be, now."

"Why Daddy?"

"Because damnit, I said so."

Deeply puzzled and amazed at just how much ancient Indian knowledge my Daddy had been keeping to himself, I ceased digging, looked up to my towering father and said, "How do you know Daddy?"

"Because it's a mule strap. I put it there when I was not much older than you."

One more "Why Daddy?"

I looked back up, through the breeze blowing through those old pecans, the sun rays showering down through the deep green leaves and gray bark until they shadowed the edge of my Daddy's strong face, feeling his protection as he towered above me. That's when I saw my Daddy cry for the first time.

There was a huge tear rolling down his left cheek, smearing the dust of what we had just uncovered, where another had already fallen. And as Daddy stared way off into the late 1930's he sweetly, softly said, "So my Daddy wouldn't beat me with it no more. Leave it be son. Just leave it be."

"How come?"

"Because son, sometimes, we have to leave buried things, alone. C'mon, let's go see Uncle Burrell and get us a cold Co-Cola and some peanuts! Want to?"

Glenn graduated from high school when he was just barely sixteen having been put ahead in school upon first starting. He was the prodigy of our Uncle Oddo, a World War II Marine veteran born on Nantucket Island, who lived in a misery of retirement from illnesses and ailments courtesy of his service in radioactive Japan. For years he had made Glenn look up everything he was taught in school, outside sources only, away from textbooks, and prove to himself what he was being taught was the truth. To question things and never accept hearsay. He literally showed my Brother the magnificence and wonder of his own mind and taught him to not merely enjoy it but how to embrace it. Over the years Glenn truly became an intellectual genius and for the rest of his life, everything he read, saw, any information that came into his knowledge, became data that could be recalled in an instant. I would grow to love Glenn's mind like I loved him. It became my own personal mobile Smithsonian complete with the hippest tour guide ever and free admssion. All I ever had to do was ask. And listen.

My extracurricular education with Uncle Oddo however was very brief. One afternoon I ran into his and Aunt Elsie's house, back behind Granny's.

"What'd ya learn in school today there buddy?"

"We learned about Joan of Arc."

"Ya know, Joan of Arc and Florence Nightingale were the same person."

"No Sir. They were not."

"Well smart-ass, how do you know? Prove it to me," as he slid a brand new Farmer's Almanac to the edge of that little table, till it was hanging off the edge dangling above my eyes, like a treat just out of reach.

"I don't have to. I already know it."

Too tired, old and sick by now to mess with it, Uncle Oddo took a nice drag on that Raleigh cigarette and replied, "the hell with you then," and went back to the Nightly News with David Brinkley and slipping in some Schlitz Malt Liquor before Aunt Elsie got home. I did notice though, I swear I did, that daily body count coming out of Vietnam always made him mighty quiet. And sad as all hell. There it was even then, the fog of the Cloud of Death.

Being the first born, when Glenn turned sixteen, Daddy bought him a brand new blue Chevrolet Malibu with a white leather top. He had it all now. The good looks, the intellect, the sarcasm and finally the sweet ride. Complete with the latest eight track tape player, Brother need not be reminded daily how cool he was. He knew it, loved it and wore it on his sleeve. To this day, the girls still say, "He was gorgeous." He wasn't one of the "Dudes." He was "Dude." Glenn drove like a bat out of hell every chance he got. I remember once, upon picking me up from little league baseball practice, high as a kite, he stopped at the service station in Eureka,

I thought to get gas. It was for M&M Peanuts for the Munchies. Upon leaving, Brother floored it, proceeded to play chicken with a two ton loaded corn truck only to drive off the road on their side and go around the truck! I was thrilled at the sense of danger and the all-knowing wisdom I had at nine years old that my Brother always knew what he was doing and could pull anything off! He was a gentle, wild, magical mystery in my eyes. And the coolest hippie that ever "hippied."

The other best part of this time, was Brother and his drums. Glenn had started playing drums and hung around for the forming of the first hippie band 'round home, Hip Pocket, with best friend Dennis Head and Jeff Grimes, both world class musicians. His love of music was to this day the deepest connection I have ever known anyone to have, bar none. Music was deeply spiritual to Glenn. I got my own first marching snare for Christmas around age three to satiate me. Glenn would do the cute "Hey, look at my little brother trying to play," thing, but by the time I was five he couldn't keep me off of his drum-set when he wasn't around. This one small lack of control was titanic for Brother. I soon learned to practice and play, with Magalene my steady lookout, when Brother wasn't around. First sign of a red Farmall tractor or Brother, and I was off the drums, the sticks back in their place. Each time I pulled it off Glenn would walk in the door, see me sitting innocently in Daddy's recliner and just stop, stare at me and disgustingly say, "Uh-huh." As Glenn departed for college, one afternoon, he opened my bedroom door, looked at me and said, "The drum set's yours." Like it was a biblical directive from the Apostle Paul or something. I vividly remember the intense understanding that a real gift had been given to me, instilled in me, and it was in fact, sacred. Over the coming years, Brother and I would forever be bound by our music and communicate through it as long as he lived. I found out later my cousin Teresa had been in the kitchen with Mama one earlier Saturday afternoon when Glenn stopped by on the tractor to take a break. He would often go straight to the drum set and play a few seconds, and then go his way. Then one particular day, as another drum fill ended, Teresa said, "Gosh Aunt Sallie, Glenn's getting good!"

Mama replied, "that wasn't Glenn. It was Chris," right about the time my brother entered from the hallway. Many, many years later, in Nashville,

Tennessee, I would ask my Brother why he gave me those drums at such an early age, and pushed me as hard as he did over the coming decades. And he would give me an answer that had never crossed my mind. "'Cause I knew by the time you were five or six you had that something I didn't, and I knew I was suppose to push you." What a Gift of a Brother.

In the fall of 1972, Glenn exited for Burlington and Elon College, leaving me at home, all six years of me, with Ed and Sallie. There were some moments of childhood magic left to experience. The long weekends when our farm was *the* place to be. My parents seemed to be the odds on favorites when it came to my cousins and they all jumped at the chance, any chance to come spend the weekend at "Uncle Ed and Aunt Sallie's!" It was a living, breathing southern sitcom. And of course there was always church. Sunday morning and evening, Wednesday Night Prayer meeting and choir practice, Ladies Auxilary and a revival either coming or going. Vacation Bible School, Christmas and Easter Sunrise services. Our lives revolved around the church. If you weren't at church, somebody was soon looking for you or witnessing to you. If you were nowhere to be found, then you must be "up to no good" and the gossip train would crank up and get running full steam ahead.

Glenn rarely came home from college, and when he did he would do everything he could to avoid any and all interaction with our parents that was humanly possible. And he was great at it. He was a whisper here, a shadow there, until it was just me. He always brought a stack of albums and would check off the songs on the back I was to learn on drums, and he was deeply serious each time. He was also usually high. And I mean high. I would learn decades later, on his death bed, his high school nickname had been "Fog." It kinda pissed me off to hear it as the unexpected, uninvited truth we already know but don't wanna accept, so often does. But the truth is what it is, whether we like it or not. It's all in how you take it.

I never ever saw my Daddy raise his hand to my mother. Ever. Never even an attempt to do so. And believe you me, Sallie Mae pushed every button that man ever had, daily, twice on Sundays, and Ed Brown did the same to her. Mama always said she would kill him if he did. Who knows. As time went by Daddy seem to highly favor the phrase, "God-Damnit

Sallie!" There were many times I thought, here it goes! Never happened. She was every bit as tough as Ed at least as stubborn, possibly even more. Those lessons ole Dent had taught her growing up were now coming in handy for her as a wife, and I starting wondering if Mama was out and about sometimes secretly squatting, you know, on someone special's grave, taking herself a leak in his honor. They were in fact, professional arguers. The best, ever. And Daddy and Glenn were forever at each others throats. If one was in a room and the other entered the tension would swim over you like the heat flames rolling off a used pickup truck out on the blacktop in late July. Many years later I would finally uncover the weird concoction of affection my Brother had for our mother. A deep love and respect, simmering with a distant, dismal disdain. And why.

Glenn entered college barely as a sixteen year old, but by the time he graduated, he seemed to have aged ten years and to have disappeared from my life, except for the very occasional drum set lesson as he rolled his pot seeds out over the *Live At the Fillmore* album. The hole left by Glenn's absence seemed to shine much more light on me than I remotely felt comfortable enduring. I suppose my parents did what all unhappy people do. Try and fake it as long as you can till you figure out why you are miserable and how to not be anymore. Magalene remained my Rock of Ages. The canyon between my parents eroded with an increasing urgency, as my child's mind sensed "something is wrong" and of course it must be, "my fault." Hence the little Savior complex was methodically instilled in me. Daddy seemed to always be working late, hunting late, working on a broke tractor late, doing anything late as possible to avoid coming home. Mama lurched at Sundays and Wednesday night choir practice and Ladies Auxiliary meetings like a smoker trying to quit leaps to a cigarette. Her ultimate escape was her beloved bridge games, with sisters and close friends, as we spent more and more time with her family in Goldsboro, particularly at Aunt Louise's and Granny's. I can still hear that gray, granite gravel popping underneath her Bonneville when Mama would fly the coup.

When it came time for me to start school, my parents had done what so many self-respecting, middle age white people did back then. Sent me to an all white, Christian, private school. Of course, it couldn't legally be all white but trust me, of course it surely was. Annoyingly so. Due to my late birthday and special tutoring by Brother and cousin Teresa, I too would start school early. They tried to move me up the same year, and I vividly recall my brother leaning against our new obnoxious, but oh-so-cool for the times, '70's orange counter top, not pleading but informing my parents they were about to ruin my very life. He spoke like I was his because I was.

I hated Goldsboro Christian School. Oh I excelled from the start. But hate it I did. Keep in my mind my older brother was now a sixteen-year-old full-fledged gorgeous hippie screaming down the road of my mind in that sharp-as-a-whistle blue Malibu with the white leather top.

The saving grace for me was my first grade teacher, Mrs. Lucas. Oh... my...God! We were in love the moment our eyes met. Well, I was. Swept off my feet. She was gorgeous, smoking hot and sweet. Of course she adored me, how could she not, with all the fresh picked roses and apples I would frequently bring to suck up to her. She is the first woman I ever *fell* in love with. My entire first grade year is like a Diane Lane love story with this sneaky little fellow, a mini-Richard Gere, a hidden forbidden love, unpredictable, outrageous, but meant to be. Each day, every day, all day, in her classroom, I envisioned my self cuddled up, nestled if you will, amongst the safety of her breasts as I conquered cursive and basic preferred social skills as accepted by sound Baptist doctrine. Advanced for first grade, huh? So I attended and excelled, as I thoroughly abhorred the additional rigidity of the school. My one saving grace was returning home each day to the recluse of my drum set, my hippie brother and the best albums of the hippie period.

Just like my brother I was raised in that country church a few miles from our home. Our pastor was so far above it's pay grade it was beyond funny. Mr. RL Ennis had been President of the Free Will Baptist College in Nashville, Tennessee from 1943-1949. Back when Bear Bryant rented a room upstairs while he was an assistant coach at Vanderbilt. Now, many decades later, Mr. Ennis was nearing the end of his life. He was truly a wise sage. He was far past the need for accomplishment and stature that all men needlessly place upon themselves to "be a man." The only reason he was our preacher was we needed one and he happened to be available. Every third Sunday he helped another smaller church so we went to Parker's BBQ over in Wilson! I loved church. I mean I loved church. Because, I loved Mr. Ennis. After Uncle Les and Uncle Burrell, he was my third strong grandfather figure. His sermons, the Word flowing off his tongue like fragrance from a honeysuckle vine caught in a casual but self-assured summer breeze, this is where I first fell in love with the spoken word and the sheer power of language. And the Gospel Truth. I would sit on the front row every Sunday, all by myself, until the weekend he pointed out to the adult congregation, if he could get them to pay attention like I did, we'd all be getting somewhere. I was simply staring at him, lost in the strength and mystery of his cadence, likely having no true understanding of what he was talking about, except I knew, deep down inside, this was authentic and important. Once I realized the spotlight was on me, that was all she wrote. I went straight to the back row, playing the part of the shy angel with hidden horns, sitting beside my older, smoking hot, female cousin, Barney. Mr. Ennis would often say he regretted scaring me. I thought God Almighty himself had sent Mr. Ennis to point out to the entire church what a complete worthless sack of crap I was. But I loved him, deeply, till the day he died. I still do.

MOJOS, MUSHROOMS, and a man named JESUS

Now, for the Free-Will Baptist white boy, the first altar call is maybe the first defining moment towards manhood. Well, other than the moment in my Aunt's bathroom while "dookie-ing," when I discovered not only my Uncle's Playboy hidden inside the Field & Stream; but the fact that it wasn't a stick pony's head rising between my legs. No Sir, that was My Mojo. Rising! MY MOJO! My very own Pee-Pee-er! That thang rose right on, all the way up, on its own. I will always think the smirk on Granny's face, when, some hour later I emerged from the bathroom, was proof positive she knew what I had discovered. The meaning of this life. Maybe it was that titillating tipping point of guilt that sent me down to my first altar call.

The altar call. This sacred act defines us. It is that moment when you either feel the conviction of the Holy Spirit, or go "down to the river" cause your cousin Jimmy did. (*I was a little younger. I thought it was the coolest thing ever when he went "swimming with the preacher" at Victory Baptist the year before.*) Or it's the first time you understand and publicly acknowledge that you're a piece of crap that is not only redeemable but have already been bought and paid for, by the blood of Jesus Christ. In other words, you're kinda like one of those old-school, glass soda bottles. You have a deposit that has been placed on your life. You're redeemable. It's up to you to return it to the store and claim it's value. "Once saved, always saved." That's what we believe. I like that. It takes a little heat off your backside and gives you some breathing room. But it does not give you the right to live like you've got a free pass from the Hell-Bent Highway Patrol.

So, while I was enthralled with older girl's behinds and anything else I could see, I was falling much more deeply in love with this experience and man named Jesus. It was that one "something," bigger than myself, that was missing in my soul. A mysterious truth a child understands but cannot put into any words. And doesn't need to. Because of faith. And at the age of nine, I made my first trip to the altar and whispered in Mr. Ennis' old hairy ears, I had accepted Jesus into my great big, open heart. And I was not just sorry, I felt really guilty for all the bad stuff I had done as well as all I hadn't had time to yet. The next week we all went to the Billy Graham Crusade at the Charlotte Coliseum, with Mama's sister Marie and her husband Johnny's family. Mama said it was okay if I went down to Mr. Billy's Altar Call, all by myself. Granny was sure to be impressed and approve of my worthiness with an even deeper favor if Mr. Billy gave me one of his green pieces of paper that said "Jesus and me, we're good!" This was back when a parent, a mother mind you, would let her nine year old leave the back of the auditorium and disappear into a sea of people down at the altar. Knowing not a sick soul in sight would bother you. I was fine when I first got down there. Fine when I signed their "Newest Sinners Saved" book. But then, something even sweeter than Jesus himself hit me, hard. Trapped in all that musty body heat of hundreds of strange sinners I'd never met, wailing and wondering if they got it "all right" with God, way down there up in front of Mr. Billy's altar, I spewed about half a dozen or more Hot Krispy Kreme Original Glazed all over those sin stained folks. Me and Uncle Johnny had been tearing through some Hot Original Glazed K & K's! I immediately felt much better! Saved, if you will.

I loved church. In fact Granny made the proclamation when I was a small child that I would be a preacher. That one didn't take. Or maybe it scared me off, who knows. Like Mr. Ennis, oh how I adored my Granny as well. And she did adore me. I got off the school bus almost every day from Kindergarten through the third grade at Aunt Louise's where Granny lived with her. And most of my childhood we seemed to be there a lot of weekends. When I was smaller my parents would go out dancing and I'm sure drinking in the wet county, since of course our's was dry and I would stay at Aunt Louise's. The older I got the more we were there, without Daddy. Always without Daddy. I got so damn tired of hearing "where's your Daddy" I often wanted to reply, "where's *your* Daddy?" I'm like nine, ten years old. Last time, in fact every time I ask Daddy where he's going he says, "going to see a dog about a man, son.'" That is one interesting man and that dog must have had a lot to say, cause Daddy ain't here, y'all! You ask him, when you see him. Just stop asking me. I wanna play!

My fourth grade year I grew my hair out long for the first time like my brother's and attended Eureka Elementary where my Aunt Mollie and Aunt LaDell were teachers. My blond hair, now as long as my parents would allow, meaning "long enough" and me, when wearing an Elon College t-shirt, I was one with Brother. We were hippies. And we did what all good hippies do. We submerged ourselves into the music of the day. Into the depths of the great soul music of the sixties, into this new modern rock-n-roll and of course by the mid-seventies, the sounds of southern rock. "Eat a Peach" was our motto. I disguised myself each day as a sweet polite child, eager to please any and every one, and avoid any pitfalls that might lead to ass whippings, until Brother came home from college. Each trip he would bring another stack of albums for me, complete with instructions on which songs I was to learn. We ran the gamut from jazz to rock, soul to singer-songwriter to southern blues. Thus began my first real years as a musician, with my Brother at the helm as my gratifying guru. Never complimentary, always pushing me, challenging me to be better than I was the day before. It's where I was given not only the immense gift of music but learned the art of listening and it became our private and preferred form of communicating.

It was also around this time frame or shortly after that I was introduced to drugs. No, not the baby stuff. I knew about pot, acid and mushrooms. Lord have Mercy did my Brother LOVE some mushrooms! No Ma'am. This was Heroin. It was one normal Saturday morning and I was watching Fat Albert, far and away my favorite cartoon, if only for the music and Bill Cosby's gentle genius, long before his fall from grace. My brother Glenn rushed into the den along with one of his best friends, whom he then told firmly to go to the car—and wait. Glenn pulled a hardback kitchen chair awkwardly up in front of me as I sat on the couch. Presenting a plastic bag full of a smoky white-brownish powder he told me what it was in the most personal way. Instinctively, I knew what I already felt, that just as Glenn was more than a big brother, I was much more than the baby, at least to him. We were in this thing together, for the long haul. So that Saturday morning, Glenn was sharing more than just a simple knowledge of drugs. He held the bag up in front of me and said, "Do you know what this is?"

Obviously, more interested in Fat Albert's current predicament, I replied, "No."

Brother went on to tell me exactly what it was, why he had it, and that he was scared. If he didn't return to school at Burlington with a lot of cash and zero drugs, his ass was facing severe consequences. He was in over his head, and he chose me at the wise, ripe old age of maybe eight or nine, to be his guardian. He also confessed with the sincerity of a sinner to a priest why he was doing what he was and that I would tote a serious "whooping" if I ever did the same. I was to always go to him for advice, and I did, until the day he entered a toxic coma and could no longer listen or speak. Through his eyes and soul, I understood what was going on and why, and from that day until the August before he died, I was afraid, worried, that I would lose my only brother to drugs, prison, or the sort of death that comes to a troubled soul that can find no solitude, no peace in this world. And I would never share this story with anyone, but once. And even then, only for us.

The next few years rolled by like a blur. I was approaching ten, and my parents were in a landing pattern of turmoil and chaos. All they did was argue. About every freaking thing. About the dumbest shit you can imagine. Even as a child I found myself perplexed at how two adults could have every conversation be a raging southern squall of an argument. If Aunt Marie Lancaster was still here she'd verify it. Wore her out too. And she loved Mama and Daddy. "Son, they never argued about the big stuff, but they argued about every little thing you could imagine." When Aunt Marie said that to me one day at her home a year before she died, I replied, "Aunt Marie, they didn't argue 'bout what matters 'cause they never had time. They were too busy arguing 'bout everything else." One of the endless things I have always loved about both sides of my extended family, why I have such a deep respect for them, is neither side ever stopped loving or trying to love my parents. They may not have understood them. Approved of their actions. But they never stopped loving them, even if they failed to show it sometimes. And we all do that. Can I get an "Amen?"

Mama and Daddy had drifted so far apart, all that was left was a chaotic chasm of one argument after another. With Glenn gone, suppertime was especially fun as we sat in silence. Daddy always seeming to be holding the coming "boiled dinner and cornbread" into a boiling rage just under the stainless steel lid of his cooker, steam leaking out his ears. Mama sitting in stunned silence, always starring deep into her sliced tomatoes or corn pudding, or dead straight ahead at the wall as if the mystery of marriage and motherhood lie hidden inside the heart of a home cooked meal or that dark pine paneling. The best dinners were when Glenn came home and they performed Act Three of "Dinner in Denial" for the evening, a cascade of fake smiles and nonsensical chatter about anything except reality. The kind of talk that people try and pull off but their voice, a few notes to high and fragile, always betrays them.

The Bicentennial Celebration of 1976 came and ended with me playing a drum set solo and "Wipe Out" on a flatbed underneath the great oak tree in the back corner of the baseball field at Eureka, with Mr. Jimmy Head tearing up an electric guitar. And me being "discovered" by a man named Mr. Jimmy Wooten, who walked up to my parents and after introducing himself apparently said, "Your son has a talent he is not aware of yet, can I work with him this summer?"

That summer, Mr. Wooten pushed me through all the music books for junior high and high school in six, thirty-minute lessons. Good thing God had sent another saint because suddenly, it was 1977. And I was headed into the eighth grade at Norwayne Junior High when an atomic bomb detonated between my parents. Home was Ground Zero. I didn't see the flash. Never did hear the boom. But I would damn sure see the mushroom. Feel the fallout. But the thing is, I always, always knew that I was loved. Even nuclear fusion can't kill love. Not real love. Neither can heroin. It might kill you, one day, down the road. Not love. Love endures.

THE BOMB

I wouldn't be worth my weight in a pillar of southern biblical-storytelling salt if I didn't somehow weave this tale into our family "eulogy" and spin it your way. Plus, I bet you don't have one of "these" lying around your nearby swamp. Besides, I can't think of a more appropriate way to introduce one of my Daddy's all-time favorite sayings while I continue to devour acceptable literary "rules of engagement."

Thanks to the Cold War, things got super frigid around the world around this time. Four days after President Kennedy took office, *(three months before the infamous failed Bay of Pigs invasion of Cuba)*, a B-52 Strato-Fortress bomber from the Strategic Air Command, took off on a 24/7 routine Unites States Air Force airborne-alert flight. Some ten hours into the mission it suddenly broke apart and crashed maybe three miles from our farm, the way the crow flies. Oh yeah, it was carrying two Mark-39-K nuclear bombs. As Daddy would often say, "I shit you not."

The plane developed a fuel leak which was noticed during an in flight refueling attempt. It was promptly aborted and they were instructed to fly out over the ocean to dump all but enough fuel to land safely at nearby Seymour Johnson Air Force Base. Never happened. The leak erupted, spilling out some 37,000 gallons of fuel in less than three minutes. The aircraft then broke apart in mid-flight, some of the crew ejected, others simply sucked out of the aircraft, and two mind you, two Mark 39 nuclear bombs hurtled toward our quiet, quaint little neck of the woods. Most everyone was awaken within miles and minutes due to the explosion of the plane

ripping apart and scattering over a five mile radius. Some of the men, teenagers at the time, like Carl Jr.'s daddy, Mr. Carl, were members of the newly
formed Faro Volunteer Fire Department, and fought the massive jet fuel
blaze. Most everybody else was on their knees praying and pleading, cutting last minute deals with their Maker. They thought the Cold War had
come to our cotton fields in a Carolina Red Dawn. I suppose it had.

One of the bombs landed intact, safely in a field, thanks to a deployed
parachute and a nearby tree catching it, and was recovered nudged a mere
eighteen inches in the ground. The other bomb however, disintegrated into
the edge of a nearby field and swamp, burying itself somewhere between
50 to 120 feet in the muddy ground below the Nahunta Swamp water table,
depending on who you believe--take your pick. UNC-Chapel Hill or the
Pentagon.

This second bomb, more importantly, the casing housing the uranium,
to this day, has never been recovered. Of course the Pentagon lied about it
for decades. But thanks to the persistence of many, including Dan Rather,
60 Minutes and some of the original Air Force recovery team, they finally
and slowly spilled the beans. After saying for years the bomb casing would
hold the uranium "indefinitely" they finally admitted, at best in those
swampy conditions, maybe "twelve to twenty five years" was a more reasonable expectation.

If that's not scary enough, the first bomb landed with all but one of the
six arming devices in the fire position. That's what I just said. One safety
switch, ONE, kept a 2.5 megaton nuclear warhead from "stirring up the
swamp" as we might say. Once again, in unison, congregation, stand and
say it with me. "I shit you not."

To this day, we still have a suspiciously high amount of weird, unex-
plainable cancer cases around home. Some say it's the uranium. Who
knows? Least the warheads didn't detonate.

The moral here is, we came mighty damn close to having a new Bay of
North Carolina and none of us being here.* One of those bombs was 250
times more powerful than those used on Hiroshima or Nagasaki. Some
have even said one explosion would have exceeded the detonation of all
ammunition in history. The important fact is it didn't explode. But sixteen

years later, in 1977, a division of atomic proportions did detonate between my parents. And an inescapable mushroom cloud of divorce and denial created a radioactive fallout across all of our lives, an implosion, from the inside out. Cupid's broken arrow found a bullseye in the heart of our family. And something finally flipped "the switch" on this bomb.

*("The Stockholm Institute has called the Goldsboro incident perhaps the single most important example in the published literature of an (nuclear) accident which nearly resulted in a catastrophe.")

1977

The T-total shit truck of all shit trucks hit the fan in 1977 at our place. Out yonder at "Uncle Ed and Aunt Sallie's." It had been a long time coming. Between Grandaddy's passing and this year, we lost mostly the expected ones, the aging. Uncle Burrell and sweet Aunt Bessie departed for Heaven as close to each other as they could. Each time Aunt Bessie would enter the room, blind as blind could be, wearing those eerie darkened green glasses, and her beautiful long white crown pulled back in a Depression-era style, one could tell she still lit up Uncle Burrell's world. And he couldn't hardly see either. She was the light of the room and all he needed to see each day. They were truly so sweet and the definition of precious as well as how to cherish someone. It is where the scripture "love her as Christ loved the church" first made an appearance for me. I'm telling you it was rare for Aunt Bessie to ramble back in the front room of their Waltons-style big farmhouse, and Uncle Burrell not literally rise up out of his own chair, out of the respect only love creates.

Because I do not remember anything about Grandaddy or his funeral back in 1967, Uncle Les had been my first experience with the wonders of a southern funeral. After experiencing my first real funeral with Uncle Les leaving, the next several seemed to be a time of storytelling and reliving the good ole, awesome, crappy days of the depression. "Hoover's Days" they called them. Man did my folks love doing that! My parents spoke so eloquently and fondly of how hard those days were, yet I think they already sensed deep inside, we were gradually losing the most special part of life. Each other. Things were improving. Cars were faster. Everyone had a television. We could watch the President murdered, his killer axed, and keep up with the latest moon shots all live on three networks. God Almighty I miss those days with all the crap on tv now.

So here we were going into 1977. I was eleven years old and though Daddy decided to stop farming for the most part, to give his attention to auctioneering and insurance sales, I still got to work on the farm. My older cousins Carl and Mike Kirby were coming of age as farmers and among the many farms they leased out and tended was ours. I loved it. Loved every single solitary thing about farming. The long hours, the tobacco gum stuck to me like tar and feathers, working hard and together with people you love to accomplish something. Being so tired at quitting time, a good supper and a bath was all she wrote and she wrote it well. I even loved using that hard-ass Lava soap to clean up with as it literally pulled the hairs off my arms!

Daddy and Uncle Harold had been raising bird dogs-English pointers-a few Setters, for many years. They raised them not only to hunt but for sale. We ate wild quail many a night at our table. But now, something seemed amiss somewhere. Mama was growing more and more uptight, suspicious-Daddy angrier and angrier, and from the telephone conversations I "accidentally" overheard I began to pick up a thing or two. Ed and Sallie were not in the best of places.

Around this time our world stopped twice, in one solitary day, to mourn the loss of Elvis the King, and our beloved pastor for the King of Kings, Mr. Ennis, as they went home to be with Jesus the same day. It was also when I began to witness the worst arguments. It took a few years for them to swell and grow, for that hurricane to begin its roar. One of Mama's favorite phrases from this time seemed to be, "Well, piss on it then!" Mama became less and less, soft and spiritual, and more and more bitter and Daddy was what we like to call "ill as all hell," all the time. By now, supper together was in complete silence, if together at all. I can still hear the echo of those damn silver forks hitting our china in a silence so loud you'd think it was gonna bust your eardrums. Before long there was no hiding it. By this time everyone had seen Daddy leave the house pissed-off for God and Country, squall his tires out the driveway, and Mama erupt into tears so many times, it was honestly an expected high point of the weekend's

activities. The tension wasn't merely palpable. It was pathetically preten-
tious. The rare times Daddy did leave, not pissed off, when he was leaving
he'd turn to us children and say "Y'all play pretty and be particular now. Ya
hear?" To this day I'm not quite sure what all that means.

The iconic, straw-breaking argument had already happened a year or
two earlier. An aunt and uncle of mine were visiting from upstate. He was a
very successful contractor, and his personal travel-suitcase/liquor-bar was
proof positive of that here in the quaint, greater Antioch Community. I was
busy entertaining cousins with one request after another on the drum set as
they sang along and danced with the stars. I remember going in the kitchen
several times during breaks in my "performances" and being shooed away.
I noticed particularly my Daddy and Uncle beginning to speak in slow
motion like a 33 1/3 vinyl record being played at the wrong speed.

I was on the drums when I heard the fight explode. All I could hear
was Mama shouting "Ed, Ed! Calm down!" And Daddy going off on my
Uncle for supposedly bragging too much about his success in the presence
of Daddy's deep insecurities. Hell, I don't know what happened. I didn't
really care and still don't. But once again, everyone fled the house leaving
me there with my intoxicated father. Mama was so upset she thought I was
in the back seat with Lisa and the rest of my cousins. She returned ten minutes later to retrieve me, bawling for my forgiveness, and off to Granny's
we went.

There had been a few fights before this one when Mama would leave all
to pieces, that I wound up with Daddy, sitting on the back porch, a Smith
and Wesson 32-Short pistol in his hand. A time or two he even mumbled
something, not to me, just to life, about him being better off... dead. This
night however, once Mama fled and the fight's noise disappeared, I came
out of hiding. I saw my Daddy standing in their bedroom, staring at himself in the bathroom mirror. Except even then, I could tell he was looking
at the part you can't see in any mirror. The inside. Something was haunting
him and driving him crazy. A something he could not live with much longer on this planet.

I rambled up to Daddy's side, feeling totally safe for me, not so much
for him, and softly asked what was wrong, as he slowly but surely came

back to me and the realm of basic sanity. He squatted down and told me he how deeply he loved me and for me not to worry. Everything would be "all right." That's why, to this day, I despise when I am going through some serious crap, for someone to look me in the eye and say it will be "All right." Just tell the truth for God's sake. It may hurt like hell. It might even kill you. It may haunt you for all your days. On the far side of the river Jordan, then and only then will some things be "all right." Made right by God Himself. That's the truth. So just tell it that way. Like it is!

They had built a life for themselves in their ranch home. Complete with a formal dining room and living/music room with crystal chandeliers hanging high above a shiny drum set. We had nice furniture and cars, nice trucks, and tractors. Daddy was spending more and more on the farm yet he wasn't farming. Mama seemed to always be in trouble for spending money. They were not only not in love anymore they honestly couldn't stand the sight of one another or themselves. And the best part was they were both always right. They were born four days apart for Christ's sake. That has to be some sort of astrological, apostolic nightmare. I don't need it explained to me, I lived it. They built a life alright, big enough for some folks but not big enough for themselves and each other. There had been a time they loved each other deeply. I had seen it. There were early days of them still flirting, but those had long since evaporated like the dew off a new tombstone. Their marriage was dead. As a doornail. And this family was the funeral bill.

So, they separated, Daddy moving out, taking all of an uncomfortable five minutes to sit down and explain to me he couldn't explain what was going down, which he couldn't with Mama all up in his, you know, his shit. All I really remember is getting upset and looking at him and he simply wasn't there. Emotionally he had already left. I knew that even then. Of course Mama was one dramatic episode after another of a nervous breakdown. She was an extremely strong woman, but as I would learn from her early in life, sometimes being strong is the very thing that makes you weak. In fact, your own strength can and will kill you, if that's all you lean on. Trust me. You're gonna need a lot more. Your definitely gonna need "each other." And especially... God.

Let me make it as simple and painless for you as possible, for I promise you, they complicated the hell out of the simple act of divorce. Shortest version is, while they were divorced by 1978, the actual divorce settlement would take the better part of ten years. I said, TEN years. Even I knew how ridiculous this was by year three. The mushroom cloud first rose to the heavens when I was ten and the ceremony, the end of the service if you will, wasn't over until two months before my twentieth birthday. It consumed all of us. Except for my Brother. Glenn was always off doing his own thing, consuming whatever he must to bear the pain consuming him. And one day, that would get him. At least the physical, earthly part of him. As well as a part of us. Pain is always a circle. You never hurt alone.

Our mother got it in her head, due to certain activities of our father leading up to the divorce, that she should not only be entitled to alimony and child support, but to half of Daddy's farm as well. That's right. His Mama's farm. The one he inherited at six years old. Not only would that never happen in eastern North Carolina but they would thoroughly successfully piss away the farm and it's value, by remaining in court all those years. And spend the better part of twenty years blaming one another but never once saying one word about what "they" could have each done. It is a damn shame. But thank God it's "dead and done with." Over and buried amongst my emotional unmarked graves. Not everything you mourn the loss of deserves a headstone. Some deaths are a welcomed relief.

Once they were separated and through the first hearing, it was obvious we would go to trial. And oh Lord of Israel, what a trial! Even the better part of the Greater Antioch Free Will Baptist Community would get swallowed up in the mire of it all, and I would take the stand at the age of eleven, right on the heels of our next significant funeral.

They were well into the trial and Mama had to meet with her lawyer early every morning before court: thus I was always in tow. This particular morning he informed her the desired outcome wasn't looking good. In other words Daddy, had done as good if not better job of making Mama look like shit, as she did him. In front of our entire community, all our people and family, my parents made complete asses out of themselves. I was so "proud" of them. I found it interesting that as the trial progressed, the accusations grew more and more outrageous. Daddy now stood accused of multiple affairs over the years and one in particular that was in the here and now. Secretly, tucked away though, I knew a little sumpin'-sumpin'.

Gentlemen, if you are having an affair, don't take your son with you to her house at night and ask the little fellow to sit in the car, under the guise of "Hey Rooster, you wanna go and get a hot fudge sundae at McDonald's? Let's go get us a hot fudge sundae and a cold Co-Cola at McDonald's." That is a quote. I promise you he's gonna see much more than you think. I sure did. Eyes peeled like a hawk. Little boys are curious. Remember, they "pick up quick." And I had never told anyone. Not even my brother. Daddy had dropped by quite a few times with me in the car. What he didn't realize is I had a crystal clear shot through the living room window of what was going down. Plus, Mama had said so much out loud, upon finding receipts in coat pockets and other evidence from Tarboro or Kinston, instead of wherever he was supposed to be, that I already knew what the deal was. Daddy had several "heart attacks" the last few years he was married to Mama. I was there for two of them. Mama scoffed every time that subject came up. This is all I'm gonna say about this. They divorced and he never had another one, until one came to take him from a hospice bed to a heavenly home. Get mad if you want to Mama, but the truth will set us all free! Just saying. They stressed each other out. They stressed themselves out. They STRESSED me out. They bathed and basked in the glory of each argument, trying whole heartedly to out do the last one. To say that something this time that would injure the soul. Neither one was ever wrong. It was amazing. Even all these decades later, I can hear them from my childhood bedroom, going at it like a month of bad reruns on Turner Classics.

My parents even threatened to subpoena who ever wouldn't volunteer to come to trial in support of their Lost Cause. We're talking siblings, first cousins, church members that are your kin folks. They would have subpoenaed God if HE would have come. And there were many, if not most, who stood their ground and refused to take sides. It was a genuine, bonafide, epic southern circus. This is also when I became amazed at how well some Christian folks can bend the truth, lie that is, under oath. So I spilled my beans to Mama's lawyer that morning in the hopes it might help her, if I got on the stand. Mama was dead set against it, but me wanting to be Mama's little man and take care of her, along with her sister and lawyer whittling away at her in my support, she finally gave in. It was a poor choice to say the least. I didn't know that. At eleven I thought I was a Little Ed Brown. Indestructible.

That day, as I had the entire trial, I sat on a wooden pew with Magalene tightly, lovingly holding my hand. I was equally petrified and dying to get my chance to "tell the truth." Really. Who in the hell puts a kid on the stand? If we had only had GoPros back then. They called me to the stand and the courtroom gasped. I remember that box seat and the Judge like it was yesterday. They swore me in. Her attorney was gentle and kind, loving, protective, being very careful not to upset me, asking only questions about Mama's housekeeping, her normal activities and a basic synopsis from me of the current situation at home versus our "normal" situation of the past. Finally he asked me about the nights in the car and what I had seen. And what I had heard at home and elsewhere.

"Now buddy, yesterday morning, did you tell your mother and I, you had seen some things you had never told anyone, that you wanted to tell us?"

I will always remember looking up into both of my parents eyes, split down the middle, by me in a witness box. They looked like pouting children, who knew they were in trouble, wearing some sort of pathetic lost look on their faces, as I firmly replied, "Yes Sir, I did."

"Would you be okay with telling us about the first night to begin with, how it started, where you were, who you were with and what you saw?"

I could see my Brother in the background, sitting on a pew, leaning forward. He made it more than obvious he was there to protect me and Brother was locked and loaded, ready to go on somebody's ass if this got out of hand.

"Yes Sir, Daddy asked me if I wanted to go to McDonald's for a hot fudge sundae...," and I began retelling that first evening and what I saw from the car. And eventually from outside the car on other visits.

"So son, you are telling us, you were suspicious enough yourself, on other visits to this house, that you actually got out of the car to sneak up outside the window?"

Oh, the look on those faces. Bust-ed!

"Oh Yes Sir. One night Daddy was wearing his burgundy pants and short sleeve white shirt with the blue tie I gave him for Christmas. And she was wearing...," and on I went, proudly describing with the detail of a veteran homicide detective, all I did see through two very young, innocent but clever eyes. When we got to the good part, "So you saw your Daddy, on numerous occasions holding, embracing and kissing a woman that was not your Mama...," that seemed to be enough for their side so Mama's attorney lovingly and abruptly said, "Well thank you for being truthful here today. You are a brave, brave, little man. No more questions, Your Honor."

I was feeling all proud, like I would surely get the gold star on the refridgerator this week for being so smart, detailed and honest, when Daddy's fancy-pants lawyer with the Attitude finally got his turn and did what all good lawyers do. "Interpret the law" with a fresh, new, sweet and sour, lemon-scent approach. Twist the truth. I had squatted and lay a huge divorce turd right in the middle of that courtroom floor for my parents to explain away, and the stench was getting ripe, right about now. Daddy's attorney began to ask the same questions in a completely different way to force the answers he wanted. Problem was, I was a child. And children are the most honest folks on earth. Life is not very gray when you're a child. It's Heaven and Hell, hot water and cold. Chocolate pie or no chocolate pie. Getting your ass whipped or not. A great day or a shitty one. Hot fudge sundae or Daddy kissing Ma-ma-Mia through the window. Children... remember... EVERYTHING! I vividly remember seeing my Uncle Henry leaned up against the back wall, and with the steam I saw slowly coming out his ears and the look in those eyes, I was assured he was there too for added protection.

Daddy's attorney, we'll call him Mr. Foghorn Leghorn the III, arrogantly rose up, hiking those suit britches up, like he was sent there by God Almighty to pull in the reins on this runaway wild family mustang, that somehow got out of the family pen. "Now boy, I say, boy, you says you, ahh, you says you went with your Dadd-ay to get a hawt-fudge-sundae, when he got home from wuk. How do you know your Daddy didn't stop at a cousins house or one of your...," and I lit in to him like a proper little Tom Sawyer is suppose to when it's time to kick a bad man in the shins and upset the apple cart with the truth! I refused to be "told" what to say or how to say it. I refused to add or subtract one single word from my expert witness testimony.

As Mr. Leghorn pushed me to alter my answers I refused to let him bend my little ass over backwards and get me to say something that wasn't true. At one point he asked the Judge to instruct me to just answer yes or no. I instructed the Judge that if he would ask me in the right way I would even be happy to answer, and for this I received glowing attention, smiles and a nice ripple of laughter approval from our homegrown, subpoenaed audience. I appeared to be "cute" to them. It was not however to me, Uncle Henry or my Brother. Finally the Judge was adamant about a "yes or no." As Daddy's lawyer began to badger and bully me, I began to get majorly upset. The kind of upset that is equal parts angry and afraid. The lawyer pressuring me to answer the question, riding a child with the purpose-ful confusion and projected anxiety of a seasoned adult, well, I did what all seasoned eleven year olds who are put on the witness stand, at their par-ents' divorce circus, in front of everybody they love, will likely do. I came unglued. The pressure of me being responsible for "the truth" between my parents began to crack me in half. I kept checking in with my Brother's eyes as he leaned against the wall in the back. I could see the anger flaming his flaring nostrils. I knew there was one person who would get me out of this fix. Cause that's what brothers do.

Just as I erupted into tears, my brother jumped up like a bouncer and made a bee-line for me. In today's world he'd get shot. Multiple times. Simultaneously, the Judge angrily said, and I do quote, "I believe we've all had about enough of this. The child will step down and be tended to." Tended to? Hell-Fire! Tend to them! I didn't start this mess! My brother grabbed me and whisked me into a secluded staircase where my Uncle Henry was the first and only other person who came or was allowed to come. Uncle Henry meant business. I believe he would have stomped both of my parents asses if they had tried to get near me. Those two calmed me down and assured me I had done nothing wrong. It was that very moment, sitting in that courtroom, my parents staring at me, one on each side of the Grand Canyon of No-Love between them, that I believe I was torn. Ripped down the middle, exactly in the middle, between two things I loved dearly. My parents. I always would be, least as long as they lived. I don't find it the least bit funny that there is an empty grave left in our family cemetery, between my parents, for me. I have firmly stated, "I shall not be pulled between them in death as in life." You can cash that damn check at any bank you like.

The best part, was for some reason that day, I had to leave with Daddy. "Thanks Mama." As we got on the elevator, Daddy's attorney stopped the door from closing and said, "Ed, you need to send that boy to Duke! He's a natural born lawyer." I wanted to kick that SOB in his middle-aged Cracker nuts! I swear I thought about it and even lifted my left foot. Later, outside on the courthouse square, on my soul, Daddy looked at me when he had an audience and said, "Daddy forgives you for lying buddy. He understands. They made you do it." Do wahhht! I would have kicked him in the shin AND you-know-where if I had remotely thought I could have escaped a public whipping.

The first trial of Ed and Sallie Mae was a pure cultural phenomena in lil ole Wayne County. The stuff divorce legends are made of. Out in public or back home in our community, I felt an embarrassment that became my Blanket of Shame that the devil lied and said was my personal homemade quilt, and I must wear it every day for the rest of my schooling days. It doesn't take twenty-seven years to admit you despise one another. Or forgive each other.

Let each other go with dignity. They would continue, both parents, to appeal any decision that did not go their way, even some that did but not good enough. From trial to trial, year to year, it flip flopped back and forth. Daddy had to continually borrow money on the farm to pay lawyer fees as my Brother pleaded, fussed, and told them all they were doing was pissing away tomorrow to make up for today. My brother, a part-time bartender at the Country Club even told my parents he as well as other workers had seen and heard their lawyers having dinner together and discussing the case--how to drag it out and make more money. Our family was finally pronounced DOA... dead on arrival. We were a brilliant-bad-sadistic-southern joke.

What had really sent this dying of sorts, over the abysmal edge of child terror, was the sudden, unexpected death of Uncle Harold during all the divorce festivities. He was Daddy's cousin and truest best friend, part of our family and we his. Uncle Harold had gone fishing, alone, down at Pamlico Sound. They found his boat, hours later trolling in a circle with no one in it. Not long afterwards, the Coast Guard discovered him, floating face down, done with the struggle of this life. November 16, 1977. He was forty two.

My entire life was changing before my very eyes and it seemed unwarranted, unfair and wrong. It also seemed way past time. My parents were splitting up; my other favorite "Uncle" was dead, and I stood there in the middle of my uncle's living room, in the shadow of pale yellow lamp light and immense grief, simply astounded that this life could change that fast. I stared at his green recliner, now empty. I clearly understood that Uncle Harold was dead and would not be coming back. My Brother Glenn wasn't there that night. Maybe he was off at school getting high. I was honestly never mad at my Brother for not being around. I respected him for it! Because baby, if I had been that good looking, with a 1972 blue Malibu, damn if you would have been able to find me either.

A few days later as we exited the Antioch Original Free Will Baptist church, with Uncle Harold's body, I cried so hard I could barely see how to walk out of the sanctuary. I cried for everything I loved, Uncle Harold, my cousins, my family, I cried for me. It was my first honest experience with the raw pain, life can suddenly toss in your lap. Once they lowered his casket into the ground, none of us have ever been the same. Life changes us. Purifies us. Losing someone like Uncle Harold you don't get over it. That aching will always be there, the shadow of his absence. I learned that letting go is a lifetime process, and though I may have lost some of my innocence during that period, I experienced my first taste of real life. Always bitter at first. The sweetness comes much more slowly, taking its own sweet time.

The last time I saw Uncle Harold, had been just a few days earlier, at noon on Sunday, when Daddy picked me up from church. As we pulled out Daddy said, "Look son, Uncle Harold's waving at you." I can still see him in his dark pants, white shirt and soft khaki jacket, his left hand up in the air and the biggest smile you've ever seen. I turned around in the seat and waved to him until we turned right at Musgrave's crossroads and he disappeared. I recall feeling like I was never gonna see him again. Whenever I think of him, although it still stings, that smile washes away everything except the truth.

And the truth is, once again, I loved my Uncle Harold, 'cause he first loved me.

My family disintegrated before my very eyes, God Almighty and the whole of Wayne County in 1977. We were officially four individuals just living life. A shattered family. Key word here though is family. God loves that mysterious ways thing. LOVES it! Remember everything in life has its gifts. Bitter slowly became bittersweet. And with every death comes a resurrection. That and some damn fine funeral food.

FRIDAY NIGHT LIGHTS, THE QUEEN OF ENGLAND, AND JUMPING COOTERS

W hile the divorce in practical terms was final the second year, in legal and emotional terms it would dominate our lives for another eight years. In and out of court, more lawyer fees, and always this constant cloud of southern community embarrassment hanging over my head and life. At least in my mind. I would stay by my Mama's side until I was fifteen. Until I literally couldn't take one more dramatic nervous breakdown of hers and Mama threw my clothes out the bedroom window because I had gone to Daddy's to stay for a few days. The important thing here is, I simply didn't know what to do-how to help her-though I desperately wished I could. Daddy on the other hand, though under constant stress, had moved on with his life and was now happily remarried. A repressed anger born of resentment towards my Daddy had slowly began to simmer into a boil with me, fueled on by Mama's constant blaming and blazing bitterness. Where in the hell Brother was, I have no idea, but I was sure glad to see him when he came rolling up.

Daddy was a lifelong deer hunter and kept his hunting dogs out in the old training pens behind the farm house where Mama and I still lived, while he enjoyed a new marital bliss, living in nearby Pikeville. The one thing a Walker deer hound does not know how to do is shut-the-F-up. And Daddy with his booming tobacco auctioneer's voice, was the only voice they'd obey. Remember now, Daddy ain't on the farm. His dogs are but he ain't. A brilliant idea if I do say so myself. One night before one of my high school football games, all hell broke loose. The dogs wouldn't shut up and it was driving Mama literally crazy. She'd open the sliding doors of the bedroom she once shared with my father, and now found herself trapped in, and scream at them. At one point Mama even slung open those doors and started peeling off rounds with a pearl handle .38.

Undefeated, with a critical football game the next night, I finally fell asleep, with play assignments and visions of another victory dancing in my head.

Suddenly Mama burst into my bedroom yelling for me to shut the hounds up! Once again, not only did I know I couldn't, I also knew the more you yelled at them the worse it WAS gonna get. I informed Mama of this simple, scientific fact. Almighty Holy God Himself couldn't get those dogs to shut up. Daddy, and only Daddy could.

Our first-ever-knock-down-drag-out argument ensued, and in a righteous teenage fury I jumped up, put on my jeans and football jersey and drove my car to school and parked. All I wanted was sleep, and anything was better than howling deer hounds, a screaming mother, and pistol shots ringing through the night air and your ears.

The next morning, as I lay sacked out in my car, our football coach and surrogate father, Coach Dave Thomas, banged on my window, demanding I get out. Our custodian Teddy had seen me outside so early and assumed I was drunk in the parking lot at school. Once we wound up in the coaches' office, Coach realized I was sober, as I told him the truth of my night's adventures. After listening, he asked me to step outside his office for just a second. Minutes later he had me return and told me he had just spoken with his wife, whom we all called Mama Pat. I'll never forget what he said next. He looked me square in the eye, married, the father of five on a high school coach's salary and said, "Son, you can come live with us right now or anytime you want and we'll figure something out together. We are here for you. We don't have much but we do have room for you in our lives." I remember my insides screaming, "Hell yes, Coach!" But my mind immediately thought, "I cannot embarrass my parents this way. They would never forgive me." Perhaps the truth was I was afraid I might not ever forgive myself. 'Cause a southerner never runs from his Lost Cause, especially when it's his own family. And this began my deep, abiding love for "my" Coach and Mama Pat. I rarely think, much less talk about them, without shedding a tear. I may not do it in your presence or theirs, but they always fall.

The next day, returning to the farm after school prior to our game, I turned in the back driveway to discover my bedroom window open and my clothes thrown out into the backyard and strewn across the bushes. I was a mixture of furious, hurt, and oddly enough, disappointment in myself. I knew I was the only one Mama could count on, maybe too well, and I had let her down when she needed me most. The moral to the story is, enough stress will make you do everything you said you never would. Mama would never forgive herself for doing that to me. Whenever it would rarely and accidentally come up in conversation through the years, she would break into tears, look me in the eyes and ask me to forgive her again. Most people can't do whatever the hell they want to you and get away with it. Mama can. I knew when she did it she didn't mean it. Mama and me, no matter what "may come," would always be alright. We still are. There's another nail you can drive in this coffin.

High school football literally saved my life. The combination of a great Coach who truly loved all his players, and a team of guys who had been playing and winning championships together since little league gave me an immediate sense of belonging and bonding I desperately needed. I would not have survived my high school years without these guys, and I'm not being poetic. I won't bore you with dramatic tales of shotguns and shells falling out of my lap, when Mama drove up in the yard. But I will tell you those guys, my brothers, would get me to my feet, in more ways than one on many, many occasions including football games and life. And to this day, we are as close as any brothers could and should ever hope to be. We'd all take a bullet for the others, no questions asked. And Coach, is forever our leader. As he told us every day, at literally every practice, "It's a great day to be alive men! Blood running through your veins, lungs pumping air! Let's learn a little about football and a whole lot about life." We did and it has been a moral, emotional and physical compass for all of us our entire lives.

I had made the football team in the seventh grade but had to quit after a few games to be in court with my parents. Mama literally drove her

Bonneville out on the practice field one day to tell me, in front of my coach and entire team. Quitting a football team is not something any red blooded, southern, American boy ever does. Unless you want to be branded a panzi and trust me, you don't. I knew my truth. I knew I was having to deal with shit no kid should ever have to think about. And no kid could handle. I knew my parents loved me dearly but they were stubborn and self centered. Even I could see they were both blinded by the worst darkness: their own bitterness of their assumed failures. And somewhere inside, they too, were wounded children.

All through junior high, I longed year after year to be part of the football team. Daddy wouldn't have it. I needed to "learn how to farm like your Brother did." My musical career had blossomed in school, and band concerts made me an instant celebrity, if only for a week yet I longed to play football with my friends. Finally, thank God, I made it to high school and the tenth grade. And I made up my mind, sitting there one Friday night with the high school band, watching and hearing those pads slap across the field, the grunts and hits echoing up in the stands, and I bravely stated, all to myself, "I am playing football next year Daddy, if you beat the living shit out of me." I practiced it. The next day I told Daddy I needed to talk and delivered the same address. Daddy smiled and said, "Well go play football son," like it was the first time I'd asked. Go figure. Parents are so strange.

The summer rolled around and broke into the fall; I made the team. I knew beforehand I would be a few years behind and had made an internal commitment to learn faster than anyone else. The previous four years I had checked out every book I could find at the county library, studying and memorizing Coach Robinson (of the San Diego Chargers) book on mastering fundamentals, among many others. The guys instantly took me under their wings, demanded all I could give plus more, and took the time to help me catch up.

I finally felt a part of something strong and positive, something that mattered deeply, because I was. We were a family. The team went 9-1 my junior year, losing the last game amidst a major controversy that has a bitterness that lingers to this day, least to us. Ask anyone who was there, on either side of the field. It was freaking ridiculous. Kenny scored. Twice if I remember right.

Needless to say, we went into our Senior year with a pissed-off vengeance. We knew in our souls we owed it to Coach and the guys before us to get it done, and we did, game after game, victory after victory. Until banged up and a bit confused, we failed to listen to our Coach, the one who got us there, for one goal-line play, losing the game to Southwest Edgecombe. We were... devastated. We had the whole she-bang in the palm of our hands and blinked. But we kept on keeping on, doing as we had all season and for several years, holding hands in the huddle. Every play. At practice. In games. Offense, defense, special teams--we held each others hands "huddling up." And the beauty of that is, thirty five years later, we still are. And I wish every high school player could have that, but they don't and won't. 'Cause every kid didn't have "Coach."

That same year, visiting football practice at East Carolina University where Coach's oldest son as well as another graduate of our school we looked up to were on the squad, I made another transformation. After being Dave and Don's guest that day, a group of my teammates and I were walking under Ficklen Stadium asking college guys that played our positions questions. I was walking with one of their offensive guards who was called Hound-Dawg, Dirty-Dawg, some kinda dog, when I heard our quarterback, Golden-Boy, another of Coach's sons say, "Look yall. There goes Hound and Lil' Hound. He looks like his little brother." Thus, Hound Brown was born. And believe you me I was ELATED to leave "Chris" as far behind as possible. I became "Hound."

Thanks to high school football, the death of our family took a back seat in my life, except for the severe anxiety I tried to hide and manage every day, any way I could. If not for the distraction and outlet of the game and our team, I honestly don't know how or where I would have wound up. Daddy was happily remarried and stayed busy building another good life with Linda his wife, as Mama continued her self entrapment in the deceitful pool of bitterness. It was as if Aesop had written a fable solely for my mother, a combination of the Fox and the Grapes mixed with the Dog and his Reflection. There comes a time, right or wrong, right AND wrong, where "why," simply does not matter. Especially if it's defining your present and future. You deal with what is or choke on your own bitter grapes while falling through the false reflection of unforgiveness that self-justification silently constructs in the eyes of the heart.

So while our family had passed on, the drawn out "funeral" of the divorce lingered around the family visitation room a few more years. There were deaths, notable ones during this time, including my beloved Uncles Doc and Cap, and Uncle Buck Edmundson. Uncle Buck. Killed a mile or so from the hospital one dark early morning going in for kidney dialysis, by an unlicensed driver/dumbass with his damn headlights off. Damn near killed his son Eddie-Rae too. Still pisses me off. A towering, big man, Uncle Buck was a southern gentle giant in my eyes and I will always remember his brown pinstripe suit, the funeral wreath cut out of styrofoam shaped like a Walker hound and the fox-horn that lay in his hands. What I remember most besides his jet black hair though, is that laugh and the soft spot he and Aunt Helen always held for my Brother and me. For the most part I did what all teenagers do. Ignore their family on the outside while it gnaws and eats them up alive from the inside out. Family deaths were no longer the sentimental, heart warming pageants of a magical childhood but the theft of a secret date up in the cornfield with your girl in a back seat or another Saturday Night Live with the Boys, blown out of the water. They became what death eventually becomes in our lives, a rude interruption and a necessary chore.

I would not be doing my long-winded southern spinster part if I did not share this next tall tale of the truth as well. The funeral of greatest significance I recall during my high school days and first one of such stature I could not attend, was that of our great aunt, Mama Ellen, my grandmother's sister and basically a grandmother to many a cousin. She had raised Uncle Henry, Daddy's brother from an infant. Mama Ellen as everyone called her, was maybe what, four-foot-nine, on a good day. She sat on Coca-Cola crates and a pillow so she could drive herself to church in her gold Electric 225 with the white leather top, which she did successfully well into her high eighties. Each Sunday, Mama Ellen sat in the same spot in the Amen corner, reserved for our aging Saints. Every child was drawn to her sweet spirit and firm discipline.

From the time of my first funeral until now, we brought the bodies home first, casketed, for a wake-visitation in the home and usually laid out in a living room, den or even a converted garage. I was the last of that final generation who reveled in doing this. Mama Ellen was the last of her generation to be brought home. And what a southern scene it was.

I was not there but every soul I have ever heard tell the story tells it basically the same. Mama Ellen, was lying in repose in her formal living room, the family forming a circle as the preacher called all into a final prayer before moving the body to the church. All eyes were closed, except for those of my Brother and all the other smart-ass, older male cousins, who were being cool and standing in the back with him. One of our family members had a lifetime struggle with severe mental illness. Her loving husband stayed devoted to her, keeping her home with him, doing whatever it took, caring for her till the day she died. But this day she somehow escaped the watchful eye assigned to her and made her way to the front standing with the preacher and the casket.

As the reverend ended his prayer, she raised her hands up in the air and declared with a yell.

"The Queen of England, the Queen of England! Here lies the Queen of England!"

Mama Ellen's daughter, our Aunt Mary, was standing behind the boys and pinched one on the ass to stop the snickering, saying, "We will stop this right now, won't we." It was not a request. I guarantee you they all stopped, immediately, most especially my Brother, who was nearly thirty. Mama Ellen, the last of the old generation was gone, along with most of them born before and at the turn of the 20th century. As my high school years began to wrap up, her passing was indeed a clear sign we were nearing the end of an era of original innocence for all of us. And truer words may have never been spoken, for in many ways, she had been, our Queen of England.

Mama Ellen was royalty and to this day still is. Just mention her sweet name and pay attention to the misty eyes in the room.

Speaking of funerals, of true words being spoken over sweet names, there is one that always comes to mind. Mamie Pearl Champion Stallings. Our Granny. Mama's Mama, and the only true grandparent I ever had. She was a meek woman, saintly in appearance and attitude, sweeter than home-made pear preserves. She was all about the Gospel and unconditional love. As my song, My Granny's Name, says, *"the sun rose in her eyes, for sure she hung the moon, she put love in her apple jacks and always spoke the truth. I try and live my life to this day, in the memory of, my Granny's name."*

If there are any saints, and there are, she is one. Our childhood spent with Granny was magical. Running in to see her, hopping up in her lap, the smell of sweet snuff on her breath and you knew nothing in this world could ever harm you as long as you were within the confines of Granny's lap and her graces. And you were always in Granny's graces.

Granny lived with her oldest daughter, our Aunt Louise, in a cute English style cottage with the "Yard from Hell." This yard had the biggest, most immense trees producing more leaves each fall than imaginable or should be legally allowed at the state or federal level. My cousins and I raked and bagged them every year together, bitching and moaning the whole time while loving every minute of it. There was the every few hours or so sighting of Granny stumbling out on the side porch to smile, wave, and love on us. She used the blooming dogwood tree each year to explain the mystery of Christ's love for us. We did something weird, beyond comprehension in today's world. We played together. Outside. We played hide and seek, took sides, fought, made up and soaked in every solitary second of the sanctuary of Granny's presence. She loved us, and we loved her right back. There it is again. That loving someone first thing.

Granny was already old in our eyes those, but as I entered high school and she entered her mid eighties that dreaded, declaration of doom kept coming up. The resthome. Why in the hell they call them resthomes, I'll never know. Cause neither you nor Granny is gonna get much rest at one. I was furious at the thought; I was not merely opposed, it was treason of the heart in a family this large to even think of putting Granny away. But reality was reality and eventually, after several failed attempts to keep her home, Mama and I even trying one last time to hold onto a past out of reach, I came home from school to find her lying in the hallway, and off she went. No Ma'am, she was not happy. The worst part was the taking away of her snuff. I hated going to see her there because of the immense guilt I felt but, Granny did what Grannies do. Made you feel better about yourself. Especially when you shouldn't or don't know how. Grannies are redeemers. Can I get an another "Amen?"

While our funerals are guaranteed to deliver epic humor that will last this lifetime, when it comes to old folks, some of the most priceless stuff happens in those last, no-so-good years of living. Not that long before Granny died, Mama and I came up with a brilliant idea. Aunt Inez was remarrying at Granny's place, The First Baptist Church. Now Granny hadn't been able to walk for several years now. No problem. I was a cock-strong ex-football player and still a devout weight lifter. Plus, I was extremely intelligent. I mapped the whole operation out, logistics and all. We would simply get a wheelchair, and I would gently pick Granny up, if the need arose, all two hundred and twenty-five plus pounds of her dead weight.

I was benching in the high three-hundred pound mark by now. I could certainly handle "Lil' ole Granny." The wedding went off without a hitch, except for Granny getting upset at the very beginning and crying because she wasn't sure where she was or why. We comforted her and moved on. The fellowship was awesome, and with the reception concluded, Granny was so tired you could see her slowly slipping, dripping and drooping further and further down in her wheelchair. It was time to take Granny back.

I wheeled her out front just as Mama drove up. The entire wedding reception standing behind us, on the sidewalk, with cheers of "We love you Granny!" and (the most popular resthome lie of all) "We miss you soooo much! We're coming to see you! Real soon!" What this actually means is, we all know you'll likely be dead soon enough, and we'll come see you in your casket.

With the car door open I knew I would have to literally pick Granny up, out of the wheelchair, her completely unable to move her legs or hips, and somehow lift her far enough into the car so her hind end was safely on and in the car seat. With an honest and honestly worried, "Are you ready

Granny," off we went. She was scared and started to tremble and let out a soft moan of fear,

"Oh me, oh oh me, dear Lord, oh me."

"I gotcha Granny, I gotcha. Don't you worry, I got ya! " Only lie I may have ever told her.

"OooooooHh me. OOOOH me!"

I knew we had a serious problem as I turned and went to set her down in the seat. That was when I first remotely realized, Granny can't move her hips to slide, like at all, and "Oh my God" I'm about to drop Granny on the driveway of the First Baptist Church in front of God, Jesus, the Holy Ghost and the worst judge and jury of them all, my entire family! Oh hell no, I wasn't. I went for it. I grabbed that precious woman like God's own personal sack of gold and lifted her all the way up far enough into the seat where I knew she couldn't slide out. Again, I was wrong. As in "dead wrong."

I knew Granny and I had a catastrophic complication because as we entered into the car door frame, I had to lift her back up again while leaning inside the car, and her dress, now caught between my arms and her legs, starting rising up. No, I mean "RISING UP!" Rising clean up past a place no Christian grandson should ever find himself and be expected to ever remotely recover emotionally or psychologically. Despite fighting her dead weight in that old polyester dress sliding against my every effort, I lifted her safely into the seat, her dress now hiked up far past the actual family tree, my face being forced mere inches from it due to the angle of the lift. A picture you can't erase and need to. At the same time, Mama was entering into the driver's side as Granny was really shouting, "OOOhh--me, Ohhh ooo MY!!!"

As I let Granny down Mama said, "what's wrong Mama?"

Granny, being a true Baptist saint, unable and unwilling to lie declared:

"My cooter done jumped out!" Then winked at me.

Mama didn't ask.

The only decent framed picture I have of Granny is at a family reunion in that very dress. And when I walk by it, you damn right, I still laugh. And I know she does too.

OPERATION SANTA CLAUS

We got Granny's cooter back under control and I graduated from high school somehow without splattering my brains across some dark pine paneling out at Route 1, Box-108, Pikeville. For the first couple of years I was as lost as a coon dog on a quail hunt in downtown Manhattan. I knew what I wanted to do, I just couldn't figure out how to do it. And my heart and mind was lost at sea in an ocean of confused, raw emotions that were now not so slowly consuming me, never seeming to be able to escape the cesspool of quicksand known as my family. After a couple of failed attempts at picking a major in college, I eventually returned and fully embraced my life's calling and compass in music and began working on my bachelor's degree in music performance. After auditioning and accepting a scholarship and transfer to the University of North Carolina at Greensboro, I finally felt like I was finding my own way. I had a great teacher who reminded me of my football coach in many ways. Dr. Cort McClaren was young and hip, very intense, and demanded your very best, that best you haven't even discovered yet. I had completed my first year in Greensboro and was loving it, when I suddenly decided I would have to sit out the fall to do my job. Take care of Mama.

My parents had finally settled in court the year before and as part of the agreement, I had to move Mama off the farm. Wouldn't have been that big a deal if she hadn't found out on Wednesday, and waited to tell me Thursday evening, that I had till noon on Saturday or else. Yeah, exactly, "I had till high noon." Not a thing packed, never the first yard sale with a farm family living there for seventeen years. I called my best and oldest friend, Stewart Baker, who helped me get $50, rent a truck, and get it done.

Mid morning on Saturday, when I saw my Daddy standing out by the shop, hands on his hips, all puffed up like some gunslinger named, Devil Dan, I had had it. I "gruffed" at Mama, told her to follow me, and I lead her out the back door towards my father. It was the maddest I had ever been in my life, the beginning of an out-of-control temper destined for "great things," and the first time I successfully cussed at both of them. I let them both have it, all nineteen years of me.

I said, "If you two are so blind and selfish, you can't see what you're doing to me--then y'all go move all this shit. I didn't marry either one of you."

There was a silence in that Carolina sun none of us had never heard before. Then it was broken, by me walking away shouting back over my shoulder, "and WHERE THE F#$@! is my Brother?!?"

Trust me. If you are from where I am, you clearly remember the first time you cuss in front of your parents, and don't tote a major ass whooping. I went all to pieces inside, but my back stayed straight as an arrow, as I walked like a man walks when he's crying mad, and telling you, "you don't want none of me, not right now. I can promise you that." I had already become a professional at being able to shoulder anything, emotionally. I literally believed I could do that. It was my duty. I was a young fool bent on proving that to himself and everyone else.

When Mama erupted into a squall of tears running towards the house, hands cupped over her mouth, and Daddy didn't whip my ass, right then and there, I knew I had gotten my point across. And I knew, they knew I was right. I loaded everything out of that house into that truck in less than thirty six hours, except for the freezer, loaded with food. My good friend football brother, Phillip "Grizzly" Jordan came with a dolly. After he left, I was too embarrassed and ashamed to ask for help, so I picked up an upright piano, end by end, inch by inch, until I had drug it up the aluminum ramp into the truck. At that moment something tore in my back, and thus began my lifelong battle with a bad back, and the bad habit of trying to shoulder things far beyond my strength. I finished permanently ruining an already unknown, deformed spine and hip in the following months by breaking my hip twice without knowing it, till I was thirty-nine years old.

I also didn't realize till twenty-one years later, but during that same three days, my high school sweetheart and I were torn apart by an unavoidable, outside source. It was quite a week speaking for myself. Epic and southern. There is an invisible fine line between love and hate and my friends, please, stay clear of it as much as possible. My parents hated each other at this point. And I hated that.

Oh!! I almost forgot. Immaculate Conception. You're gonna love this one! Take a bathroom break if you need one...

This was also the time period Mama told me how I was born. I came home from a church film showing of a guy who worked for a waste company handling abortion clinics. It upset me so bad I had to go stand out in the foyer. Upon arriving home Mama asked what was wrong. When I told her, she reminded me about always asking about a few certain bridge partners of hers that stared at me with such depth it made me very uncomfortable. How Mama was told to abort me at least three times, due to age and exposure to German Measles I believe. She was thirty six when she gave birth to me. But she had refused, even when she had to wear a brace to support her now sagging womb. She went on to inform me that three of them all got pregnant during the same few weeks but the other women aborted. Of course my Mama couldn't. Why, you ask? 'Cause I had been sent by God Almighty. A Savior Child. Her marriage to Daddy was already in shambles so, "for some reason, I don't know why, I asked God to kill me or make me pregnant." And wouldn't you know it, they hadn't had sex in "quite a while." There ya go! I was Immaculately Conceived, born of a non-virgin, wrapped in semi-swaddling clothes, sent to come save my parents' marriage. And I couldn't even do that right. No wonder I am so easily and frequently sent on free Guilt Trips. Back to our previously scheduled program...

Mama took her divorce settlement, and moved to Wilson, where she immediately sunk it all in a failed solo business attempt, that wiped her out financially, mentally, and spiritually. In less than three years, she was living in a small duplex apartment, back in our hometown, after I had moved her six times already. Well, me, Stewart, Neil, my cousin Lil' Billy and anyone else who loved me enough to help. I learned the hard-ass way early in life, just how deeply my "friends" loved me. I hope they know how much I love them. I'm not always good at showing it.

So, I'm rocking in college and then find out, "your Mama's not doing good, son." And she wasn't. My protective heart rose up and I got a job with my high school brother, Neil's father, James Mercer. I had also been a bouncer now for several years at a large rock-n-roll venue called Roadies, so I picked up more work there. I didn't mind being home since I could hang out with my friends working out, and see major national acts every weekend at Roadies. I spent a lot of time with my friends, the rock band Sidewinder, and was inspired greatly by drummer Jim Shephard, as a person and player. Sidewinder taught me how to be a professional and do it right the first time. I paid much more attention to the music than I did to handling trouble in the club, which is saying a lot. To put it short and sweet, a lot of asses got kicked … "where Bands make it Rock and Roadies make it Roll!" But I had to live somewhere, so I relented and moved in with my brother just up the street from Mama. My sweet childhood relationship with my brother had now turned sour as well, as I attempted to grow into a man and he was killing himself slowly with drugs. It would only be for a few months, hopefully Glenn and I wouldn't kill each other, and I was half-a-mile from Mama. It was the perfect setting for "t-r-o-u-b-l-e."

Gurley's Gym was on main street in Goldsboro, owned and operated by the truest, kindest, and strongest man I will ever know, in ever way. This strength included power lifting, a growing sport of which Mr. RL Gurley was a founding father, and expert at molding boys into men. Almost all of my high school football brothers worked out there, with many other friends, and they were winning state team championships and setting state records in the sport. It became my home, as I was gradually learning to avoid my parents as much as an adult child, who's sunk in the quicksand, of a shitty divorce can.

This one particular Monday night, on January 2nd, 1987 I was doing my final training before a big bench press meet the coming Saturday. Lifting with Neil, and another huge guy named Will, I prepared my approach to the bench for my final lift. As I turned to go, Mr. Gurley said, "telephone Chris." I went and answered and a strange voice said inquisitively, "Chris

Brown, Chris. Is this Chris "Hound" Brown?" I said "yes" and they imme-diately hung up. After wrapping my wrists and chalking my hands, sniff-ing ammonia, and returning to the bench in the mental and physical rage required before a heavy lift attempt, I noticed three guys leaning in the front door, wearing identical blue coats with large white letters on them that said, "SBI." State Bureau of Investigation. I felt a bizarre, chilling sweat wash over me and thought, "No way. There can be no way." Way.

That previous September, one night as I prepared to go to work at a new bar called Chevy's, I very reluctantly asked my brother if he could loan me $5 for gas, as he sat on the couch watching Duke play NC State in basketball while "Scarface-ing" cocaine out of a bowl with no straw. I had always despised drugs, eloquently taught to do so my drug doing brother! And this night, I was over it! I made some smart ass comment to the Universe's King of Sarcasm. Glenn replied and the argument ensued. It ended with me telling him a real man doesn't sit on his ass and do cocaine out of cereal bowl and him thoroughly challenging my manhood. "And your too much of a "puddentang" (not the word he used) to do it." Handing me the $5, along with a half gram of cocaine wrapped and hidden in an M&M's Peanuts' bag, he instructed me I would pay him back and do him a favor. I was to sell the coke. What in the world possessed him to do that and me accept the challenge, neither of us will ever know. I took it and walked out the door. Mistake Numero Uno.

Later on this same night, we had already broken up several fights as I walked around the bar with cocaine on me and the cops now in the build-ing, all around me, talking to me. So I thought what every first time drug salesman thinks I'm sure, "You need to unload this and now." So I did. Problem is, as I stood outside in a dark alleyway with a guy I'd known well since junior high, the kind you know does drugs and keeps his mouth shut, something strange happened. I had heard my brother discussing Drug Salesman-101 tips many times and Rule Number One was don't ever accept money from anyone other than your buyer. Standing in the dark-ness, as I checked all around, to be sure no-one was looking, I drew from my right pocket the half-gram and handed it to my guy. As I did, I looked far down the alley way to my left, just to be sure we were still good. And there, appeared a bearded, middle-age man stepping out of the bushes, going out of his way to let me know he was identifying me. I started to snatch it out my buyer's hand, when simultaneously, I felt a jab to my right. I looked down and my friend's girlfriend was handing me the $40. The same girlfriend I had angrily grilled him about when she appeared in the alley un-invited. The one he told me he had been dating for "quite a while" and "She's cool man. I know her, man."

Mistake Number Two. Taking someone buying drugs at their word. Problem here was he didn't know she was an under cover Sheriff's Deputy from Onslow County, the SBI *(State Bureau of Investigation)* had brought in for extra operatives, while they conducted a three county sting called Operation Santa Claus, the largest in history in our neck of the woods. And that's saying a lot. The primary gift I would receive from this was a felony conviction. A damn felony conviction on a first offense $40 sale of one-half gram of cocaine. Another of Daddy's sayings, I've found highly useful over the years is, "How, can you be, so damn stupid?"

I...was...devastated. The night of Monday, January 2nd, 1987, as the SBI continued to stare and approach me in that packed gym, my mind was racing through the past months. My brother had been a highly success-ful, evasive target for several years now, and frankly it was just as much a miracle as Glenn's savvy that had kept him safe. They quickly informed me I needed to come with them. "Right now." And, "you know why, don't you?" I played dumb and nice and asked if I could retrieve my clothes. In the adjacent back room, stalling for time, looking a way out as I leaned over to grab my clothes, I looked under my left forearm to the century old back door for a possible escape route. My heart sank into panic but I was cucumber cool on the outside. There, leaning in the back door, each with a foot propped up on the high door jam, stood two more SBI agents with that shit eating grin that says, "Gotcha."

We calmly left the gym, and went outside, where I was immediately informed I was under arrest for the possession as well as the sale of cocaine. They knew I was a "good guy" and felt no need to handcuff me, read me my rights, and said, "Let's step across the street here, and see what we can find out together, Hound." All I could think, obsessively, over and over was,

"You have *got* to be shitting me." One time. One sale. First time. ONLY time. And I'm the one who gets nailed. Unbelievable! As we walked literally across Center Street to the police department, I immediately pushed the disbelief down inside me, and went straight to the absolute fact, that I knew what they were going to use to threaten me and why. After fingerprinting and booking me, I was rushed into a board room of sorts where at least ten officers sat and stood, local and state level narcotics LEO's. Sitting directly across from me sat the "girlfriend" from that night. I then knew, for sure, this was happening and I was about to get screwed to the wall.

She smiled, choked back a laugh and said "Good to see you again, Chris." I on the other hand showed absolutely zero emotion, and had already reminded myself I would not say one word until the inevitable happened, and then I would inform them, we're not playing *this* game. Several more smart-ass comments later, aimed at luring me into talking, the SBI agent in charge got to their real target. In an authentically, believable "kind" voice, I refused to fall for he said, "We know you're a good kid who's made a huge mistake. You know this. We've watched you nearly six months and we're all on your side. All we want to talk about... is your Brother."

I did what any real family man of my roots would do. I looked into his soul and silently said, "That...will never, ever, ever happen," without uttering a word. The agent pushed on as my eyes caught a local narcotics officer, who graduated from my high school and knew my brother and I, well. He was leaning against the wall, it seemed purposely, back behind everyone. I looked at him just as he looked at me, both of us thinking the same thing, just be cool, watch your step, and don't make a bad deal worse. Finally and sufficiently irritated with the SBI agent still running his mouth, and trying to make me blink and spill some beans, I proudly looked up and said one and only one thing. "I ain't got shit to say, till I talk to Gene." Dude. I grew up in this courthouse. In the system. I know every good lawyer within a fifty, square-mile radius and enough statutes and techniques to head off to law school. Act like an adult. You ain't gonna badger me into giving up my own brother.

Clearly exhausted with this charade the agent said, "Who in the hell is Gene?" Our homegrown officer, almost proudly said, "Gene Braswell, just one of the best trial lawyers east of the Mississippi. I told you, no Wayne County boy is gonna roll over on his own brother over a half a gram... or half an ounce." I spent the next three days wearing the one color I don't look good in. Orange.

The major crackdown on drugs was inevitable here at home. Goldsboro, located twenty five miles east of I-95, was now well known for decades as a major distribution point for the drugs of the times. In fact, the largest heroin bust in history, that would stand for I believe twenty six years-- part of the Frank Lucas/American Gangster story-- involved the Vietnam War, nearby Fort Bragg, our local Seymour Johnson Air Force Base, and the myth of military coffins loaded with cocaine and our very own homegrown gangsters—the Atkinson Brothers. Plus now, Ronald Reagan was not only simply saying "Just say No," he was saying "No More." The laws had literally just been changed and drastically expanded, for lesser and greater crimes, allowing for many more arrests and higher charges with no possibility for expungement, due to the cocaine epidemic sweeping our country. And most of it on the east coast, was coming from the Medellin Cartel, to Miami, up Interstate 95, to be "cut" in our neck of the woods, where you could hop right back on the highway and be in New York City in hours. Quiet, lil'--ole, sleepy Goldsboro, North Carolina. Even folks that never touched a drug knew that.

Walking in the courtroom two days later, handcuffed to another inmate, I heard a girl on the back row say as I walked by, "Chris Brown? You gotta be kidding." I felt the same way, Shoog. Then I, the former President of the Class of 1982, C.B. Aycock High, stood in front of one of the judges from my parents' numerous divorce proceedings, as he explained to me I was facing a maximum sentence of forty years. Since I knew that was both technically true and total bullshit my knees didn't shake. But they would.

Playing bridge at Mama's, Aunt Inez saw me on the news the night I was arrested, and had to tell her. This was the second night of arrests and arraignments. The jail couldn't hold all of us. The next day Granny told Mama when she walked in the rest home, "Chris is in trouble. He is in danger. Go find him." Yet she knew nothing. Perhaps the first thing I ever heard all of Mama's family agree on was the fact that Granny could not know I was busted. It would be too much. And it was at the time my greatest fear. Thank God, Daddy was on the tobacco market in Ohio far, far away. I had enough to worry about.

James and his sweet wife Connie, stood my bail and welcomed me into their home, a safe haven, where I was absolutely protected from anybody, most especially myself, for the time being, and prayed over by a holy woman and man every single day and night. They saved me from self destruction and I will always be grateful. Not many people would put their house up for collateral on your bond, when they've just paid it off. That's the kind of folks I come from. People who understand forgiveness and redemption. As well as survival. Still makes my eyes leak to this day.

It was hard on my parents, those six months, embarrassing I surely knew, for their son to be staying with someone else. I had gone from angel to the Official Black Sheep of my family. And I had experienced enough already to know, yes, we love each other, but we need a break from one another. In six months, I returned to college where Dr. McClaren became my other surrogate father and pinned my butt to the "responsibility wall." I was on a "One Strike" and your ass is outta here policy, and I LOVED him for it. My lawyer continued to move my trial date, looking for the best judge for me. One weekend I began to have an intense vivid dream. The same dream three nights in a row. I was a small boy holding Granny's hand as we walked down the sidewalk, that I knew would take us to Woolworths, where she had often walked me as a child for a milkshake. At the end of the walk, down a dark hallway with this beaming light, there stood two adult male figures that I could not make out. After the third night of this dream, I drove home unannounced, to discover Granny was in the hospital dying, and they hadn't told me. Everyone always said her and I had ESP with each other, and we did have something special.

Walking in her hospital room that night, we both knew this was our last visit. She was worn completely out from eighty seven years of life, yet she reached up, held my hand and comforted me. Literally, the only thing she said was, "Son, I'm tired. I'm going home." We said goodbye with our eyes and hearts and not one more word. It was simple and perfectly beautiful. The next morning, back at school, I woke up in a cold sweat at exactly 5:03

am. Once again I had the same dream, except this time as we approached the end of the hallway, I could make out the two male figures. It was my Uncle Doc and Uncle Cap, the first two of Granny's adult children to pass away. She smiled at me, and letting go of my hand, went with them, and I understood where she was going. About ten minutes later, my phone rang and I interrupted Mama to let her know before she could tell me. Granny was dead. She died at 5:03a.m.

The day of Granny's funeral, before it started, I hung in the front foyer of First Baptist with two other "pallbearing" cousins. We just stood there staring at Granny, lying in her casket, far across the massive sanctuary, waiting to seat people. One of my first cousins, who had been struggling a bit for years, his hands stuffed in his pockets kept mumbling over and over and over... "I just can't believe it. I can't believe she's gone. I feel like I'm not in my right mind."

Without so much as a breath, our other first cousin replied, "Hell, tell us something we don't already know." We gathered around her precious remains at First Baptist and sang her favorite hymn in unison. "I come to the garden alone." Then we thanked Almighty God for our Grandmother and buried her body but kept her memory. There's only one way to say this. Letting go of Granny... is hard.

Granny's funeral was the official end of that era of rollicking adolescence. But it was also a time of intense gratitude and the gradual beginning of a new life. Late the afternoon of her internment, clinging to a tent pole and headed back to school, I felt complete sorrow, a weeping one down in your bones. I watched that sun set, and hushed the child in me that was clinging to a sweet old woman's graces. The growing man in me, hit the road, and prepared to buck up and face the music of my coming punishment.

They say the Saints plead before the very Throne of God on our behalf. I sure wish Granny could have spoken with the judge, and maybe she did. A few weeks after Granny's passing, I got the phone call from my lawyer. With more of my good luck, the Great State of North Carolina had just passed, the First Offender's Act, meaning even on a first offense drug sale, you had to serve time of some length at the judge's discretion. And no expungement for me. We were going to court A.S.A.P. Delaying it, the outcome would only get worse.

The Grand Jury added two counts of Conspiracy so they could indite me, forcing me into Superior Court and a plea bargain. We were thinking they would drop the sale charge and let me plead guilty to possession. The morning of court they pulled the offer. Just before my case was called up my lawyer came straight from the Judge's chambers and asked me, in the courtroom y'all, if we could come up with another $3000. If so, I wouldn't serve hardly any time, perhaps only one day. With my mother, Aunt Louise and James and Connie Mercer squirming beside me, I firmly said "NO." I would not be coming off more money for a weekend of high class golf for the judicial system. Yes, I was proud of myself.

So there I sat in front of the judge. He started off by saying cases like mine were a tragedy. By all accounts, I was a great kid, but one who had made a serious mistake. One he would make sure I didn't make again. When the prosecuting district attorney, who knew my brother well and had known me since I was twelve, began the softest attack ever made on an accused, the judge spryly asked, "Mr. Ferguson, are you defending Mr. Brown or prosecuting him?" It's on record.

My first cousin, John, at the time a detective with the City Police sat off to the side in an empty jury box to show his support. In a matter of minutes I was standing to be sentenced. The judge called out my sentence, "three years incarceration in the Department of Corrections and five years probation."

As Justice rattled on, there was no mention of a split sentence, meaning the three years would be suspended and a shorter sentence imposed. That's when my legs starting shaking like Forrest Gump teaching Elvis how to dance. And that old sweet, familiar family thought was racing through my head, "You have got, to be shitting me."

Finally he suspended the sentence, giving me ninety days time to serve, which I would do, over the summer, at the completion of my school year. I spent that summer, wearing orange denim overalls, courtesy of the Gibsonville Prison Farm in the North Carolina Department of Corrections, still pondering how the hell this happened to me! There would be no military for me. My plans were gone. I even had to later turn down a final audition for *The President's Own, the U.S. Marine Corps Band* as well as *Ft. Meade's Army Band,* two of only four VIP military musical posts at the time. I wanted to fly helicopters anyway. I knew for sure now, I would be a professional musician. Back then, it was one of the only places no one judged you for being a convicted felon. I would build my life with music.

My brother had raised me from my earliest memories with music. Schooled me, coached and challenged me. I excelled at it. It came extremely naturally for me. Sometimes, maybe even too easy. Plus, my oldest first cousin, Tricia, had married Bruce Joyner, the original drummer for *The O'Kaysians*. His gold record for the Number One hit, "I'm a Girl Watcher" hung on his wall, his psychedelic swirl Ludwig drum set in the next room. Bruce had also served in the Army and I idolized him as well. Ever since farming hadn't been an option for me, I planned on going to college, then the military and finally pursuing music maybe in six to ten years. $40 and one bad choice changed all that. Thank God, Granny never knew. It would have killed her. But you know, she would not, have shamed me. Wasn't in her to do that type of pettiness. The summer of 1988 I would spend at Gibsonville, on the road crew, cleaning up hog shit and finally, believe it or not, as one of the two head farmers running the place from the shop. Lemme tell you, in 1988, three million dollars worth of hogs was a lot of hog shit. And if you ever get the chance, volunteer to take the little piggies headed for Bacon Heaven to the slaughter house in Siler City. Then you'll understand what real guilt is.

I made it to the summer of '88 and after having a cheeseburger and a beer, my brother dropped me off in downtown Greensboro, where I was instructed to turn myself in and begin my sentence at the city jail. They would process my paperwork and me. I walked in and handed the young, female officer my paper through the window. She had no idea what I was talking about and soon began to discuss it with several officers behind the glass. Finally she called my name, and when I got up to the window, said, "Aaah, we can't take you. Nobody here knows what this is all about or what to do with you. You'll have to leave and come back tomorrow."

Not being well, a dumb-ass too, I replied, "No Ma'am. I can't do that. I am a convicted felon with this sentence to pull, and all the details are on this (one page) document. If I leave, I am committing another felony. The judge was crystal clear about that." Brothers and Sisters, you CANNOT make stuff this good up! Several times we went through this, her somehow getting dumber each go-round. She finally bowed up and said, "get away from this window! You need to leave this lobby, now, and come back tomorrow! Or you WILL be arrested!"

I went back over and sat on the closest bench, refusing to leave but being very polite and acting like I should, all convicted looking. Officer Crazy-Woman-with-Bird-Shit for-Brains, came flying around the corner with a cop a little older, one who looked like he had some sense. The gal started getting serious about me leaving now or, "she was gonna lock me up." That's what I've been trying to get you to do for the last hour and a half, Honey.

Finally, finally, they "locked me up!" I was tickled to death! After a good ole strip search with a bend over and my new orange outfit, I was placed in a cell block meant to hold maybe sixteen people, I was the twenty sixth guy. There's no other way to say this, than to say it, because if you had been me, trust me, what happens next sucked! I was the only white inmate in there. I didn't mind at all. They all weren't sure until they "cased me out." I was shortly pronounced "cool."

The biggest guy in there, about six foot six, at least three-hundred and fifty pounds was running the place. Let's call him, Bigfoot. He was a pro, you could tell by his arms and prison tattoos. We watched television all afternoon, played cards and then suddenly, Bigfoot turned around at exactly 5:30 p.m. and looked at me and said, "Gonna let my man there watch Andy Griffith. I know he likes some Andy Griffith. I love that Barney." The other inmates started making a rumble and Bigfoot, I swear, stomps his big ole foot down and yells, well... hold on here. I know I've pushed the "envelope" already, so we won't say what Bigfoot said. Mayberry came and disappeared with a familiar whistle and finger snaps and then the evening news began.

I'm just becoming comfortable with my new surroundings; an iron bunk and cell, filled with pissed off, uneducated, angry, orange men, when, (get ready to say it with me) I shit you not, I looked up to see the damn Klu Klux Klan leading off the broadcast with a live protest-rally downtown, DOWNTOWN, RIGHT NOW, right outside our windows. The very afternoon I had to start my sentence. LOVE to meet that Wizard. For eighteen days, I was stuck in that dank, hard, hole of crap, while my paperwork went to Raleigh, and finally they came and shackled Public Enemy # One, Hound Brown, and took me out to the prison farm.

When we pulled up in the prison van, I saw Daddy standing out there with the Warden and I wanted to absolutely kill him! I was twenty two years old and had been pissed off at the world already for a few years. And I had grown very street-smart the last few of them. (Well, besides selling a lil' cocaine. It happens.) This was not my first arrest. I already had a number of assault and various fighting related charges on my record from being a bouncer, mostly dismissed, and I mean who's really counting? My point is, it wasn't "sweet Lil' Ole Crisco" showing up there. When I stepped off the van, shackled to my attitude, the Warden took me off to the side and said "We don't normally do this, but I'm allowing your Dad to speak with you for a short moment." Gee, thanks.

As I stepped into Daddy's presence and he began to go into "Daddy routine," where Ed's in charge and it's "all under control," I shut him down like the lid on a body headed for a closed casket funeral! "Daddy, I love you but for the LOVE OF GOD IN HEAVEN!!! Please leave before you make me look like a complete pussy, in front of an entire prison population, and I have to fight my way out of here all summer, before I even get through the door! PLEASE! Just go!"

Besides a couple of minor fights and me taking a short crow bar to a huge eighteen year old idiot's back late one afternoon in the Captain's truck, two significant things happened on that prison farm that summer. One Saturday my Brother finally came to see me. I had told him absolutely "do not come see me" but we all know how well older brothers listen to the baby in the family. So Brother came anyway. Shortly thereafter, Daddy showed up and immediately, here came the same old, tired tension between them with me feeling the responsibility of being the human band aid. Literally the second Daddy started talking, Glenn went into his go-to

"Asshole for Daddy mode" towards our father, and Daddy hadn't done a thing. Hell, he hadn't been there two minutes and they got into it! With them sitting on the same side of a pine picnic-table arguing about something in the outside world I couldn't care less about, and me on the other side, I stood there in complete disbelief. All I was thinking was, "lemme get this straight. I'm in here pulling time, I kept your ass out prison and you two self-centered SOB'S can't visit me without arguing?" I loudly, firmly interrupted their southern squall with, "Goodbye."

As they tried to stop me I whirled around, and as lovingly as I could said, "No more! No more man. I am DONE with this shit! Y'all wanna hate each other's guts, tear each other apart, till Jesus Christ Himself breaks the Clouds of Glory, have at it. I'm done!" And with that, for the very first time, I stood up for myself and may have taken my first real steps as a man. At least to becoming one.

My last month at the Farm, late one beautiful, orange, blue and white Carolina dusk, I stood at the crest of a field with the Warden watching the sun set as we oversaw some fixes on crop irrigation. And out of nowhere he said, "Son. This ain't none of my business but I'm gonna tell you something. Your Daddy loves you. I mean he loves you. Sooner or later, the day will come when you have to set some things down. For yourself, as much as him. One day, you're gonna have to tell your Daddy how you feel. And you may even discover a few things about yourself as well as some peace of mind."

My heart quit hurting. I "swear" to God. For a short time, my heart actually quit hurting right there in that cotton field. I may not have buried it all there, but at least I became aware a proper hole needing digging, where I could lay some of the brokenhearted part of that burden to rest. I discovered, I do believe, for the first time, what true forgiveness feels like. Because of my Daddy. There's an "Amen" for ya. Then I memorized that sun set and turned my back to my first unmarked grave. I came off the Prison Farm feeling resurrected. I truly did. I went in determined to make it a positive life experience, no matter what, and I departed feeling stronger than any amount of weight you can bench press could ever make you feel. I left with my very own solid backbone. I left that place a young man. I never did see Santa Claus but I did receive these life changing gifts.

PART TWO

SCRIPTURE READINGS
SERMONS AND EULOGIES

HEAVEN DON'T HAVE NO WEEDS

Nearly a decade of life whisked by with only the occasional family funeral, and little drama. Well, that may be a lie, but we gotta get going here, the cars are getting jammed up in our funeral procession. In fact, the only one I remember during this period, was the first one I missed that hurt my heart. My older cousin, Jenny. She had suddenly developed a brain tumor and fought bravely, valiantly for several years, before finally passing. I left college, was in several successful bands, and after spending about a year or so at Lake Norman, working for my Uncle Bud and with his sons, Mark and Freddie, I took a gig with a live theater show in Williamsburg, Virginia at *The Old Dominion Opry,* to save money and gain more experience before making my big move.

Produced by a former Nashville hot-shot guitar player, Sid Hudson, the band included numerous older Nashville studio session musicians who had been slowly pushed out of the scene there. I gained invaluable experience working with guys who had actually toured and recorded with too many country and rock legends to begin to mention. More importantly, I met a sweet, beautiful, long-legged blonde gal from South Dakota, Anne Marie. An aspiring artist and great vocalist, "Rose," as we all affectionately called her, Rose and I fell in love in Williamsburg, and made plans to move to Music City, USA to chase our dreams together. I moved to Nashville, Tennessee on September 13, 1992, the morning after my tenth-year high school reunion, Anne Marie came out later in the year and together we took on Music Row.

I saw the sign, Nashville City Limits as it passed by my window. I arrived with $189.00 and a quarter-tank of gas. I was two truck payments behind; when I left, in a week or two it'd be three. I was on my own chasing a dream no one in my family really understood but I was at peace. At nearly twenty-seven years old I didn't have a "job," but I did have a purpose. And a calling. It was always a calling to me, not a "dream." Dreaming is for children. A grown man or woman, knows what God put them here to do, whether they ever do it or not. With little more than most of my family's blessing, a soul's passion, and a constant inner voice, I was proud of myself for the first time. I may fall flat of face but by-God, I'm going for it! I had gained enormous experience the preceding years, majoring in music, playing in various bands and touring up and down the east coast, making great contacts with up and coming monster musicians and now young artists signing major label record deals. At the constant suggestion of my old college roommate and former bandmate, Ben Folds, who had moved to Nashville with a publishing deal, I finally made the leap. Within three weeks I had my first gig, and the next decade of my life would justify every tobacco row I ever suffered through and turn my pipe dreams into a reality. When I stood on the soil of Scotland, woke up in Australia, or survived Canadian blizzards freezing my butt off on a tour bus, my people went with me. And the first time I played the Grand Ole Opry, I imagined the spirits of poor Carolinians, my own Mama's family, huddled around a cheap radio after working all week in the field. I could smell the cornbread, BBQ and homemade cobbler. I could see their ghosts, dancing. I was proud from some hard work, backbone, and survival, and where I come from, there ain't a damn thing wrong with that.

In the spring of 1993, after only being in Nashville six months, I landed a job with a young man from Athens, Georgia; a new modern pop-country artist on Capitol Records, named John Berry, and started my career. I was elated! It came about like almost all good things in life do, seemingly out of left field but a direct result of doing the right things with the right kind of people. Preparation meeting opportunity and a star or two lining up correctly. A chance encounter and conversation had resulted in me being handed a cassette tape for an audition, which I learned riding around in my Ford Ranger at night with no where to practice, nailed the audition and landed the gig. For the next five or six years, we traveled the entire country and all of Canada touring full time and performing at country music festivals and events, with opening slots on major tours with the likes of Reba McEntire, Clint Black, and many, many others, as well as scores of theaters nationwide. I got to see America, all of it, for the first time on all-night tour bus rides and I loved it. I was doing what I knew I was put on this earth to do with passion and purpose. John, one of the best singers to ever walk this planet, period, quickly enjoyed several Number One hits as well as several top tens, and the ride was growing in intensity as 1996 rolled around.

We were performing in Indiana at a theater when I received the message from our road manager Robin LaRue Majors. Before cell phones and the internet, it was pay phones, calling cards, and your significant folks having the info on your whereabouts on a thing called, "a piece of paper." My Aunt Rachel had finally succumbed to her battle with cancer. Her children told me all about the service over the phone, and I was truly devastated, deep inside, that I couldn't attend. It's something you don't miss. The funeral of someone you love and that has loved you, molded you. Especially a woman of Aunt Rachel's holy magnitude. A horrible feeling.

Aunt Rachel was the purest spiritual woman in all our farming community and church. Everyone knew it. She was that rare one that walks the walk so well, she rarely has to talk the talk. She led by quiet example, a meek but strong willed woman, truly overflowing with an honorable, genuine humility and what I recognize as the Holy Spirit. A devout Christian, she raised a family of five with her husband Uncle Barney, who had passed away years ago in 1975. As I sat on that tour bus that day, reliving every Aunt Rachel memory I could find and grab in my heart, the ones that stood out the most were from childhood.

Aunt Rachel was my Sunday School teacher, an extended family member, our families were intertwined the way farming in the good ole days always bonded families. Just up to the point of being illegal in many states of lesser greatness and integrity than our North Carolina. Uncle Barney died from a sudden heart attack when I was in the fifth grade, and there we were, standing in their living room, mourning the loss of a truly beloved man. I remember the intense sadness and grief on his oldest son Carl's face, that weight of responsibility only the love of family can and always does create. But what I remember most is Mr. Spruill.

An elderly poor black man, Mr. Spruill had worked for Uncle Barney nearly all his life. He seemed to already be ancient in the face. He had that gentle, weathered look that a life spent working outdoors, a hard life, produces and that cannot be faked. There we were, the entire family and most of our church congregation, supporting Aunt Rachel and her kids, and the doorbell rang. I adored Aunt Rachel from my earliest memories so I did what all little boys do and hung on her skirt. I walked to the door with her, and there standing off the front porch was Mr. Spruill, in his finest denim overalls, white shirt, tie and old tattered black dress coat; the best one he had, his hat held in his hands, along with his entire family. There were huge tears streaming down his rich, dark face, for he loved Uncle Barney as family.

He had rung the doorbell and quickly stepped back off the porch. Sadly, in those days, this wasn't odd, you see, Mr. Spruill was "black." Aunt Rachel's entire living room was filled with our white, Free Will Baptist congregation. My entire childhood was spent around white and black families. Every day. Our lives were intertwined from birth. The sad part was we still lived in a time where it was an unspoken rule, but rule none the less, that black people were rarely allowed in a white home, unless of course they happened to be "The Help." Yet despite our faults and sins of past generations, we loved each other, we truly did.

I stood hugging tight to Aunt Rachel's skirt as she opened the door and with a grateful, mournful awe she said, "Oh William. He loved you too." As if it were her first nature, because it was, Aunt Rachel then said, "Come on in. I know you want to see him." Even at the age of nine, I could clearly sense the gasp in the room most of the white ladies wanted to take and a few did. The Christian white ladies. I could feel the tension from the men. Clinching his hat and holding in his grief, with a form of kindness and inner strength tempered by survival emanating from his eyes, Mr. Spruill said, "Thank You, Mrs. Rachel, believe we'll stay out here."

She would have none of it and opened that door wide open, clean to the hinge's limits, the way I imagine God does His Heart for all us, for all the world to see. This was no show, no pretense, just her immediate instinctual, loving nature. It didn't cross her mind, whatsoever, what so and so might think. Because it didn't. Aunt Rachel stayed too busy walking with Jesus than to waste her time here with anything other than uncondi-tional love. Though Mr. Spruill refused and remained outside, protecting Aunt Rachel, that awkward, Dixie-moment was forever stamped into my little white mind. I could sense, no I experienced, the sheer holiness of it. Because you could see in his eyes, he knew the Gospel Truth as well as Aunt Rachel. They were busy loving one another. People, you cannot hold love and fear in your heart at the same time. It won't work. There's not enough room.

I recall being quite confused as a child. I mean we were all God's Children, right? But the contrast between home, church life and a deeply Christian community and, like it or not, I was there, I lived it, heard it, saw it, smelled it, and still remember the after-taste—of a hypocritical rac-ist society in denial. It disturbed me even before I knew what it was. But Aunt Rachel's love and respect, her doing the next right thing, was forever stamped in my heart. And what impressed me even more was the respect, love and kindness I saw in Mr. Spruill's eyes.

My earliest memories were mostly of Magalene holding me, fixing my skint knee. Of sitting with me and reading Bible stories, teaching me to read and write. I had a wonderful, devoted Mama, who ate me up like "sug-ar-pie," but Magalene was every bit my Mama as a small child. Magalene's own mother had died very shortly after she first started helping raise me. My Mama loved her like a daughter. I am not being poetic. This very day, at around seventy-two years old, Magalene will tell you I love her and I am hers. She became my "other Mama." But the racist, backroom, smart-ass remarks I would hear over and over growing up, out in the field, at the store, in the bank, at church, bothered my little soul. Because its suppose to. Be careful, please, what you say 'round the children. Their hearts are listening as much as their minds.

I'm not fondly rewriting history with some memory from Uncle Barney's parlor wake. I'm simple saying, the racism of the south poisoned us ALL. Most of all, all of us little children, black and white. The mental lines of division and spiritual lies of separation were drawn for us all, long before we could fathom things like slavery and the Civil War. Integration and Civil Rights. I am just so grateful, always have been, that as a small child I was exposed to the unconditional love of honorable people of color and whites, one as much as the other. And I'm still grateful that it bothers me deeply, at any level, for any reason. Because I simply know, in my heart, as you do, it should. We are all born of the same Spirit regardless of what this world does to us. Thank God Almighty, Aunt Rachel planted that seed of love and hope inside my little cracker heart that night.

Another reason I admired Aunt Rachel so deeply was what she had done at church one Sunday during my parents divorce. As the proceedings became more blaming and bitter, Mama became estranged from the congregation, largely made up of Daddy's folks. They all felt caught in the middle, afraid to say or speak much of anything to Mama at church and frankly, I never, ever blamed them or held any resentment. Don't let your dog shit on someone's porch you love, and leave it there, expecting them to feel good about it and you. Clean up your own mess. However, when you know someone is hurting, let them know you do care. Cause they can't see that in their broken state. Mama was as afraid to speak to them. Regardless one Sunday as Aunt Lottie softly played, "Just As I Am," I looked up from the back row and saw my Mama being the only one walking to the altar. And people I freaked out. Freaked out! I had no idea what was going down. After whispering in our new preacher's ear, he directed the music to stop. You could have dropped a pin on the grass and it would have been heard.

"Sallie wants to ask, if she has sinned against anyone, offended anyone in the church or community? If so, she wants to own it, apologize and publicly ask for your forgiveness."

No one moved especially me. No one except Aunt Rachael that is. After a few long seconds of silence, I want you to know Aunt Rachel walked up there and held my Mama and said, "I have failed you as a Christian woman and friend. I am sorry. And I ask for your forgiveness." This may be the only "lie" that woman ever told. She was probably the only person in Mama's life that hadn't hurt her by accident or attitude. See, here you go folks. Once again. A moment of grace. Trust me, it's always amazing. Every year, Aunt Rachel had an immaculate, huge garden on her farm. And not one single weed. This is why I know. Heaven don't have no weeds. Not with Aunt Rachel there.

Less than a year before Aunt Rachel's passing, Anne Marie or "Rose" and I were married in a quaint little Methodist Church outside Franklin, Tennessee. The only church congregation to successfully sue, and actually get paid, for being destructed by the Union Army in the Civil War. And what a perfect place for a young Catholic and Free-Will Baptist to take their vows. Seriously. It was an epic beauty. Ann Marie was my new family now, and we were very happy during this time. And what better to suddenly drop in on the blushing, cooing Newlyweds than death. Only married for a few months, what else but a good ole fashioned, Christian-based, southern funeral, could provide the proper ceremonial atmosphere that our very first major argument deserved. "Oooh death. Oooooh death." Sing it Dr. Stanley!

UNCLE HENRY'S ROSE

A retired Coast Guard navigator, and my Daddy's only surviving sibling, Uncle Henry was bigger than life. His tattoos mesmerized us, his demeanor kept us at bay. He possessed a wit and sadness so deep it reflected into a twinkle in his eyes. He was Cool Hand Luke and Clint Eastwood all rolled up in a homegrown smoke. His unspoken spirit whispered, "You ain't gone' break me," and just in case some fool thought they could, he kept an arsenal of guns beside his front door. Nothing fancy, just a few high powered deer rifles, and an assortment of shotguns, automatics and pumps. And for the real smart-ass, a sawed-off 12 gauge. The bulge in his pants? Oh yeah, don't forget about the .22 derringer pistol in his pocket.

Uncle Henry had developed a drinking problem slowly along his life's journey, and eventually it kicked in, fully committed to the destruction of his family, like the symptoms of all deeply wounded people usually do. Some men drink to silence their demons; Uncle Henry drank just to piss his off. More than likely he got up in the middle of the night to kick one in the ass and tell it to go to Hell. Hard as nails, he was softer than a pussycat in a feather bed. I freaking adored him, for so many reasons. But I'm sure I loved him so, because once again, he had first loved me.

About two years before Rose and I were married, Uncle Henry had been diagnosed with esophageal cancer. Eventually, it did the devil's work that cancer does and grew throughout his body like interstate kudzu, until it claimed that part, and the only part of him it could, for its selfish self. We had recently seen Uncle Henry on a Christmas visit back home to Carolina. He was not doing well then. He'd been sick for a couple of years now and the effects of cancer had ravaged his body. His mind, when clear, was still sharp as a tack though. Now, on our honeymoon, we wanted to stop and see Uncle Henry if it was okay. I called ahead and he sounded actually good, for a dying man. But by the time we got over to his place, he'd just taken a shot of morphine. He could barely speak and Ann Marie and I had to get on the road to South Carolina for another wedding rehearsal. I thought, "He'll never remember us dropping in on him." Wrong. About an hour later his youngest daughter, Lisa called and said "Daddy just called and he's mad as hell with you, just letting you know. He said you said you were coming back by and you didn't."

Listen to me folks! You never know when that last chance is gonna come. Don't tell a dying man you're coming and then never see his face again. Some things you don't get a do-over on in life. Uncle Henry knew we loved him. But, just try and do what you say you're gonna do, that's all I'm saying. Take that little bit of "extra time" to love. God Almighty, do I miss him and men of his make and model. Men that held you to "the letter" of your every damn word. Men that were well, men. And that twinkle in his eyes. He was a "card" if God ever dealt one.

February came and staying in close contact with his children, I knew we were down to weeks, maybe even days. Knowing it was coming, I had picked out my first, grown man, really sharp suit, a nice dark olive, because I wanted to pay my respects in class. Problem with any suit on me though, is we have to get the coat to fit my shoulders and chest, so the pants legs are always big enough for two of me. You have to split them and have them tailored. Evidently it takes a little bit more time than triple a promised "jiffy," for a nice tailor job in Nashville. Going on two weeks now and I was still, not patiently waiting. It will be ready tomorrow for sure. Then the call came, like they always do, when your pants are down. Around your ankles.

Now maybe midwestern Catholics do it different than us Free Will Baptist, I don't know. But I was in a torrid panic. Here it is late afternoon and Uncle Henry is dead. We're eleven hours away, easy, in Nashville. My precious, new wife is telling me for the tenth time "just wear what you have. It will be fine. No one says you have to wear a suit." I never said they said it. I did. I finally erupted into an angry proclamation, stomping my feet and shouting, "I am NOT going home and burying MY Uncle Henry without wearing a suit! You wear a suit! That's what you do back home. You're born. Eat lots off BBQ. Die. And wear a damn suit! In the casket, outside the casket, toting the casket, you wear... a... suit! With a tie!"

We managed to get the goods the next day and hit the road, only to have a flat tire in the middle of Bum-Chuck, North Carolina so we missed the entire visitation. The next morning we walked into "our" funeral home, the one my family always uses, Seymour, and viewed him one, last time. When I say they don't make 'em like that any more, you better damn well believe it. This soft, thin-skinned world couldn't handle men like Uncle Henry. If we had a few more "Uncle Henrys" around, I guaran-damn-tee you some of this modern day nonsense would cease to exist. Or there'd be a lot more funerals. And more suits sold. The knock out game? Yeah, try that one on Uncle Henry and be sure, and let me know where to go view your body. I'll even wear a suit. And tie.

Uncle Henry was not one for any kind of show or attention, but a quiet, reserved man. One whose personal honor you could sense, simply, by the way he consistently carried himself. A man who did not shy away from his faults and fears. I will always believe he willed himself to make it to February 29th, so we could only mourn his passing once every four years. They played, "Go Rest High on that Mountain" and as I sat beside my Brother and the other pallbearers, he squeezed my knee as we cried along with his own children, and I remember thinking, "It's all changing man." We were getting older. Boy, was I in for a surprise.

I missed home. No ma'am, I mean, I MISSED home. I missed our real North Carolina vinegar-based BBQ, Sundays and familiar faces, Friday Night Lights and pulling for the boys to pull it out. I missed my friends, the best ones I would ever have, that any one could ever hope to have, in this lifetime.

I missed homecomings, even missed attending funerals and hearing awesome music. Somebody "good" is almost always gonna sing "the Special Music" at our funerals. Hell, some of us scope the obits, to see who's performing this week. I missed, HOME. Where you can go and love on someone who first loved on you. Uncle Henry's funeral unsettled something in me I was never able to quite put back in a convenient, quiet place. It began to leak out of me.

Uncle Henry's children and he grew closer than ever at the end of his life. And a peace of the soul was delivered for all, the way only an achingly slow death can bring, rather demand, with tempered honesty and genuine forgiveness. When he died, I bet a dollar to a doughnut, the demons cried along with the angels. Uncle Henry died like a man. With dignity. And that my friend, you have to earn. He had developed his own hybrid rose late in life and they are beyond beautiful. Red as the blood dripping down a wooden cross. After he died his children took cuttings off those rose bushes and replanted them in their own yards. It is the perfect memorial for a man who never gave up, fighting the good fight, even when he was losing, fighting for his children, for closure, for peace, till the bittersweet end. Every rose has thorns. Perhaps that's why they're so beautiful. But to me, they look their best, like Uncle Henry did. The way God made 'em. Left blooming in their God-given glory, free, to be themselves. Unjudged. Uncut. And simply, adored.

A mere month later Aunt Elsie succumbed to her cancer rather quickly. God she was truly something special. Artsy, independent and cut from a different cloth somehow than all nine of her siblings. I mean she was older than Mama, and she thought Jesus Christ Superstar was cool. When it came out! She even owned a copy and would "turn me on" to it every now and then. Aunt Elsie, was plain-ole-Cool. Her funeral was the first one that brought us back to Granny's place, First Baptist Church, and it did not escape my steel-trap mind that nearly an entire decade had passed us by. It was also the last damn time I had the excruciating honor of bearing a casket down that long, double set, of concrete stairs and steps, out in front of the church. My knees were already killing me and I was only thirty one years old. Trust me, every set of pallbearers that ever toted a casket down those steps had someone who said out loud, "The idiot who came up with this bright idea oughta have his ass whipped." By the last time I would have such an honor, they would move it to the short stairs out the side. Still not easy mind you, but a helluva lot better than toting a three hundred pound casket, plus whatever Uncle Pork-Pie or Aunt Lil-Debbie-Cakes weighs, down thirty to forty steps.

SMASHVILLE

I returned to Nashville knowing full well what I was missing. The people that I loved the most, that loved me the most, life was passing us by too quickly. It wasn't the BBQ I longed for; it was my people. And once again, something began tearing at the seams and stitches already loose inside my heart. My career continued with more touring, recording sessions and my now, deep fascination in the craft of writing. Songwriting and writing in general. Something buried deep inside a vault in my soul almost, seemed to hear a new inner voice that suddenly had more to say than frankly, I could understand much less document daily.

Every single solitary musician that ever comes to Nashville, whether they admit it or not, dreams of playing the Grand Ole Opry that very first time. It's the mother church of Country Music. An American Institution. To stand in the Circle, to perform where Hank, Patsy, and Elvis performed is indescribable. It's an achievement of what originally fuels all performers. One of the heart and soul. One, no one can write you a check for, or give you a fake gold record to hang on the wall. The first time you stand center stage in what we call, "The Circle," it is the kind of validation no one can ever take away from you. Because you earned it. Finally our turn came the spring 1997.

I flew Mama to Nashville that Friday. It was more important to me that she be there than the fact that we were actually performing on the Opry. Mama had always believed in me and I wanted success probably more for her than myself. We toured the stars' homes and her eyes lit up like a little country girl at Christmas sucking on hard candy while I obsessed over how to write hit songs, become a session legend, make a million dollars and buy her Graceland. Hopefully within the next year. We went out to eat, shopped, and she told the same old stories I would never hear enough. I wouldn't recognize this until later, but for the first time I saw Mama as a happy little girl. I could see her innocence.

You only have about fifteen to thirty seconds to take your spot. This is plug & play; The Grand Ole Opry, the Mother Church of Country Music. A split second before I counted off the song, I glanced over my shoulder. Mama was sitting up on the stage behind us in the VIP seats. I remember thinking how appropriate it was that the seat Mama sat in was an actual church bench from the original Ryman Auditorium. I barely heard the applause of the audience and didn't notice who else was there. I just zeroed in on Mama's face. The tears that were rolling down her cheek would mean more to me than any raise or gig I'd ever have. After our portion of the show, I took her by the hand backstage and escorted her to the Green Room for an Opry tradition. There, Miss Louise, a beautiful, sweet, petite, woman served us Pink Lemonade. We had made it. All of us.

My wife and I bought our first house later that year on the edge of Brentwood, Tennessee, a fast growing, hip suburb of south Nashville. By the early 2000's I was writing every day, my confidence steadily growing. We were not touring full time so I was staying in town more, getting some great studio time as a drummer, co-writing with some fascinating folks and even touring part time with other artists. There were a few major gig opportunities, the ones that can change your life overnight. Those that usually only come around once or twice, if ever, in your career, but they too died on the vine at the last minute, which deeply fueled my instinctual passion to really get serious about writing. Plus I was recognizing a "voice" in the things I did create, and it wasn't mine. People seemed to like it and the truth is, so did I.

The next several years were a swirl of the first good years of marriage, when the romance is still in full bloom, that first home, remodeling, favorite Christmas ornaments. Of football-grilling parties and that mid 30's feeling that you've actually found a solid way of building a life, all your own. Your way. But like Al Pacino says in Devil's Advocate, "Vanity. Definitely my favorite." Whether I thought this or not, my actions were telling me and others, I got this all under control Yeah, right.

TILL DEATH DO US PART

I had been taking care of my mother since I was a child. Though we were deeply close, we were even more unhealthily bonded together in this dysfunctional relationship that far too often for me felt like some sort of matrimonial commitment I certainly never made. She hadn't been doing good since she retired early from her ongoing battle with chronic physical pain. I don't know how many car wrecks or back/neck surgeries she'd had by now. Honestly I quit counting back in the eighties, the second or third time the top surgeons at Duke said, " we believe we have this type of thing all figured out," only to do another failed surgery. As time went by, I needed to be there for her more and more. Mama had always been there for me. And I truly never felt like I owed her anything. Never did. Doing anything for my Mama was a high honor to me, regardless of what the peanut gallery thought. For Christ's sakes, she brought me in this world. One thing I had made up my mind about fairly early in life was I would never, ever, apologize for taking care of my own Mama. But the frequency of "helping Mama out," translated correctly, began to mean sending Mama money on a regular basis, and it was starting to chip away at my marriage, as did Ann Marie and I growing further and further apart without even realizing it. It happens. It does. To good people. And it did to us.

Suddenly my Brother started having more problems by 1999. Back when I got busted, Glenn had actually gone in for rehab treatment in Charlottesville, Virginia, where he met and fell in love with an all-around beautiful being. Paige, who was early in her own career as a drug rehab counselor, and Glenn were married in 1994. By the end of '99 they were divorced. Out on the road one night, after a show with John and Wynonna,

I got another phone call. Down in Waycross, Georgia on the tobacco market, after being clean for probably the longest stretch of his life, my Brother suddenly decided an eight-ball of cocaine and bottle of high dollar Rum might ease his pain. He had a heart attack. I lost the sister I'd never had and at times thought I'd lost my own brother. It was around this time, that I began to seriously and slowly, unravel deep down myself.

One fall evening, I got a call that my Brother, a ticket-marker on the tobacco market in Kentucky had instantly gone blind while driving and wrecked. A day later, picking him up, it was confirmed he had the diabetes, and no insurance. It was back to our place in Nashville with him.

I remember sitting at the table with my wife and Brother, discussing any options we had to his being uninsured. Health care was no longer debatable, unless he wanted to gradually start losing small body parts. I recall me standing up to him for the first time ever and telling him, this is the way it is. You are welcome to live with us, but you are going to a doctor tomorrow and we are paying for it. One thing Glenn never allowed himself to be was a helpless victim. He would walk through hell, high as a kite, barefooted on broken glass to avoid it. He would do all humanly necessary to avoid it until, almost inevitably, he became one by default. Another family trait.

Sitting at that table that night I clearly remember feeling overwhelmed in a way I never had before. Daddy's health wasn't good. Hadn't been for years now with his heart and track record for smoking, drinking and eating pork. Every time I looked down and saw his number ringing in, I thought he was dead. Mama was, well, Mama. My responsibility. My joy. My burden. And now, here I sat with my older brother, somehow sensing both of us were not seeing something, right in front us. In just a year, we would face it together, in a hotel room in Hickory, North Carolina. For now, boy needs insulin. Get it. And I have to be very successful, very quickly. My family needs me. And we're gonna need real money.

I spent the next year and a half doing two successful tours with three well known artists, John Berry, Susie Boggus and Billy Dean, a great show featuring an entire performance of nothing but number one hits. One night, post show, in a hotel room in Hickory, North Carolina, I noticed the back of my Brother's white t-shirt was dotted with all these different-sized brown, rust colored looking dots. Some small, some pretty big, and the number seemed to grow as the night passed. On another rushed trip to the bathroom, I asked him what it was and he ripped his shirt off, a fear in his eyes and voice I had never witnessed, and said, "Look at this shit man! And the doctor keeps telling me it's diabetes. This ain't no fucking diabetes!" After he dropped his pants revealing over half to three quarters of his body caked in infection, sores, psoriasis, looking like it was rotting slowly from the inside out, I knew as well. No, this ain't "the diabetes." Grape Nuts ain't gonna fix this.

Glenn was never one to shy away from much of anything. Most especially the truth. That evening, we sat there, two brothers, openly talking about his lifelong dance with drugs and replayed it over and over, decade by decade, playing detective. What was this and where did it start? Both of us thinking the worst. He had something bad and it was killing him. We made a solemn decision in that hotel room, that for now, this was between us and no one else. When I left him that night, I knew in my heart I was not simply closing a hotel room door. A part of our lives was closing down soon, forever. But, Brothers are brothers, and Mama's boys are the same, till death do us part.

HOMECOMINGS

O ther than a good funeral, down south, there is one yearly event you can count on to keep you grounded. And I mean, grounded. Like a grave. Homecoming at your home church. Trust me, if your butt is out of line, we'll let you know, at homecoming. In front of God, country and Aunt Hazel. Once a year, we all go home for one Sunday and everyone is required to bring food. Real food. Homecoming Rule-of-Thumb Number One. If it ain't good enough for a funeral, it ain't good enough here either. This old southern tradition is revered by young and old alike. Over the years, those sweet memories of homecomings past, always come and whisper to your heart,

"Come home, come home,
Ye who are weary, come ho-o-ome.
Earnestly, tenderly Jesus is calling,
calling oh sinner, come Home."

Home. That safe place where you remember and are reminded who you are and why, as well as who you're not, and why as well. It's where you're loved and celebrated despite of and because of being the only you. No matter how screwed up you are. But growing older, homecomings start to change. Faces you could count on disappear each year as new ones, you can't remember to save your life, arrive. The world gets busier, life faster, and even homecomings, like everything else in this life from work to love, barring Jesus, eventually seem to betray and turn on us and become something totally different. Too often, the exact opposite of what they've always been. At some point, for each of us along our soul's journey, we start to notice and gradually admit to ourselves, (while trying to hide it from the world), that life is having its way with us too.

I started to make it home for homecoming only every few years or so. And I slowly noticed they didn't feel the same and neither did I. It was homecomings that had taught me early in life, you can always come back home and now were teaching me, no, not really. Maybe home never is that simple safe poetic place we think it is. Or perhaps, as well as preserving the tenderest part of our hearts, it's also the only place that can touch it, poke it, and expose to us exactly where we hurt the most and why. Regardless, by this point I had lived long enough to know for sure, at some point we all get lost in life and go back home, in some fashion or another, to find ourselves. Or at least the part we think we've lost along the way, when the life we have been building blows up in our face. By 2003, mine was blowing up like a restless forgotten Mark-39K atomic bomb, someone left in the swamp, and the harder I tried to fix it, the worse it got.

Since as long as I could remember, my family unit was this well of immense love, a chaotic living conversation, our very own constant drama only we could author. By this point, Daddy had been remarried over twenty-five years and had built a strong family unit with his wife Linda, now called GiGi, and was enjoying grandchildren. Papa, as he was now known, was this sugary, sweet old man, the master storyteller who kept your anticipating toes curled and by now, far more than comfortable living with any life regrets he held in his soft, southern heart. Save one. Mama was a living case study of pain management and prescription meds, and the Gospel of Jesus Christ mixed with up to date box scores and stats for the Yankees. She was both that deeply spiritual woman as well as that consistently unpredictable saucy one that you and even the preacher had grown to sense and savor. She was an enjoyable trouble.

Brother was changing physically every month right before our eyes, still doing this unavoidable, slow-turning of the soul, that old southern boiled dinner slowly getting out of control. Where bitterness and sweetness take their time, deep inside, boiling over only when you stop paying attention, and even then mix with the deep love of what matters most in life.

My marriage had been in trouble for a while, and I did what I was suppose to do. Hide it from my family. I hid it from myself for as long as I could. I would not repeat the cursed act of divorce. I had been convinced, committed, since I was thirteen that I could and would create my musician career as well as have a solid simple home life. I would marry a sweet, beautiful, loyal woman who adored me as I did her. We would have at least several children and I would be the best Daddy in all the history of the South. In other words, I would correct all my parents mistakes, I had so effortlessly judged, with my all original, cleverly planned, perfect life. Why? Because my "heart was in the right place."

I would make my brother proud of the years he spent teaching, challenging, and guiding me musically. Daddy would beam with pride at my solid home life and adore his grandchildren I had dutifully given unto him, running up to his legs for a five dollar bill, and carrying on our Christian name. And Mama? I would buy her Graceland. No, not *the* Graceland. Her own version. A house paid for, money to enjoy life, break her bonds of disability and poverty, and keep her ever closer as she aged, always doing a son's sacred duty. Be Mama's boy.

My wife had been close to Mama from our dating days and Mama adored her. But over the decade, as our marriage began growing up, our own responsibilities mounting, Mama was a growing issue. She wasn't taking care of herself. Eventually, one weekend at her place in Raleigh, we looked at each other and knew why. She couldn't. She was the most depressed being I've ever been in the presence of, still breathing and quoting the scripture of deliverance. It was either Nashville or Goldsboro. I eventually moved Mama home from Raleigh once it was clear I couldn't move her to Nashville and keep my sanity, my marriage and my career. I had taking care of her from a distance, down to an art.

In 2001 we moved her into her small apartment back home in Goldsboro, where she had bitterly prophesied for years she would only return in a "pink nightgown and a casket!" Her bitterness was all encompassing, and Wayne County represented the sight of the original crime and sin. By now, I knew more of "the truth." Mama struggled with her failings in many ways deeper than any of us. That's what strong, Christian women do.

Try to bear all the burdens of the family on the back of their hearts. But life decided for her and that was that. Before long she was calling me, thanking us for placing her there, close to her own family and Granny's church. She hit it off with the new preacher immediately. Pastor Glenn Phillips went to visit Mama for the first time at her new apartment. Turned out they were both Duke Blue Devil fans, in a place where Carolina Blue is the color of a pride that borders on an annoying mental illness, firmly rooted in many of my people. Not us. To us they're a cult. To them we're nothing more than Devils. Our family had always been deep, dark, rich, Duke true-blue. She'd hit the pastor jackpot, "a First Baptist preacher who's a die hard 'Dookie!' And a good one too!" That's what Mama said when she told me about him, crowing like a prize gamecock leaving the cage. They instantly liked each other. When Glenn was at the door leaving, he thanked Mama, smiled, winked, and said, "I thing you're gonna be trouble."

Though my music career was solid; I was now a veteran at it, I was also in a tricky time of major transition. Well into my commitment to become a successful songwriter, I recorded my first original album, *Next of Kin*, in 2003. Later in the year I was hired as a sound designer and became a co-writer on a commissioned work with a very successful Americana composer & Nashville String icon, Conni Ellisor. In October of that year, the world premiere of *The Bell Witch Ballet* graced the TPAC performing arts hall in Nashville. The experience opened doors inside of me I had been trying to rip open for years, as a writer, a human, and a soul. It was what we creative folks call "cathartic." Though that sounds incredibly romantic and courageous, and believe me it is, what it really means is you finally ripped open the closet to your very essence as a human being and your skeletons are buck dancing and howling like wild little Indians around the campfire of your soul burning up. And that year, I finally, methodically, came completely unglued from the inside out. I hid it as long as could, stuffing the fear of failure in dark places, until slowly but surely, one by one, witnessed person by person, the panic attacks surfaced. Until I began having them at home in front of my wife. We had developed some sort of strangely dedicated, deeply loving, dysfunctional existence. Fiercely loyal to all the business of marriage while the emotional, physical and most of all, the spiritual aspects withered away and died. Both of us had repeated, subconsciously, the imprint of divorce from our own families and woke up one day wondering who the hell we were, where we were, and why. We did what all divorcees eventually do. Got a divorce. And I finally learned my bitter truth. There aren't certain types of people that get a divorce. It just happens. And all the emotional trauma of my childhood, buried proper-like inside my soul, all I had overcome and healed, came howling up from a shallow grave and slowly, devilishly, ate me up alive. Stephen King would have loved it! The one thing I had never experienced was feeling like a complete failure. Now, getting a divorce, committing the Ultimate Sin of my Mind, I had redefined the meaning of failing for all coming time. Even Jesus wouldn't look me in the eyes now. That devil loves a lie!

As 2004 raged on and we went through a most amiable divorce, if there is such a thing, (*There is and there's not. Something else in your life has died. Death always has a price*), the day eventually came. Anne Marie called me as I headed to the farm one afternoon to let me know, it was done and we were now divorced. Daddy was in one of his over-the-top, let's pretend and ignore reality, sugar-sweet moods, when I entered the house that day. He could tell something was deathly wrong and kept annoyingly trying to talk with me.

"Just talk to Daddy, son, tell Daddy what's wrong." I gave him every warning a grown man could give without taking out a loan on caution signs. I mean I was forty years old and in no mood for much of anything. As I turned to the fridge and he spoke of himself in the third person yet once again, I lost it. Before I could even think I was well into an explosion of the rawest truth ever with my Daddy, "You wanna talk now? After thirty-fucking-years, NOW you wanna know how I feel!?!

And I started at the beginning, going from my childhood, how he, my Hero of all heroes, had abandoned me, how I had felt as a son and lil' brother when he and Glenn left me to deal with Mama. I went through the entire divorce, covering literally our entire lives in a matter of seconds. How I went from the deepest, reverent love as a son, to literally almost despising the sound of his voice, fueled on by Mama's constant bitterness. How deeply that had devoured me, how guilty I felt for years. Finally I said,

"And then I became a man. I got married and I understood our family and life for the first time, through your eyes. And how in the hell you lived with my Mama, and God knows how much I do love her, but how you dealt with that woman for twenty-seven years, damn if I'll ever know. Cause my ass has dealt with her ever since. And it's just about killed me." Folks, the truth, no I said the Truth, will set you free. I wish to this day, every son could have a moment of reconciliation and resurrection with their father as I had that day.

As November rolled around another deeply embarrassing irony came up. An old high school friend, Chris Wheeler had nominated me for our high school's Hall of Fame. That night of the induction, I couldn't have possibly felt any worse about myself. I found out that very afternoon for all intensive purposes, for the time being, I might as well be bankrupt on paper. I managed to go from stellar credit to the cellar in a year. Not over-come-able, but it would be mighty tough given the family circumstances I was facing and choices I'd made.

There were four inductees that night, including Shelton Robinson, the only football player from our school to ever make it to the NFL. Significant, as I had ridden the school bus with Shelton during the fall that my parents split up. Shelton was a gentle giant and admired perhaps even more for his fine character and gentleness than his top-shelf athletic abilities. I would wear my junior-high football jersey, the short time I had one, on Thursdays, and Shelton, a senior, wore his on Fridays. He was a star. He began saving me a seat after two brothers older than me, "The Evil Bass Boys," started ganging up on me. I stood up the best I could, and then one morning, as Shelton sat across from them I walked up and stared at their grinning faces, and of course, the only seat available, directly in front them. Our daily morning picking session commenced. Suddenly, Shelton's deep voice said, "You can seat with me," with the slightest smile. Shelton slid over to the window giving me the sit right beside them. My chest poked out like a lil' bear and I looked those "mean ole Bass Boys," in the eyes and shared my shit eating grin. "Yeah, dumb-asses, mess with me now!" Folks, take your opportunities and God's Gifts when they come.

So this induction ceremony was enormously special to me. And two of my three favorite teachers were there. The ones that changed and saved my life. Coach and Mrs. Kitty Barnes, a fiery, red-head literature teacher newly retired whom everyone either revered, were scared of, or both. I freaking LOVED Miss Kitty. She made me a writer. The only genuine writer's tools I have today were all bestowed by her. Since I was musician/songwriter, they asked me to perform during the dinner. It was a special night. I managed to make it even more special by, don't laugh, blowing out my one good knee right before the banquet started. Aunt Nymph let me borrow her cane, and then I accepted my Falcon Hall of Fame statue and stood there, limping in front of my hometown people, feeling like a fraudulent failure. Here they were honoring me for my accomplishments in Nashville and I was wounded, bleeding, broken in every way. Physically, emotionally and financially. It sucked. I felt like a liar. And to top it off, Mrs. Kitty attended and came striding up to me afterwards. I had told a story how she gave me an A on an essay and after questioning me after class and discovering that was another of my last minute, final and only drafts, marked through the A with her red pen and gave me a C+. She handed it back to me, looked in into my soul, almost hurt and said, "Don't you ever bring me anything but your best work. You are too talented for this." So that night we had a reunion and lo and behold she still had the paper! Had used it as an example of good essay writing till she retired a few years before. When she asked me if I remembered what the essay's subject was and I didn't, she replied, "Spearing in football! You have never read a more eloquent telling of the physical, mental and even spiritual reasons for spearing. It was three pages of masterful BS." Then she told me how every single morning Coach and her met in the teacher's lounge to check in and see how I was doing. You never, ever know who your angels are in this life. But with God as my witness, they're there. Doing what angels do. Divine Intervention.

Earlier that year, when my marriage dissolved, I had been reunited with my first-love, high school sweetheart, Whitney. I hadn't seen her in over twenty one years. She was working at a place called The Perfect Gift. I mean, to be sure, this must be a direct sign from God. I did what a first time divorcee who's lost in life, going broke, with his whole family dying, should do. I remarried as quickly as possible that December, adding two step-daughters I was in love with as well, into my life. But the real truth is, I was living, breathing "stressed out," and I continued my lifelong performance of wearing the "I'm fine," face.

Also earlier that same year, I met a young, super talented artist and we hit it off immediately. In fact the day after I had told my first wife I wanted a divorce, at a theater in Dothan, Alabama, the young Zac Brown smiled and said, "Hey man, I just met your Lady. Your Lady's cool." I replied, "Yeah. She's truly a wonderful person. We're divorcing," and continued walking to the tour bus. Irony is the blood that pumps through my veins.

I imagine, like all adult children who are pulled home later in life, I wasn't exactly sure what I was doing. I only knew, I had to be at home at this point of my journey. I couldn't tell you why, didn't need to. I was burnt out on a spiritually boring, artistically dull Nashville, and was now completely focused on writing and discovering my own artistic thing. My entire family was sick. I knew in my heart they were dying so time became sacred. And I continued to see this wondrous day of healing I had always dreamed of for us. My Daddy would admit he beat Glenn, Glenn would really, sweetly forgive him, Mama would magically lose her deep resentment towards my father, (which I, of course knew was actually her refusal to accept any responsibility in their divorce), creating really some sort of deeply corrosive, bitter, strange hate/love. See? Our journey would finally all make perfect and divine sense. And I, the family baby, immaculately conceived, would no longer be stressed out every waking minute of my life, and a hidden nervous wreck every time I entered a room that two or more of these people I called "family" were in. The family disease and pain, the deep wounds would heal, and the "ransom would be paid in full." It was perfect! A southern Calvary for the Family Soul. If only our lives really did play out like a great biblical story of redemption and sacrificial love for little children. My Day of Reckoning would be Calvary alright, a dixie-based Golgatha itself. I would learn what the love of family really means, and the weight of it would nearly bury me, along with them.

I continued to tour part time out of Nashville and restart a life back home. Suddenly it was the fall of 2006, and we learned in the span of a few days, for sure, my brother was dying as was our mother. And Daddy was a death, dying to happen daily. The year dragged on, a bad New Orleans funeral march, played out of tune, marched out of step, as I watched my brother's appearance rapidly deteriorate. Mama became more of a full time job of managing her narcotic pain meds, Valium, Xanax, and trying to help her from not waking up one morning all relaxed and dead. Then the spring of 2007 rolled around, and Zac called. Feeling very connected in a rare sort of way, from the moment we met, Zac and I had stayed in touch for several years and finally decided to get together for a serious talk. He had built his homegrown Georgia band into a southeastern powerhouse. The whole package was there; the songs were great, the major, hip Nashville producer involved, the momentum of the industry machine of distribution and support up and running, and so some sort of major success was clearly beyond obvious. I joined the Zac Brown Band in April. I played my first show with them at the old Georgia Theater in Athens on a sold-out Saturday night, and for the first time in several years my musical life seemed to make some sort of sense. The problem was I had to drive nearly eight hours each way, every week to fulfill my now new family duties as well as be the son I needed to be. I never lied to myself. I did it as much for me as them. I had lost a decade and a half of family time. Now that we were definitely lining up cars for coming funerals, I had to be the best son and brother I could possibly be before the southern sand ran out of our homemade hourglass. It was now or never. I knew there was one person I would have to live with when this burial ended and the dust settled. And I longed for some sort of peace I knew didn't exist. Not in this world. The kind that can only be found in your heart. The kind that makes your Soul...shine.

You never ever forget those lifetime moments. The ones that rock your world. That steal the ground from underneath you like a runaway train and drive your soul's stomach straight down the tracks of that infinite, endless, bottomless pit of a genuine, emotional hell. It was a mid August, Saturday night in Athens Georgia, post football game. Headed out of town with a close friend, Braden, I missed the call but soon heard a frantic message from Gene Banks. My Brother, spending time with a long time best friend at Carolina Beach, Bill, decided to do a little construction work. I had fussed at him, pleaded with him, he was way too weak to be in that kind of heat, with advanced hepatitis C, cirrhosis and most likely liver cancer, oh, and "the diabetes." Till the day he looked at me and pathetically said, "Man, I just want to hold a hammer in my hand and feel like a man one more time." No man has the right to deny that from another, much less his dying brother. Glenn had fallen some fifteen feet or so, trying to get on a roof, landing on a tree stump and fallen ladder, crushing his entire right shoulder, arm and rib-cage. I was told he had been seen at the hospital there and then released as quickly as possible a couple of days ago. I was f-ing furious. Thank God, Gene was at least close.

I had dropped Glenn back off at the beach just three days earlier. He wanted to see me play one more time, and had felt he was up to it, so I loaded him up and drove him across the Carolinas, down through his old stomping grounds in south Georgia, seeing old friends and having the sweetest long weekend two brothers ever had. He hung with the band in Atlanta and we ended it with a show in Charlotte, I returned him safely then headed back to Atlanta. Barely one week later, his already fragile life was hanging on by mere threads thanks to one bad step on a cranky, crappy ladder.

The emergency room, seeing my brother was stage four liver disease, now with massive injuries; a crushed collarbone, shoulder joint and upper arm broken completely in two in numerous places, simply said, "Here's a sling, we can't give you pain meds, (*cause you're dying*) so go home and call this orthopedic doctor on Monday and make an appointment." He had stood the pain already for two days, and then, knowing he was in trouble, drove himself back to the safety of his closest friend, Gene, in Greensboro, where he was living. Maybe a four hour drive, my dying, injured Brother made it all by himself in about ten hours. If you could have seen him, how in Heaven's name he did it, I'll never know. The thing about liver disease is, when it shuts down, so do you. His liver and kidneys couldn't handle the trauma he had suffered on his entire right side; his arm through the shoulder and complete right side of his face had turned black. Not purple. Black. Like death-black. When I walked in his hospital room eight hours later, he simply looked at me wild eyed and said with a quivering voice, "You better get ready. This is it man." I knew he was right.

We spent the next ten days at Moses Cone Hospital in Greensboro and then I checked him out Sunday evening and drove three miles to a hotel room. I thought he was gonna die in that room that very night, but the next morning we headed for Durham and his people at the Duke Liver Clinic. His doctor at Duke, Dr. Muir, was the head of hepatology and the Coach K of livers, least to my Brother. After an initial exam, he put one hand on my knee, one on my Brother's and said, "You boys are in a pickle. What are you gonna do?"

The outcome was obvious and clearly exposed to us that day. It was only a matter of time. I would hear the phrase "forty-eight to seventy-two hours to ten days" until it nearly drove me insane. I let Doc know, "You're all he's got. I'm not taking him out of Durham," until as Glenn poetically said, "It's time for the six pack and lawn chair at the beach." Glenn's belly had swollen rapidly those few days and he looked like a nine-month pregnant woman about to pop. Like all hospitals, Duke wouldn't just take him in and treat him since hospitals generally don't want the dying on their floors. So we were told, take the pain and swelling as long as you can and then go to the emergency room at Duke Hospital. It was the only way we could get him admitted and any relief at all.

Hours later in another hotel room, I sat on the bed, nearly at attention and in utter awe as I watched my Brother stand there, naked, upright, his back against the wall, and fight the excruciating pain of paratinitis. It was the most ridiculous and unbelievable feat I've ever witnessed. It felt like a self-imposed, unnecessary crucifixion. Finally, as he began to urinate on himself fighting the pain, my eyes fixated on his, thanks be to God, my Brother looked at me gently said, "Let's go, man. Now, I've had enough." He was so exhausted and weak from the physical fight, I honestly didn't think I could get him in the truck. A short time later, in the emergency room at Duke, two young interns, sizing him up with that standard, "Oh bless his heart, this guy is toast" demeanor, asked who his doctor was. When he replied, with great Duke Pride, "Dr. Muir," they reacted like it was the Final Four and Coach K was expected any minute. I don't know if they were interns or what, but you've never seen mere words, and less of them, snatch a knot in a doctor's ass like those did.

A short time later, they performed the only procedure that could offer any genuine relief. One I would come to pray for and then loathe for him, for months. They pierced his abdomen with a large syringe attached to a long thick tube that ended in a clear one-liter glass medical bottle. We began to hope for the best and drain the foul fluid wreaking havoc on his internal organs off his abdomen. This first time looked promising as they got a liter and a half. Glenn got a room on the floor for those headed out of here and our final journey as brothers started down its long and winding road. It would be the most hauntingly beautiful ride of my life.

God, he was trooper. From that Monday night in early August until he died, I would not leave his side unless I was doing the one thing I knew he would not let me fail to do, continue my music career. So I stayed in that cold, unwelcoming room at Duke every day and night, by his side, week after week, only leaving at the last minute to haul ass to Atlanta and hook up with the boys for a show or two. Each Saturday night, after our show, I'd haul ass back to my Brother and Duke. After all, he would only be here "forty-eight to seventy-two hours, no more than ten days." I could do that. Easily. Standing on my head. When it comes to my family, I could do anything, bear any price. That's what my people do. Least that's what I told myself day after day.

Coming home now suddenly felt all too familiar in a fresh, new, strange way. Like life was purposely pouring salt in that old wound everyone knows you hide, your real birthright, instead of a cherry-picking, sentimental trip down memory lane. Homecomings never are quite the same once we've lost our innocence. But we gotta lose it someday. And isn't that a small price to pay, for your own peace of mind? For literally, the love of your family? Amen? Amen.

The one thing you can count on back home, besides my people's love, is the food. You can always expect a southern spread of heavenly-halleluja delight come homecoming. Whatever that homecoming may be. Our annual one or your final one. Some folks won't show up, new ones will, but you know before you even cross the county line, soon you will be full. Filled with family, faith, friends and food. Food for the Soul.

THE END OF THAT

About a year and half before Glenn went south, he was a walking, breathing toxic nightmare. It would take several weeks for his liver and body to become overloaded and then we would go to the hospital and they would flush him out for a couple of days. It "worked" as a short term band aid for a sinking ship. Eventually it became so routine, I literally marked the next expected crisis, every 15-21 days in my date book, for me to be on the lookout for Brother being in trouble. You see, when someone's body literally fills up with this toxic waste, they become unaware of reality. For about eight months, like clockwork I would get calls at all hours of the night and day from friends, family, police officers, restaurant workers, cashiers, and my Brother would be stranded somewhere. Most people, with any common sense at all, could immediately tell, "this guy is dying." But you'd be amazed, maybe not, at how many couldn't. Even some close friends and family, did a knee jerk, "oh he's high." What if he was? Or people would stare at him sitting in Smithfield's BBQ like he was an exhibit at the county fair. And it fucking infuriated me. But I buried it. Deep. Another unmarked grave I am well aware of and never visit on purpose. When you are "looking at" someone, see if you can see someone other than yourself, reflecting in their eyes.

Eventually, on a really good week, I sat Glenn down and showed him my notes. He was quite moved at my detailed dedication, so we formulated a plan. No matter what. We would stay in touch. I would know when he was starting to go south again before he would, so I would get to him and bring him home with me. Of course, he would become belligerent and sometimes unmanageable. But we shook hands and hearts that no matter what happened, or he thought had happened, (*a dying man is entitled to his reality. It doesn't have to be, and honey, it won't be yours. But he's the one dying. Give him enough space and dignity to do it gracefully*) we would get through it together.

Tension was as thick as the August humidity in Blackshear, Georgia. I had known the day was coming rapidly that we would have our final showdown. I had picked him up at a CVS one night. He was lost and had the wrong key, yet once again, jammed into the car ignition and because he was in a toxic haze, he thought the car wouldn't crank. Thank God, a Wilson police officer realized he was sick and not high and helped him call me. I picked him up and of course, belligerent as all hell, he refused yet again to go to the hospital. I waited until that argument was mute and I could barely get him in the car. Two or three days in the hospital and my brother would reappear in our world.

This time though he was especially irritable and angry. He was tired of being taken care of by his baby brother. It humiliated him. He took care of me. Part of our deal we had struck was, it was up to me when to release his car keys back to him when I felt it was safe. He had already wrecked two cars. His and Mama's. Sooner or later he was gonna hurt someone else.

A year or so before, Glenn had met former Duke University basketball legend and NBA star Gene Banks by, well, an act of God. You'll see. They were close in age and two kindred spirits, immediately. They didn't become friends, they became Brothers. Gene had tragically lost his beautiful wife and mother of his children, only a few years before and understood exactly how fragile and short this life is. So Gene with an open heart that had been broken by life and was actively healing, he welcomed Brother into his home as he was his Brother too. Even Gene's daughter's fell deeply in love with "Uncle Glenn." A bigger, wiser more tender heart than Gene Banks has never walked this planet. And he's hell on defense.

So this morning, Brother angrily strode up to my desk and without saying good morning or go to hell announced, "I reckon I'm going back to Greensboro. I got things to do."

I replied, "Cool, give me a few minutes and I'll take you right now."

"I didn't ask you to take me god-dammit! Where are my keys?"

The exchange did not go back and forth. I sat there as he cussed me out, up and down, and the whole time I just looked at him and loved him. This wasn't my brother. It was the disease. Finally, he got really ugly. I pulled the keys out and lay them on the desk. I said, "Your choice. Right here. Here it is. You can choose your car keys and run off yet again and wind up God knows where, maybe kill yourself if you're lucky or somebody's little girl if you're not. Or you can choose to trust your own brother and honor our agreement. Your choice. One time, last time offer, on this deal. I have a wife and family and we have two dying parents too man!"

And then I said the words, I HAD to say. The hardest and most loving ones I would ever say to him. They didn't fly out by accident. They came from that place in the heart that loves, far too much to lie. About anything. Especially dying. So I spoke the Gospel Truth. And I knew before it came out of my mouth, it would break his heart and mine. Sometimes, being broken is the only path to being whole again.

"Man. Even dying ain't all about You." That silence broke the heavens in half, that day. We both heard it when it split.

"Fuck. You." And he damn sure meant it. But I wasn't going to fight or wrestle my dying Brother down to the ground and help him dig his own grave. He was already so close to it, he didn't need any help getting there. It was a matter of time, like all things. Glenn stood up and went into a another brief cussing of how he was "through with me for good." When he was done, I began to say the second of the two hardest but most loving things I would ever utter to my brother.

"Are you finished? I know you're not yourself. I know you don't mean this. But if you can't love me enough to trust me, right here, right now, if you take those keys and walk out that damn door-I promise you, the next time you see me coming to the rescue, you'll be flat of your back and unable to argue. But make NO mistake, Brother. I'll be the one who comes. I will be the one there. And you and I both know that. Because I love You. Now make your choice and be done with it."

One more, very meaningful, "Fuck you," and he stormed out. As he slammed the back door, I stared at his keys he left on my desk and within seconds he was blaring down on the horn, like the eccentric, all original, self centered asshole he could often be, wanting me to bring his keys to him. I took it as long as I could and then went flying out the back of the house with his keys, barefoot. As I came out the door I said, "you forget something?" That scored another elegant "fuck you" right as I felt something pierce my right big toe.

Glenn was always dropping shit, especially diabetic supplies, as sick folks often do, all over the place. Never used stuff, just unopened alcohol swabs, syringes, etc. I looked down and in a brief moment of horror I saw a syringe sticking out of my bare foot. In a cold dread, I lifted my foot up with the syringe hanging out of it and yelled, "THIS... is the kind of shit I'm talking about! Fuck man! Think about someone besides yourself. Just for a second, Just for today!"

One last refrain from his toxic peanut gallery, "Fuck You! Give me my keys!"

I will never forget the look of sheer horror in his eyes. And we both knew, we would not be speaking for a while, but we loved each other and we would straighten it out. My fear went down when I found the cap, examined the syringe and realized it was unused and he had dropped several things coming out the door. I found out later that day he stopped to tell a cousin he was "done" with me. I was "old enough to know better." No shit. I was. We ain't done pal, we're just getting started. If you think for one second there is ANY power that exists, ANY where that will touch, harm or kill the love I have for my Brother, then you don't know how much I love you.

A few weeks later, Glenn called and as soon I said "Hello," he said, "We need to talk." The way an older sibling says it and you know it's not a request. It's a demand. The next day I pulled up and picked him up at Gene's house in Greensboro. I was so accustom to his anger, frankly, by now, it was boring most of the time. In a strange way, I was even loving the venom, because I knew, one day soon, oddly enough I'd miss it. I knew the defensiveness and insecurity was coming from a dying man, who was scared and who did love his little brother. We took a silent ride through downtown past the historic "Greensboro Four" Woolworths museum and finally Glenn started talking baseball and his mood lightened. He had been wanting to take Mama to a Duke basketball or baseball game for forever, as he now directed me to the new Greensboro Hornets baseball stadium. We got out and walked around peering through the gates, admiring the field. Just as I turned to head to the car, I realized the older brother "set up" had been immaculately pulled off yet once again. Here came the showdown.

Glenn started spewing real venom, purposeful poison designed to break you down until you have no choice but to agree with him or shrivel up and die. Not this time. Ever since I had moved home I kept reminding my family I was not just the little Crisco of Wonder Years gone by, sweet, innocent and vulnerable. Here for their beckon call. I was a grown man. One they had forgotten to meet. I didn't say a word. Your brother knows when you're listening. And we both knew we would never have this chance again. We wouldn't need it. We would both make damn sure of that.

The short ride back to Gene's, Glenn unloaded his every emotion on me. He couldn't believe his little brother had "told him what he was gonna do." And then suddenly, exhausted, he softened like a sinner, looked at me and said, "Man, I know you're doing the best you can do. I know you're scared. You're probably in disbelief I'm gonna die before Mama & Daddy. You are the best little brother any man ever had. And if you don't know I love you by now then... fuck it." Slight pause. "But don't ever fucking talk to me like that again." He gleemed out the window and I remember thinking, I wish I could see exactly what he was seeing in that moment. A dead man walking to his grave, peering into the Carolina morning sunshine, through it, into the very threads of time and mysteries of life. I knew, he could see what he needed to see in that moment, just the right amount of "enough," to get to the next "where" he was going. And I knew, he now knew, for damn sure, his little brother would never, ever leave his side. I waited to make absolutely sure he had said all he wanted to, needed to, out of my deep respect for him. It seemed like a lifetime went by and then Glenn took a deep breath, an exhaustive one and looked in my soul and said, "Anything you need to say to me? Get off your chest? Better do it while you can."

As I pondered deep into my heart's memory, all the fun and fights, the drama and delights of life we had shared, I was thinking, "anything I hold against you?" I could think of absolutely nothing. And then it hit me.

I said, "Yeah man. You never lifted a hand, spent a god-damn penny on taking care of Mama all these years. You totally ignored the divorce fallout. Hell, you even ignored me, when I was nine and they were first divorcing. I had forty eight hours to move Mama off the farm. I was nineteen years old with no resources, you were twenty nine, single and making a shitload of money. I've moved her thirteen times, six times in three years. I've had to borrow money from friends and my best friends have helped me move her nearly every time. But not you. She has drug me down my whole life. And you've never even called, once, to ask if you could help. But I do know why. You hold her as responsible, if not more, for Daddy beating your ass."

Like our father, our mother had said her whole life, she "never knew anything" was going on. Well, Sallie. I was fucking three and a half. I knew it. The Sheriff's department knew it. The whole county knew it from a few festive fight nights. But, Mama didn't. I got that. I understand Brother. But don't punish my ass for it.

Without a pause, with the tears of death choked back in his eyes, he looked at me and said,"You're absolutely right. And I am sorry." And that, was the end of that. Me and my big Brother had a genuine healing of our hearts and connection. We went and got a Hardees' Vanilla milkshake and listened to the Allman Brothers Band's Revival one more time. Look me in the eyes and tell me this wasn't grace? People can you feel it? Love is everywhere.

We always knew what each other was thinking. He confided about good people's well intentions that were wearing him out. About how little time he had and what he had and hadn't done with his life, and why, he shared an honest man's regret. Like you should do with Jesus. One that bends those knees, breaks you open, and heals you. And of course, my Brother always knew exactly what I should do with mine. We were honest and authentic with each other. And spent a little more time, being Brothers while we could.

BLUEBERRIES AND
BROTHERLY LOVE

The hours, days, and weeks slowly began adding up, some sort of strange cash register, endless moments of slow suffering strung along with moments of high hope, a pearl necklace for sale in the window of life, where the price tag always remains hidden behind the gems underneath the glass. And personal time, if you can steal some, is sitting in a restroom stall with your smartphone, pretending you're ignoring that one stubborn elephant who, will not leave the room. "Is today the day, is this hour," when we turn south and head out the door feet first? We would fight this losing battle the way we were taught, refusing to ever give the war the satisfaction of surrender. And we were not gonna be asked to leave.

It was clearly obvious our parents were simply too old to deal with brother's illness on a daily basis. We were all dealing with their growing illnesses and rapid decline as well as his. Daddy had severe COPD at this point, so any given week was another last-second desperate call for the ambulance by Daddy's wife, GiGi, and another trip to the local emergency room to hopefully keep him ticking another day, or week. I often wondered, why fight as hard as he did, in that kind of shape? The only honest answer I have is, although he was miserable incarnate in body, Daddy wanted to live every second he could in spirit, and at the very least die like a man. Fighting.

Even if it *was* wrapped in a fleece blanket, slumped over in a chair, chewing on a candy orange slice and Vicodin, watching *The Young and the Restless*. Just because we all have to "give up the ghost" to Death one day, it doesn't me we have to literally hand it the Jerk.

Daddy had enthusiastically, proudly refused to sign any papers about End of Life directives, like it was the Confederate Declaration of Secession of Life. It was comical, at first. We never could get him to understand it was so he could choose how he died, if he got that choice, as much as possible, and limit unnecessary suffering. Unnecessary suffering? Ain't no such thing, as "Unnecessary Suffering" where I come from. You may not understand it, but God does. If Jesus could die on the cross for your sorry ass, and leave that Gift, laying at the very doorstep of your ego and arrogance, as to whether you accept it or not, then the very least you can do is suffer through this life with some class. Don't get me started or I'll never stop. Burns me up how we treat the Son of God sometimes. Don't get haughty, I'm talking about me too.

With a mind and will molded by the echoes of the Great Depression, Daddy would just get pissed off and yell, "I ain't signing no damn papers so I can help them kill me! That's what they want to do. Kill me!" It became an ongoing sadistically comical routine with each hospital stay, pressured by the hospital administration to get him to sign. But this old dog would be doing no new tricks. We tried 'em all.

Mama was physically unable to make the trips to Duke to visit Glenn. Period. The ride as well as the trauma every mother feels for her dying child was simply too much to handle at her age. Glenn's first stay at Duke hospital lasted just shy of a month. Two teams of doctors worked round the clock to make him as comfortable as medically possible, keeping as much fluid off his stomach as they could, with endless transfusions, antibiotics, and anything else to clean out the toxins and boost his immune system. The very first morning at Duke, my Brother, ever the one for no bullshit, except his, had informed the medical team they would be brutally honest with him at all times. He expected no emotional favors. Hopefully they could learn something from him to help someone else. He would stay on top of what was going on in his lucid moments, as well as tell you what had been said when you thought he was out.

It was well into the second week before visitors began to pour in, since we had no way of knowing how long our predicament might last. Remember, "forty-eight to seventy-two hours, or ten days, tops!" We had passed the "or tops" part and headed into a third week when Daddy had his own appointment at the Veteran's Hospital right across the street. I saw this reckoning coming like a bad high school marching band in the Christmas Parade in Kenly, North Carolina. More like an ass-kicking on a Saturday night back behind Roadies. It was evident, needed, and unavoidable in every way. I considered it to be of holy importance at this point. Don't die with anger or shame on your heart. I can't imagine it's gonna do anybody any good. Most especially you.

Like all of us, Daddy had his coping skills and lack thereof. Under extreme stress, even now, he would bow up and attempt to be the "Daddy of Lore" from long ago, the one we as brothers grew up with and knew well. It was simply his learned way of enduring the encumbering stress of life when it got overwhelming.

It "goes without saying," which is why we always say it, no parent should watch their child die or see them dead first. It's unnatural, unnerving and goes against everything naturally parental and protective in nature. Regarding my Daddy and Brother, I had heard it all, plus a lot I wasn't supposed to, by this point, so let me be "crystal-Kentucky-clear" about my feelings on the following. The hard history my Daddy and Brother shared, the beatings both endured, growing up, were true. Plenty of witnesses. But Daddy loved his son, and his son loved our Daddy the same. Unconditionally. And that means, no matter what someone does to you, or doesn't do for you, you still love them, if you ever loved them at all. My Daddy and Brother shared this kind of love. An enduring one. They were not merely at odds like fire and rain, but did a mysterious dance of a hard and painful, unconditional, constantly tested love. Loud, abrasive, upsetting, ugly. Then sweet as cane sugar on a wet finger tip. But they did love one another in their own unique way, as best they could, like we all do in this life. Imperfectly. If that's good enough for God, and it is, then "by-God" it's good enough for you,. So stop gossiping about it. And for "God's sake" and mine, quit bringing it up, reliving it, every time you see me. Let the heavy skeletons stay in the closet and rest every once in a while.

Perhaps, the times Glenn grew up in explains why Daddy's correction was so over the top. Perhaps them being so much alike made it inevitable.

But I've heard the damning remarks and stood in silence as long as I'm willing.

Our Daddy was a damn good man. He was loving. Sensitive, caring. He was hurt, wounded. He was pissed off. He was a flawed soul just as you and I are. So all of those that still feel the need to damn MY Daddy to hell for the past, beware of your own damn faults. He did the best he knew how. He got a lot right and royally screwed up some things. So, Yes! For the LAST fucking time, Daddy beat my Brother growing up. Least it wasn't with a mule strap like he got. Always some blessing to count. If you can add. You will not dispense your grace and forgiveness selectively around me. God doesn't. And He knows none of us deserve it.

The damage broke and molded my Brother's spirit to the largest degree, for life. But that's the first part of the story. It did not kill it. Somewhere along our journeys we all either choose to stay wounded or decide to heal as best we can. If it takes doing it with a cliché, "One day at a time." From my experience, least in this life, our great wounds may heal, but leave us a constant reminder of the pain endured, a deep scar, a real tattoo, for a reason. If I learned anything at all from my Brother and Daddy, it was this. Always remember, there are some things in this life, tender, precious, sacred things, if broken, that cannot be fully healed. Not here. Not by you. These require confessing they happened, acceptance of the penalty, death, lamentations and an appropriate burial. The ones that wound our very soul and spirit may require an unmarked grave, that only you and you alone can locate, lest the past be repeated.

So here came Daddy for his first visit to the bedside of his suffering, dying son. He was unnerved, already in mourning: you could see the haunting spread across his weathered face, already imprinting in his soul, its shadow echoing through his very eyes, when the old man rounded the corner. There was this familiar weight on his shoulders that night, as clear as a store-bought backpack. In his eyes, you could see this immense love for his son, his Firstborn, and the unnatural look all parents obtain by seeing their children die first. A rare place where even Hope wants to curl up and die. And there it was, that same "something," our homegrown Original Sin, hanging dense in the air, longing for somewhere to hide while seeking the next spot to leap out and bite you! An angry copperhead of shame & guilt Daddy had to carry, curled up in a dark corner of his heart. A burden of generations. A broken treaty of the trust of the heart.

I knew the final reckoning was coming. I also knew it wouldn't be what any of us expected. Even dying can't screw up love. Finding the courage to speak your truth really will set you free. We may go to our graves, still disagreeing, but the act of proclaiming and owning your own truth, devoid of any other's understanding or validation, is in itself a simple act of accepting grace, the salve and salvation for the soul. But what do I know?

This was the first time Daddy and Linda had been able to visit, the ride was simply too far, Daddy was in too bad of shape to come and it was all Linda/GiGi could do to nurse him every day at home from sunrise to another sunset, and hope to find a single moment for herself. For some reason the wisdom came to me that I could not be in the room when Daddy went inside. The dynamic would change. He might feel attacked by his two sons. My Brother might assume I was on his side and use baby brother as a weapon. Or worse, think Daddy and me were emotional gangsters come to rob the little loot Brother had left. So I did what all double-first cousins do, or should, in moments of family crisis and despair. I enlisted my first available one to do the job for me. Bless her heart. Lisa was there and earlier, I had got her off to the side and quickly explained what was most likely, for sure, under God's Carolina blue sky about to happen here. Daddy would walk in behind his facade, only showing the grieving parent. My Brother and I had already discussed it and I knew Glenn had come to some sort of awkward inner treaty with this he was ready to sign. For the first time in his life, as best he could, he was finding a broken peace, by accepting the truth, openly speaking of his own antagonizing part in the long feud. But he still needed our father to admit face to face, just one time, in private, these things happened. Just, say it. Admit it. If he was to sign the treaty, say "I'm sorry," that would be a double bonus on severance pay for the soul. But admission was now, non negotiable.

My brother had accepted two truths, and he knew Daddy loved him much better than Peter loved the Lord, least as well. Daddy never denied his own son in public three times with roosters crowing. Daddy did occasionally beat the living shit out of him. Every whipping was not a beating. Daddy was not a monster. But they had happened. For far too long, one being too long, but we're talking the better part of ten years. They had damaged Glenn. He was pissed-off and angry, literally, his entire life, off seeking refuge for his heart. But the deeper truth is it had hurt both of them, deeply. Sure, it broke and confused a child, creating an anger in him that was honestly unmatchable at its highest, non-extinquishable even at a spark. It also broke our Daddy, who carried the guilt for decades, molding it into an emotional mason jar, and preserving a moldy shame to hide in the pantry of our family's heart. One where the seal didn't take. It did what all "sin" does, separated and bound us, in a family tale only we could weave and only the Divine could help us unweave together. The deepest truth however, was Daddy didn't invent this. It was handed to him as a scared-shitless, little boy himself, who didn't know what to do with it. I imagine, when you're six, you run in to kiss Mama "Good Morning" and she's dead as a bent doornail, your baby brother's been taken away, oh, AND Daddy's drunk again, tearing your ass up for no reason with a mule strap days later, I imagine that sets pretty solid in a child's soul, for quite a while. For a lifetime. In this one.

When I asked her to guest-officiate the deathbed reunion, Lisa's eyes immediately grew as big as Granny's coffee saucers, as she said, "I don't know, man." I comforted her and let her know someone objective needed to be in the room. Bravely, Lisa made her way into my Brother's room. Soon enough, Daddy and GiGi got off the elevator and visited with me a for a few moments, getting a full update on what Daddy was about to witness, what to expect, and then a silent, deeply somber, sweet but sad man made his way down that cold hallway. GiGi and I looked at each other and prayed for the best.

I gotta be honest. I did not pray. Surely all the worthwhile prayers anyone could say had been uttered by now. When you get to the place where you have "handed it over" to the Big Guy, actually done that, you don't need to talk about it and you move on. This impending interaction might clear the entire damn hospital floor, someone might get arrested, but no one would die. Least, no one we weren't already expecting to be leaving us soon anyway.

A long time went by, and finally Lisa came out, walking briskly down the hall, her head down, and reaching me she looked me square in the eye and said, "God, my God, how they talked to each other. I have never heard any one talk to each other like that! It just... it just... breaks your heart."

Amen Sister; it does. Every time. It breaks all our hearts. And Lisa, I hope you can forgive me for asking that of you one day. You will always be my Soul Sister.

I eased down to outside the room, keeping my distance, and soon enough Daddy emerged. They had made it another twenty-odd minutes alone, so I honestly thought, "I'll be damned, they got somewhere." Daddy fumbled around for a minute getting his "mess right," that's what we call it, which gave me time to grab my own and soften my heart. As I walked up, he pulled and firmly tugged his farm hat down over his eyes, trying to hide them from me. It was the only time I would ever feel this exact way with my own Daddy. A strange, southern son's, out-of-body experience to wind up feeling like a counselor or pastor with your own Daddy, of all people. I was tired too. Too tired for arguing over a deathbed. Trying to look in his eyes I asked, "How is he? How was your visit?"

The bullshit started immediately. I had come to always expect implausible denial and disguise on this subject long ago. Daddy had never, ever admitted, not once, that the beatings took place. Ever. Do you hear me? Not once! And I seriously doubted at nearly eighty years old, he was going to now. That is, barring a divine miracle, that no one here seemed willing to create enough space for. He usually defensively and immediately, shut down any conversation about it, simply left, or on rare occasions could be pushed to the expected explosion of, "I ain't never beat anybody like that! Especially my own son! It's a bunch of shit somebody's made up!" The audacity of such a repulsive, redundant, repudiating renunciation of the truth, Daddy's reconstruction of it, had long since ceased to amaze, impress or bewilder me. For at least a decade or two, I saw it for what it was. Shame. A family's shame, and generations old. A deeply injured man's way of trying to accept the unacceptable, all on his own. I may not be the smartest squirrel in this family's nest, but even I can get a nut every now and then.

Trying to avoid me and realizing he could not, Daddy finally erupted with his go-to condemnation of my brother, "You should have heard the way he talked to me? He don't love me! You don't talk to your Daddy like that and..." Not that I needed one, but I had a witness, had already seen her face, and spoken to her. Even now, even freaking now, with you two, it's gonna be the same old shit? So we ARE gonna tote this to the graveyard? Well. Y'all tote it! Damnit. Cause my knees and back are shot.

When I replied "Daddy, Glenn loves you," I might as well have thrown water in a cast iron frying pan swimming in Crisco and buttermilk breaded chicken in Hell's Kitchen. His anger, hot as frying grease, splattered into my face. Suddenly, for some holy reason, something I didn't deserve flowed through me, so I leaned down into his face, and lovingly said, "Daddy, look at me. Look at me Daddy. Trust me." I'd never talked to my Daddy like this. Who in the hell did I think I was? I knew it wasn't me because it was amazing. It was grace again.

And for the very first time in my life I saw my Daddy cry from his soul. I mean weep, brother! That honest cry, the one you know you need to have, but none of us can ever pry out of ourselves alone. A cry of Confession. Of surrender. I knew, in that moment, I could communicate with our Daddy. The truth silently pried that vault of denial open. He was tender, accessible. The veil and illusion of a man raised in the sad shadow of the Depression was shattered. It evaporated. I saw a six year old child standing in front of me still missing his mother and trying to build a life with the only shitty tools he was given, death and low self-esteem, hard liquor and hard work. Then I realized, someone had showered just enough sweetness on the feller, to make it bearable through the years. I saw my Daddy's innocence. Experienced it.

Daddy stood there emotionally naked to me for the first time, broken to the point of full access, broken by his own accord. As I gently placed my hand on his left shoulder, Daddy opened up to me in a way he never had before and I noticed out of the corner of my eye, Glenn was staring deep into my eyes through the open slits of the white shades in the tiny window on his door reading every word coming off my lips, and it wasn't until our eyes locked that he was sure I wasn't betraying him. His stare shot through me and then, realizing what I was saying, he sank back on his pillow and relaxed, because he knew his brother was not going to shove this under a cheap, emotional rug. The only thing I was interested in was getting to the truth in all our hearts, and it was now or never! And personally, I was exhausted at toting this unbearable crap around. It is a slow death of the spirit. Because, you are toting death itself.

Literally crushed and now hushed by the weight he had carried inside far too long, I felt like Daddy's heart was in the palm of my hand. And I could feel Glenn's open heart desperately staring at me through that small hospital room window. I knew, we were all in the same place, a spirit of contrition, if only for a second. I felt the responsibility of being a weak excuse for a bridge, that might hold our weight, long enough for us to cross this canyon, together, God willing. And then, I felt only love.

As sweet but firm as I could, I looked into my tired, old father's face, hand resting on his shoulder, softly smiled and said, "Daddy, don't you understand? This isn't about blame. We ain't got enough time left for blame. This is about love. Glenn has already forgiven you. He just wants you to know that, and he needs to know you've forgiven yourself before he's gone." But no one can forgive what hasn't been acknowledged. Nobody. Daddy wept. Like the Bible says, "and Jesus wept." Tears streamed down my face as well as my Brother's. And for one brief, brilliance of a holy moment, we could all three feel each other's hearts and nothing else, our opinions and emotional demands pushed out of the way.

And then, as quickly as his heart had opened, a rushing wave of high-tide pride shut it down again. His defense mechanisms, beyond his emotional control at this point in life, swirled up onto that sweet shore of openness, and swallowed it back into a lost sea. But I saw it in my Daddy. My Brother saw him break too, saw him exposed. And the look on his face said it all. Be mighty careful digging for what you want. It may not be what you think it is when you turn the dirt on the grave. May not be a perfect Hollywood example of closure, but me and my folks, we live in the real world. An unforgiving world, where we love with all our might, sharing imperfect love and seeking those brief moments when amazing grace makes the sweetest sound. I also saw the deep hurt in my Brother's eyes he felt from seeing his own Daddy's long hidden shame fully exposed in that moment. I saw the waterfall of hot tears striding down his cheeks. A genuine apology softens every heart involved. How's that go, "Confession is good for the soul?"

And that was that. Daddy and GiGi headed home and I returned to my Brother's side. We spoke not one word of it. Spent time being brothers while we could, and then he had the strangest request. He was never hungry, for anything, and suddenly he wouldn't stop talking about fresh blueberries. He sent me down to the high-end but fabulous, Duke Hospital cafeteria-food court to get him, of all things, some blueberries.

The sun rose on another day, and hours later I got in my truck for Atlanta.We all needed a little time to let some sunshine in. Days later, after a few more shows with Zac and the boys, once again, leaving Hot-lanta at four in the morning, I hauled ass back to my dying brother's side and he continued to do what all siblings of The Exalted Older Ones do. He ordered me around, and I enjoyed it. With me at forty-three years old, he was still giving me life advice from his deathbed and he even eventually made me take a vow, in front of him in that hospital room with a nurse as a Witness. I would not leave the band while he was alive. I knew the truth. The "lone dolphin" could not deal with that being laid, on his table and he knew me well. I was doing what all babies in the family do. Try and be there for everyone. Create a false sense of responsibility that is impossible to carry. The weight of all three family members rushing to the grave and me driving round trip across three states, weekly, sleeping in the back of my truck, open to the stars, at rest areas, was literally about to kill me. Within a month or so, I had fallen asleep returning, and three times driven completely off the interstate before waking up. It was a miracle I had not killed myself or someone else.

Walking in the room I saw Glenn was in the most intense pain I had yet seen him stoically suffer, still refusing pain meds. I grabbed the hospital recliner and turned it around facing him and pushed it snug, right up against his bed. Where we could look in each other's eyes, and talk, soul to soul.

"I reckon you heard all about our last visit to the Great Divide?" Referring to the long standing, chasm between our father and him. Glenn was bowing up, mirroring that unapologetic, haughty, "I'm always right god-damnit face," the direct imprint of our Daddy. I was talking to the same demon yet once again, one I knew first-hand and by first name. He'd just switched carriers to my Brother for this moment.

"Yeah, I did. Heard about it when he walked out this door, from the horse's mouth."

"Well, I'm fucking done. I'll never mention it to him again," When I uncharacteristically didn't react, he soon said," Well, I wanna know what you think?" I was floored, he asked.

I simply said, "Man, what do I think? I think he is a tired old man who is exactly who he is. I think he truly doesn't believe it happened by this point, maybe he never did or it is literally unbearable to approach. And I think, you expect him to apologize to you this one magical time, the way you want it given and that probably ain't gonna happen. Man, he didn't go to college, he was raised with a fucking mule strap, eating opossum with his drunk Daddy. Words like *therapy* and *inner healing* mean a good day fishing at Uncle Walter's pond or running deer with dogs through pine plantations.That doesn't make him a monster. It makes him broken, just like the rest of us."

Tears began to well in Glenn's eyes as I finished up, "And I think your Daddy loves you and you love him the same way. We ain't got no more time for pride, Brother. We ain't got time for this shit. " And my dying brother's face became what I consider a perfect picture of true peace. Not a Hallmark card or lame, poorly written poem on the back of a funeral program, that denies the beauty and elegance of living this painful life. One, where we see the lines we've drawn across each other's faces, dates and names cut in a tombstone, and acknowledge the damage done and the high cost of these bitter struggles. The one that kinda takes our breath, and we wonder, we can hope, perhaps this is the battle that ends the war. And Glenn sighed, smiled and sank back on his pillow, looking upward and said, "Yeah. Fuck it."

It was never, ever mentioned again. And now, I'm done with this "special music" myself. Rest in peace, family pain.

Then he did what older brothers always do. A quick pause and he lovingly said, "Go get me some more fucking blueberries."

I did. Cause I LOVE my Brother.

COACH K, GOOD LOOKS, AND THE MOMENT

That first month at Duke Hospital was a roller coaster. Two teams of specialists worked with Glenn to keep him "comfortable," which meant sit and watch his belly grow larger until the pain was too much, then siphon it off and hope for the best, that being an easy a death as possible. There was no cure for Hepatitis C at this time. No need to worry about the rest. Cirrhosis, liver cancer or diabetes. It only takes one fatal illness to kill you they say.

One morning the initial team came in and Glenn announced, "Look, I know I'm dead in the water. Can't y'all use me to learn something so the next poor son of a bitch that comes along doesn't have to go through this?" The "this" he referred to being a typical, final stage of any terminal illness-the ridiculous medical circus-circle of "keep 'em comfortable but be sure you don't kill 'em. Make death do it." If you've been there you know exactly what I'm talking about.

The lead doctor firmly replied that he was not being considered for research material. My brother lovingly said, swear on my soul, "I wasn't asking. It was an intelligent suggestion." Brother got word to his physician, Dr. Muir and after a brief visit, explaining what this might entail, he consented with the sweetest, most sincere gratitude. The journey began. They worked to get him in the best shape they could, which meant maybe we could leave the hospital knowing we'd either be running back there in, "forty-eight to seventy-two hours, or ten days," if not to the funeral home. Going into a third week, Glenn was actually doing really good. Good enough for a dying man to leave the hospital and go home, and die.

Dr. Muir requested we come by his office on the way out and got right to the point. "I've come to know some intimate parts of your family dynamics. My simple question is, what are you guys gonna do? Where are you gonna go?"

For the first time I had to put my brother "in his place" so to speak. If you know anything about dolphins, they never swim alone. Yet Glenn was a bit of "Lone Dolphin," always off doing his own thing his own way, and even lying there dying, he would somehow do death, his way. He was living, breathing paradoxical pride. The Beautiful Problem was, so was I. I glanced at Glenn then informed Dr. Muir, "I'm not taking him any further from you than I have to. You're all we've got."

Doc replied, "Good. 'Cause you're gonna need me again unless he gets lucky and just dies. Easily. Best hopes are the liver's artery rupturing, or he enters a toxic coma." That always makes for a bright Monday morning!

Glenn blared out, "God-damnit, I'll tell you where I'm going!" We both smiled that "Dude, I love you smile" and ignored him. After Dr. Muir left the room, I explained to Glenn how I was going to pay for our plan, which I had already unveiled to Doc. I had reservations maybe seven miles up the road on a nice disabled room at a weekly stay motel. We wheeled Glenn out, to my truck. In my gut, I knew we were screwed, well before we left. He was so weak and weathered he could barely sit up in the wheelchair without falling out. He had been knock, knock, knocking on Heaven's door for so long, he was tired of asking. For the past year and a half, he had looked like the stage-four cancer patient that haggled for one last round of chemo and another experimental drug, bearing that pitiful look of false, fatal hope. Now, he was beginning to look like a concentration camp inmate. A pregnant one when the fluids backed up.

The deepest truth we all learn eventually, with death, is experience means nothing. Death wears multiple masks, confusing you, gently whispering "Don't worry. I'm coming soon to bless you with a peaceful exit." While behind your back it's being the devil's advocate for dragging it out. "C'mon boys, you demons suck the very life out of them, slowly, while you can!"

My point? The whole scenario was like most drawn-out illnesses. Tragically comedic. Getting Glenn in the truck was more like getting your drunk and drugged brother quietly in the house before Mama or Daddy comes out and busts your ass than anything medically related.

I got us checked in at the hotel and lied my ass off at the desk. Because they absolutely asked me if I had a terminal hospital patient staying with me and didn't seem happy about asking. I had no plan of how I would move Glenn around. I only knew I would when I had to, because I had to do it. Leaning on me, a dead man walking, with his brother, you could feel his fragile exhaustion whispering through his weight loss and see the steel-willed determination of his spirit in his eyes. Everyone wants to, "die good." With dignity. And Glenn could feel my fear.

"God-damn man, chill out. You're gonna have a heart attack just thinking."

When I didn't reply as we entered the room, he cracked, "Damn, you didn't have to get us the honeymoon suite."

He wanted to go to the bathroom immediately and said, "Man I need a shower somehow," knowing he couldn't stand up in one. I said "Come on I got a surprise for you." When I pulled the shower curtain back, I helped him over the side, and as he sat down on that disabled seat in the tub, the heaviest tears of sheer relief and gratitude flowed freely. The man hadn't had a shower in about five weeks or more. They had drawn at least five to six liters of fluid off his belly, not to mention the normal wear and tear of dying slower than most. When that hot water gushed over him, you couldn't tell where the tears or the water started. Glenn softly uttered, "Thank You " And he meant it. I'm pretty sure that was mostly directed to God, but he didn't have to tell me he loved me. He just did. And I had told him. Hot water can work a divine miracle in a pinch.

I got him bathed, dry and back into bed. I let him know I was headed right across the street to Harris Teeter. The security guard and front desk were there if he needed something before I returned. Handing him a charged cell phone I said "I'm going to get us some water, fruit-Is there any food you think you could eat?" He wasn't interested in food; he was happy to be lying on a real bed, clean. He didn't care if he died right then. Brother drifted off to sleep in minutes and I backed out the door trying to close it silently. Right as the door was about to click, I saw those eyelids barely part and that rich baritone voice instructed me...

"Yo. Get me some fucking blueberries."

An hour later I could hear him moaning before I opened the door. In less than three hours I was wheeling him back into ER at Duke. Round Two was here. The blueberries lay in the room all week. I couldn't touch my brother's blueberries. It felt dishonorable. I watched them slowly, day by day, shrivel up and die too. For now, eat your blueberries with those you love, if you can, while you can. Nothing lasts forever. Not even dying.

At first you don't notice the change in yourself. You're foolish enough to think you can walk through this on willpower and come out the other side, maybe a lil' battered and bruised, announcing "The clipper and the captain have braved the storm." Sure, it will hurt, but you'll have time for healing later. Hours drew by like weeks, weeks flew by like they never existed. I didn't notice for the longest time I was shutting out the rest of the world. The rest of my life. I didn't understand I was shutting down my life like the beach season had ended and we were boarding up for the coming Category Three Hurricane. It was weeks before I noticed I could be standing in the packed cafeteria at Duke and suddenly realize I was hearing... nothing. In a room with family or friends, I may respond to your every question, then look up and have no idea what the topic was. Or care. All I knew I was doing, least trying to do, was the one thing I knew I had to do. Take care of my Brother and parents. Come to some sort of acceptance that our entire family was standing around the open grave of this life. And I began to fight the feeling that I was standing there with them, unwillingly waiting for permission to throw some dirt on our family's life.

Brother's second stay at Duke began peacefully enough. As soon as he was settled in a room, Dr. Muir stopped by and informed us we would be going to four teams of specialists instead of two. They wanted to make Glenn as comfortable as medically possible while they learned what they could from this sneaky, shy, unforgivingly horrific disease. Hepatitis C, a deadly virus of the liver, is much like the copperhead lying in the grass in the evening dark, just outside the throw of your front porch light. You may not know you're bitten until it's too late. The average patient at that time had contracted the virus twelve to sixteen years before being correctly diagnosed. Glenn was stage four when they found it. To be short and sweet, your liver literally rots from the inside out. And thus, so do you. There were many long hours I would just stare at my brother and plead for God to take him. Right then. Yet I knew in my heart, like everything else with Brother, dying would be no different. This would be a slow, stubborn, dreadfully drawn-out ordeal.

As the fall leaves began to paint Duke's beautiful campus into the epic beauty it is, the evergreens and pines stood out more and more against the Carolina blue sky, Duke Chapel's stones and a room of Death. With a fabulous view of The Chapel, we kept the shades drawn open and enjoyed every single sunrise and sunset in the protective silence of one another. We could go all day and night and not have to say one word to each other. This particular week he rarely talked, save the occasional, polite, "Go get me some fucking blueberries." *(He always included the adjective.)* It had long since become a darkly running joke, depending on the delivery. Late one night things were not going well and hadn't been for a bit. When you're in that kinda shape, that can absolutely mean that the someone who's knocking on the door or sneaking in is probably Death.

With tubes and IV's attached and coming out of every available spot, and a few that weren't, Glenn decides around three in the morning in a morphine- blitzkrieg, of ALL things, and I do quote, he "thinks he needs to shit." Of course, to make it easier on me, he absolutely forbade me to call the nurse for help moving, as we had been strictly instructed and already reprimanded. In fact he was already off the bed and halfway to the bathroom, before I realized it was a moot point. I got him situated on the toilet, Glenn holding onto the rolling IV stand, which now stood next to his new throne. The catheter and everything attached was flipping and flopping every which way including loose.

A few mostly unimpressive farts and nothing. I moved my chair closer to the door. Glenn wanted to keep the door shut, and I could not get him to understand, you're gonna cut the IVs and tubes in two or I can't get to you if you fall. Not exactly what the quintessential older brother wants to hear. As bad as he needed to go, "bless his heart," once he finally got situated and let his bowels burp a few times, the man couldn't shit to save his mortal life. I've never to this day seen that exact look on a man's face. That desperation, for the love of everything Holy, simply praying for a dump. Be mighty careful what you say you'll never pray for. But, being a classic Duke Blue Devil, down by fourteen with seven minutes to go, in foul trouble, Brother hung right in there, waiting it out, determined sooner or later to get, as Coach K calls them, "a good look." Ask those ball players sometime. You don't always get the shot you want. Sometimes you take what you can get, when you can get it.

Within thirty to forty five minutes Glenn was drifting off to sleep, sitting on the toilet, seemingly in complete bliss, while I stared through the crack in the door, jumping through my skin every time he fell asleep and started to fall over to his left. It would wake him up as I tried to ease in the bathroom to catch him. Each time this happened Glenn continued to shut the door. I was mortified at the thought of him falling off the toilet hooked up to all that crap and winding up wedged between the toilet and the wall. It was a critical care nurse's nightmare's screenplay. About every ten minutes or so or when he would begin falling over I would say "Glenn, you alright?"

"Yes, god-damnit!" in that loving sadistic southern drawl, was the only reply I got. Over and over. Some two hours later, still sitting on pins and needles, I pulled the recliner right up next to the bathroom door where I could relax more and still do my job keeping "point" as the Army calls it. I was sitting there staring at him, thinking of memory after memory, worry after worry, wondering how I was gonna manage losing my only brother and both parents. His eyes closed, head kind of pointed towards the ceiling, here came the next big toilet lean. To wake him and keep him from falling, I would wait as long as I could and then once again say, "Glenn, you alright?"

"Yeah. Yeah, yeah, yeah! Daaaaamn man. Hush!" Long pause.

Our pathetic prayer is answered with... well, not the sounds of silence, and Brother sighs deeply and says, " You know man-You just don't wanna miss... the moment. Your one shining moment."

Gotcha. You take the shot when you can get it, don't 'cha Brother?

Oh boy, do I ever miss him.

Glenn knew out in Nashville I had a little something going down that could be good, perhaps great. An artist friend of mine named Billy Dean and I had written a song based off a poem I had written several years earlier on a turkey hunting trip with Billy and my cousin Jimmy, entitled "*Real Things.*" Billy had called me several times while he "shopped" the song with major artists in the hopes they'd record it. We got a "hold" with George Strait's people first. Months later they dropped it and Billy pitched the song to Kenny Chesney's producer. He loved it. Eventually Kenny passed. That same day, a Thursday, Billy, a veteran songwriter and well-known star, walked out of that meeting and informed me he already had a hot younger artist waiting in the wings. When Chesney's camp bailed, Billy was on the phone with Joe Nichols. So that Thursday afternoon, Billy called and said, "They passed; Joe is cutting it as soon as possible." Four days later on Monday, Billy called informing me they had just recorded it and we would love it. And we did. Even better news was there was talk it could possibly be a third single and go to radio. For songwriters, that's the lottery ticket for a shot at making real dough. Mailbox money. For me, I was losing my one and only brother while both of our parents were in a foot race to the grave. I was about to get my first major cut on a national artist; and I honestly couldn't have cared less, other than any money that could help our situation. What we didn't know that day was it would be chosen as the title track for the album. Family was the only thing on my mind, for better and worse. But at least, my Brother had lived to see me accomplish something of significance as a songwriter.

The very day Round Two ended, I was able to get a significant advance on the new recording which would enable me to take care of us for at least a few months, whatever the Good Lord decided to give us. They had Glenn in fairly "good" shape, so we gathered around once again for the quick and uncomfortable goodbye of the nurses and doctors, a few instructions for "healthy living for the dying" and off we went. This time we made almost a week before I had to roll Brother back through that lobby and into the arms and care of the faithful Duke nursing staff. This was Round 3. And it had that kinda "ring" to it, like, this might our last round of boxing with the delightful deception of Death.

As we started Glenn's final round of treatment the holidays were arriving. Thanksgiving and my birthday were right around the corner. One Monday morning upon returning from Atlanta, I presented him with an iPod Zac Brown had given me loaded with thousands of songs for Glenn. I told him about the acoustic show we all did at Five Points in Atlanta, with Zac, Hop, Coy Bowles, Clay Cook, Oliver Wood and myself. And that I was the only person, artist or fan, in the entire place that night that did not know the show was a fundraiser for our expenses. He was as moved as I had been that previous Saturday night. He was in Heaven as he fumbled with this iPod thing and listened to music; it seemed to ease his pain and suffering much, more than narcotic pain meds. I sat silently in the nearby hospital recliner working on my laptop until I noticed he was having trouble figuring out how to work the iPod. Finally in a hostile fury, he erupted with a classic "I don't know how to work this damn thing!" I pulled up some Randall Bramblett and watched the peace and serenity wash over his face as he closed his eyes and relaxed, lost in a southern melody that seem to encapsulate his own sultry, south-bound heart.

I had been working for a while in silence as Glenn enjoyed his music when suddenly he pulled the headphones off. I could tell he had something he needed to say.

Word for word, this was it. "Man, I want you to know something. I always lived my life, my entire life, like it was semester to semester and I was still in college. Doing whatever I wanted, blowing with the breeze. But man, that ain't no way to build a life. That ain't no way to build a life. Build you a life, if you can, brother." And he put his earbuds back in.

As the final stay at Duke ended, the sojourn had become his lonesome, solo journey with a handful of us there as witnesses. We had always been so brutally honest with one another, there was zero emotional bullshit to wade through. What a beautiful Gift unto itself. The unsayable had already been said between us and bronzed our Brotherly-Bond. At this point there was absolutely nothing that could come between us. No opinion, fact, person. No attitude or circumstance. There is a holy place inside of each of us that not even death itself can touch. And oddly enough the closer you get to it, Death, blinded by its own dark selfishness, illuminates this sacred spot and gives you and those you love, a moment here, one there. A stolen moment. One of pure grace that gets you through another hour or day. It happens often enough you begin to keep your eyes open for those Good Looks and when your one brief shining moment comes, you must go for nothing but net. That's what Coach K. would say. We kept our eyes open from here on out.

HOLINESS, THE REBEL
JESUS, AND HONOR

It was clear this drama was coming to the end. I caught Dr. Muir in the hallway alone one day. He put his hand on my shoulder and lovingly, respectfully said, "It's about time for the beach." Glenn had informed him a long time ago to let him know if we could, when death was close or close enough to as he said, "head for the six pack and a lawn chair." He didn't want to miss that opportunity, if it came.

It was a Monday morning when a young, hitherto unknown, scared, intern entered the room. We figured, "New face, probably a new test."

The young doctor softly interrupted Glenn and his new iPod obsession and began to ramble. And I mean ramble. Finally Glenn said, "Son, what *are* you trying to ask me?"

They were sending him home to die. Boy did he get pissed. He angrily said, "You go tell them sons-a-bitches I said to get their asses in here, right now! Every god-damn one of 'em! I got something to say!"

Believe it or not, within minutes about six doctors from various teams walked in and lined up at the foot of his bed. I was sitting in the recliner working on my laptop and knew what was coming. One thing I learned, a long time ago, was when Brother wants to lose his shit, give Brother the space to do it or pay the price. After all, it's his shit, not mine. The main female doctor leaned over the bed to start to console and cajole Glenn and he stopped her in her tracks.

"I got one thing to say. I can't believe you guys sent this young kid in here to do your dirty work when he's never even met me. And I'm not gonna waste this opportunity to tell every one of you, you oughta be ashamed. That was a shitty thing to do and he deserves an apology. So, apologize."

And Almighty God as my witness, they did. "Now then, is it time for me to go? Let's get with it!"

Later that afternoon Dr. Muir came by at Glenn's request. He had treated us like family over this entire ordeal-Glenn had a way of getting in your heart, whatever it took, sugar, piss, vinegar or all three. They chatted for a few short moments, old friends now, laughing at misfortune and spilled milk, too old, tired and too cool for tears. You cannot be grateful and sad at the same time.

Glenn looked up at Doc and said, "I just really want to thank you for all you've done and tried to do. You've made this journey bearable for me and my family."

Blushing Doc replied, "Oh that's not necessary. It's what we do."

Brother sharply replied, "Oh yes it is! Ingratitude is a cardinal sin." And that was that. This time we were leaving Durham behind for good. I was able to talk the hospital into giving me twenty-four hours to figure out what the hell I was gonna do. I had a dying brother. I couldn't take him to the farm. It would be an emotional nightmare for everyone. Couldn't take him to Mama's or my home. We'd both be looking a new place to stay. So, I took Glenn home to Goldsboro, and rented a hotel room for the weekend to buy time. Lemme tell you something. Damn if time ain't expensive, by the day y'all. After getting him set up with food, and water and supplies in a cooler bedside to get him through the weekend, I had to immediately drive all night to Atlanta for all day rehearsal and two shows. I'd be back in less than two days, and our cousins would check on him every few hours by cell or in person. I was maybe four hours down the road when the call came from Lisa. They were headed back to Duke. My heart sank thinking I would not be with my Brother when it counted most. But, at least I knew he would be taken care of and loved. I will never ever forget having to leave him, looking back at Glenn, sitting on the bed in that hotel room, him cussing at me telling me to go to my gig, as a father. That he was "fine." I felt like an asshole. Okay, a very loving asshole. He was doing all he could to take care of me taking care of him. That's what brothers do.

While I was in Atlanta, they drew off what fluid they could from his abdomen, relieving some pain, Hospitals and insurance companies don't want dying people on the floor. Unless you know somebody. That's a fact. Dr. Muir made an unexpected visit and was lovingly blunt. He would have to leave, and the hospital didn't want us back. Doc was getting flack for, well, being a great doctor. But, it was Duke, and Duke had been good to us, and we don't whine. Brother was ready for "the beach."

I had recently been talking with our beloved cousin Jay about possibly renting a small house and living there with Brother till this was over. When I called home on Monday, I was told Glenn was safe and sound in Jay's living room in a hospital bed my cousin Lisa had rented for the long haul. And no, don't ask her, "Lil' Henry," again how much it cost, that was her and Andy's gift!

I will never forget walking in Jay's living room that day. I looked up as I entered the kitchen and caught Jay's eyes. He said, "We'll do what we can, as long as we can, Pal," holding his own growing grief and love for Glenn anywhere he could to keep from losing it. His eyes. Heart. On the very shoulders of his soul. I sensed Jay knew something I didn't. When I entered the living room, then I knew. It was different. He was different. This would be it.

There were a few weeks where Glenn went back and forth, going downhill, improving. He had forbidden our mother to come visit from the get-go. He did not want her to watch this go down, and he was right. Mama couldn't have taken it at eighty years old. So one really good week, as I was in Atlanta, Jay dropped Glenn off at Mama's for a weekend visit.

I got back in to Mama's late Saturday night, and Brother was not doing well. The toxins had rapidly risen, his color was that last hue the living hold, a bruised, blueish-gray tint of death squeezing the ever-loving last drop of life out of you. As slow as possible. Even though I'd been up and awake, going for over two days, I knew I had to stay awake in case he woke up. Sometime just before dawn, I must have fallen asleep. I awoke to my brother standing up in the middle of the room, swaying back and forth, a nose hair away from falling. He was stoned on toxins, his brain function slowed down to a crawl. I whispered as to not scare him, "Glenn. Hey Glenn." And as he sarcastically said, "Whaaaatttt, god-damnit," here came the fall. I leaped to catch him, but it was too far, too late. My Brother leaned backward as soft as a feather, straight as an arrow and fell like the stone being rolled on Jesus' tomb. Bam! The back of his head hit first, and God as my witness it sounded like a rotten watermelon hitting the far side of a dirty ditch-bank. He didn't move. I didn't either, at first. I thought, my Brother, is dead. Mama came flying out of her bedroom and said, "What in the world was that?"

"His head." And Mama sank as the if winds of Life were sucked out of her too. I couldn't tell if he was dead or not for several minutes. Gradually he came to in a concussion fog. I got him up and back in the chair, and Mama back in her room. Within minutes, blood starting pooling underneath both of his eyes, giving him two huge purple, black eyes, only underneath. I have never seen anything like it. He looked like the Demon of Death sent his top Death-Clown to be a smart-ass and paint my Brothers's face. To smear it and rub it in. I was convinced, this is it. I finally called a close friend's wife in Nashville, Kerri, a critical care nurse and asked what to do. She said, "If he is not in any pain, if he seems to be okay, just sit with him. You could be right. This may be it."

I stretched him out in Mama's recliner. Glenn seemed to be in a strange state of content but in absolutely no pain. But his breathing became shallow and far apart, like the honest sigh we give when a sunset doesn't solve all life's problems and we're more cool with that than a fake Hallmark movie-moment. The haze of death fell across his lips and face. I finally went and got Mama and said, "You need to come sit with us. Now, Mama." And we sat on each side, both of us holding one of his hands, one of ours, an Unbroken Circle of almost near mythical madness that settled into a love so pure, it flowed and dripped across my brother like a cool, lazy October afternoon. Later that afternoon, GiGi and Daddy dropped by Mama's, having been told the dire situation. Though they had never been to Mama's before, they came in and we all pulled up chairs around my Brother in a silent frail fellowship. It felt so natural and honest, it felt loving, because it was, like we had done this together weekly for years. For all the bad wrap death gets, only dying can make certain divinely beautiful things happen. That... was a moment of healing.

As the next day broke, suddenly, Glenn parted his eyes, seemingly surprised himself, almost annoyed, disappointed he was still here and said, "Damn, where is the coffee. I want some of Mama's coffee." She lit up like poor white trash getting hard-rock candy at a Cracker-Christmas and started brewing her coffee. And Mama's coffee was better than yours. I promise you that. I got Glenn appeased in the end chair at the kitchen table. Mama brings the coffee, Glenn lifts it up. "God-damn Mama!! I ain't had coffee this hot since I was with Uncle Henry on his ship."

My Brother was "back" as they say, so I did what I knew he loved! Called him on it. Challenged his memory and intellect. And honestly, I was a little past jealous at the mere thought he might have actually, possibly, ever been on one of Uncle Henry's Coast Guard cutters.

"When in the hell were you ever on one of Uncle Henry's ships?"

As dry as a cock-eyed actus in a creaky canyon, he looked me dead in the eye and with the coyness and a satisfaction saved only for a Big Brother or pied piper who knows he's right, Brother said, "July 7th, 1961."

As I went to press him on these bullshit facts, he sat up tall and proclaimed in his go-to, matter-of-fact, John Wayne, "well-ah-tell yah, pardner" voice, what I knew would be hard cold facts. "And the next day was, July 8th, 1961, smart-ass! Ladies Day at Yankees Stadium!" So and so was the pitcher and so and so lead off , on and on, he calmly, enjoyable, arrogantly and deliberately named the entire starting lineup, not only for the Yankees but the Red Sox as well. Even told us who closed and got the win. Mama sat in support, nodding her head at me, up and down, happy as Heaven as he had retrieved a pleasant memory as much for her as him. And Brother was 100%, *Marisa Tomei* in *My Cousin Vinny*, "dead-on-balls, accurate." Reason I know this, I had grabbed a pen, quickly caught up with him, and wrote down every single name and fact he uttered. The next morning I went online and checked it out. I'll be damned, if he wasn't right! Maybe the most impressive display of the human mind, intellect and spirit, that I've ever seen. Brother ended by saying, "Sorry I cussed Mama, but that's some hot-ass coffee. Thank you for making it though."

"You're welcome Shoog."

Which was always followed by the proper manner of acknowledgement. "Yes Ma'am. Yes Ma'am." I shook my head in, belief and disbelief, and sucked in that moment and entire morning for what it absolutely was. Incredulous grace.

Glenn kinda stabilized for maybe a month and then he began to swell, and I mean, swell. We had a visit previously scheduled with Doc at his clinic, contingent on brother's condition, so I called to discuss what to do. Doc actually got on the phone asking what kinda shape he was in. Glenn spoke for himself and said, "Please Doc, I just don't wanna die with all this shit on my belly. Please take it off." Dr. Muir said, "Bring him on."

The entire staff had that look as I wheeled him down the halls. That poor, pitiful look most folks give the dying. His PA shared a story I knew all too well. She couldn't stand Glenn and his acerbic wit when they first met, his mind and mouth could always draw a crowd, start a fight, or steal your heart. Now she had committed the worst medical sin of all. Along the way she had "fallen in love" with him and his dire condition told her what she didn't want to know.. "He just gets in your heart, doesn't he?" Yep.

Doc appeared and agreed to draw as much fluid as possible, with our hopes being very low due to recent attempts. Doc sent Jay and me to another lunch in a hospital cafeteria, and we returned, rounding the corner an hour later, Dr. Muir was elated. They had drawn three liters of fluid off Glenn's abdomen. The sticking point was that he was in a lot of pain and his blood pressure had plummeted.

Almost proudly, Doc said, "It went better than ever. Usually near the end, the fluid will collect and draw together. Three liters came off with no effort at all. I believe we can get more, problem is your brother may very well die on that table."

I already knew the answer. I knew my brother. His heart. How his mind worked. As complicated as he could seem to others, he was actually quite simple to me. "Complicatingly simple." Rhetorically, I asked what my brother had said. As we walked in the room, Jay, in our own uniquely acquired, traditional family sarcasm, looked at Brother and the three clear one liter medical bottles full of sordid fluid and said, "Well, Bud, you got a pale ale here, a nice German lager and a..."

Glenn unable to even lift his head, smiled and said, "Yeah, boy! I was waiting for you two stooges. Starting my own brewing company. Have a sip!" Brother used his own death to hone an already masterful sense of humor into a surreal southern original work of art.

The issue at hand was the fact our bodies are pressurized. Glenn was a certified diving instructor, so this fact made complete sense to him. He had a diving reputation, like everything else in his life. Take it to the Limit, one more time. I'll always believe in my heart and mind that Brother thought he could will the drop in pressure away, as if he was dealing with air bubbles in his bloodstream. We waited and waited until finally, he said, "Let's do it."

Doc verbally stated the obvious, I'm sure for legal reasons, that we would proceed with the understanding he could die on the table. My brother didn't care. In his mind, if there was one solitary thing he could do to fight, he must do it. A short time later we had two more liters. Five liters of fluid drawn off my Brother's abdomen at one time. It was the most horrific example of gruesome astonishment I've ever witnessed. Privately out in the hallway, Doc looked me in the eye and said, "All I can tell you is, your brother just won't die."

I replied, with the strongest conviction, "Oh he will. When the Lord's ready to take him, he'll go. Right now, he's got a bigger battle to fight."

Doc did the usual, no predictions how the end would play out. Certainly it couldn't be more than, you can laugh now, "forty-eight to seventy-two hours, or ten days," at the most. Hopefully he would slip into a toxic coma and die. However, the Doc assured me, as the old saying goes, my Brother was, "not long for this world."

An hour and half later we pulled up in Jay's driveway. Brother was so tired and weak from the trip to Durham and the drawing off of fluid he literally was, now, a dead man barely walking. As we went to go up the steps into the house, a second after refusing Jay's hand of help, Glenn t-totally busted his ass, busting open his right knee. We got in the house, Glenn in the bed, and put a band aid on what we could. At this point, that was pretty much a knee and our hearts.

The next few weeks, went by like a slow motion whirlwind. I stayed by my Brother's side until the very last minute, then headed to Atlanta for a show or two with the band. I felt supremely responsible for my Brother lying in a rented bed in our cousin's living room. I wasn't embarrassed. But I felt deep inside I should have, could have, been more successful. I should have been prepared somehow. I look back now and wonder what fool could actually think such a self-centered thing. The next month crawled by as Glenn slowly then more rapidly deteriorated. There were the daily visits by the faithful like my double first cousin Lisa's husband Andy. Every single morning, on his way to work at UPS, Andy pulled up on the curb and came in, the sun usually not even up, a slight fog in the air. It might only be a minute or two, but he was there every day to see how we were, what we needed. Too many of us talk the talk and don't walk the walk. Lemme put it another way. There are far too many Christians, from my humble experience, that are far more full of themselves or shit than they are the Holy Ghost. And I've felt that way since I was a child. The world needs more "Andy-ies."

The weekends visits greatly increased, as well as the homemade food. Jay and I never went hungry thanks to a dear high school friend, Caroline Rackley and many, many others. Nearly every day without fail, Caroline brought or sent over a homemade lunch or supper for us. Just because. We were being loved, just because. That still makes me cry. To eat homemade food somebody, who didn't have to, made for you. THAT is Soul Food.

One early, dark November Sunday morning, I came in from Atlanta about daybreak. I could feel it in the dense winter air, the impending death, and as I walked in the house, I knew we were close. From the look in Jay's eyes he was beyond exhausted. Dealing with a severely damaged back and hip himself, Jay had jumped right in from the get-go. We had home-hospice while we patiently waited for a bed at a hospice center, but they came only once a week, with another short visit later in the week to bathe him. Jay and I changed nearly every diaper on him for months. We wiped him down, bathed him, lotion, baby powder, whatever it took, wherever it took it and it took it all. But this morning the look in Jay's eyes said, "I don't know, Bud."

Glenn was in extreme pain, and we had been gradually administering morphine with a dropper for several weeks. He had somehow held off and not taken narcotic pain medicine on a regular basis. But now, there was no choice. I walked up to my Brother 's bed and glanced over at the tiny Christmas tree Jay had decorated and placed at the foot of it. For almost two months, he had not eaten a single bite of food, instead living off Aunt Louise's Boiled Custard, a half a tiny bathroom Dixie-cup at the time. A creamy, soothing, age-old concoction for the sick and ailing or the dying. But this morning, something was "different" as they say. This moment was inherently important. It had that thing you can feel as if it were fresh dirt floating in pure air, a truth so raw that to ignore it is a sin itself. My Brother, nearly begging simply said, "The Rebel Jesus, man. The Rebel Jesus."

I knew exactly what he meant and went over to the iPod connected to a small boombox and found Jackson Browne's tune. As it ended the first time, he said, "Again." And this repeated for three replays. I got in the chair facing my Brother's back as he lay on his side, writhing in pain, and tried to comfort him. For an instant I felt like that lil' blond headed boy, filled with love and in over his head again. Finally Glenn began pleading out loud, "God Almighty, whatever I've done to deserve this... I am so sorry. I am so sorry." I whispered, "It's okay," and then I realized, "Hey, dumb ass! He's not talking to you." The short distance between us slowly zoomed away, as if I were a film director pulling away for the money shot. And my Brother, wept, the way I like to imagine Jesus wept, in the Garden of Gethsemane, pleading, down on the very knees of his soul from the deepest part of Him for a way out or the supernatural strength to go on. And I pray to my God I never have to watch anyone else repent like that. Brutal, yet oddly enough it was so deeply beautiful and pure, a true thing, the truest, a man's conversing with his Savior, offering up the only thing he has left. His pride. I saw my Brother completely, utterly helpless, lying in the ashes of his life. And as the song, the Rebel Jesus ended, my eyes fell across the bed, admiring my sweet Brother, scanning his body wrapped in a cool white cotton sheet, the faint glow of old school Christmas tree lights trying to take me to better days long since gone.

I knew I had witnessed another true confession. A peace began to fall across him like an undeserved White Christmas. And for now, his pain subsided.

I walked up to Jay in the kitchen and said, "You... are a Holy Man."

Jay replied, eloquently, with the smile of a child that had been caught with his hand in the cookie jar, "Shit."

I countered with, "That proves it. 'Cause a true Holy Man would never admit it with his own lips. He'd be too holy for that." And with smiles we both collapsed around his kitchen table once again.

It wasn't long after this that Glenn decided one evening, as I prepared his evening dose of umpteen pills keeping him "alive," to wave them off. He was done with that. His deterioration seemed to cease, and he actually improved for a few days, and I knew, this was the Little Bighorn. Surrounded by only the love of family, cut off from the silly worries and frets of the living, there was no getting out of this one.

Glenn's greatest fear all along had been living long enough to lose his mind. Or as he would say, "If I start to get pickled, you promise me, you'll try and warn me of the first signs I might miss." My Brother coveted the gift of his intellect. Around this time, he began to lose the function of his arms. At first his hands became like bear paws, awkward and swollen, till they were eventually useless. He could sense the ship was going down, so he became belligerent at times. There was a cycle through intense pain, his head slinging side to side like that of a reckless mule, on to exhaustion, then an hour or three, on a lucky day, of stillness. And then suddenly Glenn would want to go see Doc. We couldn't get him to understand, there was no more "Doc," except The Great Physician as he became weaker and weaker.

Glenn had a weekly visitor who had been with us since week one at Duke. Mama Pat. Glenn's ex-wife's mother. As she said, "They divorced but I didn't divorced him, Darling." At 73 years old, walking on a prosthetic leg since she was a child, Mama Pat drove herself every week, from Charlottesville, Virginia to Richmond. She boarded the afternoon train, and I would pick her up in nearby Wilson. She would stay the night and love on Glenn like he was her own son, because he was. Her most used, go to line was, "Love you more, Darling." Mama Pat had always had a very tender spot for Glenn. She could see the scars on his heart, those permanent tattoos. She also understood his unique form of venom and could more often than not diffuse it. They adored each other, and they soaked in their time together as we soaked in their love as well. Another gorgeous true thing to witness.

Brother's legs were now not working well. He knew deep in his intellect he was failing. So one morning he rose up like it was time to go to work. His speech becoming very slow and slurred as he began to utter over and over. "I gotta go, let's go. God-damnit, let's go!" I walked him for a spell. Then Jay relieved me. Going into half an hour of him standing up in the middle of the room, saying "I gotta go" he was not going to be told what to do. Finally Mama Pat in her old school, classy, sultry, southern drawl said, "Let us walk for a while, Darling, want to?"

He proceeded to have her, one achingly slow step at a time, assist him to the standing coat rack. He wanted to put on his barn coat and favorite newsboy cap. And once he was properly attired, in his medical diapers, jacket and hat, he stood up, for two and a half hours, with Mama Pat holding on to him. Finally he said, "Okay. Okay. Time to go home." He took of his hat, his jacket, and my Brother never walked again, with or without assistance. What he did do, in my heart, was walk tall, that day. In our family, you don't quit. Ever. If it kills you, you walk with purpose and passion, head held high, to the Crossroads.

All you caretakers out there, who've been there, done this, know the awesome feeling of helplessness you feel throughout most of the "dead man walking" the Green Mile. And with that, my Brother was never the same. He did what the dying do. Slowly, he became the small ship on the horizon, withdrawn unto himself, no longer trying to wrap his head around the whole of it all. And I continued to worry, obsess about the only thing I gave a decent damn about. His Soul.

It was around this time that fluid began to build up and backup in his throat. Jay's sister Phyllis had been a nurse at Duke for twenty three years before she had to find an answer to something stirring in her soul. And just a month before, already an ordained minister, our cousin received her master's degree from the seminary in Kentucky. Phyllis and Glenn had graduated high school together, and Jay the year before, so this was a tight-knit group of people. And now not only was Phyllis, Glenn's cousin and classmate, but she was his pastor too. There were no surprises to discover in each other. There were however some mysteries of the heart to be revealed.

One evening, I was dog tired, and very stressed out. Glenn was unusually stressed and making it impossible for me to suck the fluid out of his lungs with the device Phyllis had been smart enough to acquire weeks before we needed it. Suddenly she came in unannounced, and as she walked in the room said, "Here Shoog, let me help you." Glenn immediately calmed down as Phyllis proceeded, and I literally collapsed in a hard-back chair at the foot of Brother's bed. Slowly our eyes met, and we started another of those unspoken conversations like we'd always had. I could literally feel him talking to me. My Brother looked so deep into my soul in that moment, he showed me a tender spot, even I didn't know I had. I uttered "So that's why you did it." And tears started to roll down both our cheeks.

Phyllis inquired, "Did what sweetheart? What did Glenn do?" in her soothing, loving way. So I proceeded to tell how Glenn called home every week when he went off to college. He knew what time Mama had choir practice on Wednesday, so every Tuesday night he would call home and talk to Mama, shoot the breeze, and then say, " Let me speak to Chris."

As I would take the phone he always said in a don't-bullshit-me manner, "You alright?"

I always said, "Yeah," cause in that moment I was. Long as I knew my Brother's eyes were on me.

"I'm gonna call you tomorrow night at 6:45 on the nose. Now be there damnit, answer the damn phone or I'll tear your lil ass up."

"Okay."

He always ended with, "I love You now!"

And thirty plus years later, staring through what was left of my Brother and seeing his soul and he seeing mine, exposed the way only dying seems to do, I had an answer for Phyllis' question. And myself. I ended with, "He was calling to make sure I was alright. That I wasn't getting the beatings he got." My Brother, crying at the sound of discovery, tears rolling down my face, I ended with, "'Cause he would have killed Mama, Daddy, or anybody else if they'd ever laid a hand on me."

Glenn, filled with breath of acknowledgment, sank back into relaxation in the bed. Phyllis looked over her glasses and sweetly, reverently said, "How noble is that?" I replied, slowly, deliberately, "Pretty fucking noble." A pause.

"Glenn used to say to me every now and then. Damn bro, you *can* be slow sometimes to be kin to me." And we all laughed and cried.

Glenn could no longer talk, or sit up, even with assistance. He was imprisoned in his tired body, bound to a bed of pure misery. On our last Sunday night together, I was alone and preparing to give Glenn his morphine. He was having severe trouble swallowing. We had been putting the morphine in apple sauce, and now even that was drying and crystalizing on his tongue. He kept staring at me with a strange look I hadn't seen before. Like, "Jesus Christ, do something. Kill me please."

As I prepared the pain meds, I looked deep into his eyes. He was pleading with me, nodding to put more medicine in the dropper. He started blinking his eyes sharply shut, then opening them wide again. I asked him, "Are you asking me what I think you're asking me?"

My brother nodded yes. I sank in my chair. I sat there with a full bottle of morphine, knowing he was begging me to help him go. To overdose him. I could feel him pleading for the rush of warm relief morphine brings, for it to spread across his body and envelop him until he evaporated across the horizon. And on my soul, I wanted to do it. He could tell by the look in my eyes, I wanted to free him. I just... could not... do it.

After a long pause I barely mumbled," I'm so sorry." I didn't have to tell him I wasn't man enough. He understood me better than anyone. (The Truth is, I was *more* than man enough physically. Spiritually, was something else. That was all that stopped me. I couldn't play God with my Brother's life). He looked back at me and slowly batted his eyes, and smiled. I gave Glenn an appropriate dose and sat in stunned silence until he drifted off into another narcotic cloud. I held it together till I knew he was out, and then I cried the way you cry when you have failed the only real thing this fallen world has to offer. Those you love. And I prayed he would die. I knew Glenn wasn't mad at me. I wasn't even mad at myself. I cried anyway. Simply because I knew how deeply my Brother loved me and how deeply I loved him. That's a gratitude that comes like a tsunami. A love that just washes all of life's bullshit far, far away.

There are occasional quiet moments in which I feel like I failed him and then, eventually, I see my Brother's smile. That was our last "conversation." One that needed no words, cause when there's nothing left to say, that needs to be said, you hush talking. By Wednesday night, he began slipping into a toxic coma. Easily, peacefully, so it seemed. My brother was indeed, about to die. The salty-sweet taste of death was beginning to settle on the tongue so to speak.

FROM CHAPEL HILL TO HEAVEN.

I believe I've made it clear me and mine are Duke fans. Lemme "perspective" that for you.. Where I'm from, you're either UNC– Chapel Hill-Carolina Tarheel – pale, pasty, sky blue OR if you're like us, you're true Duke dark navy blue down to your blood. A Goat or a Devil. The reason this is significant is it's significant. It's one of the world's oldest most intense, name-calling, butt-brawling sports rivalries dating back over a hundred years to the first fistfight... they started. Eastern North Carolina, Tobacco Road is all about ACC basketball due to what we use to call the BIG FOUR (UNC, Duke, NC State, Wake Forest) all being within miles of each other. UNC and Duke are still seven miles apart and each year we meet for a mandatory two conference games minimum, usually in the conference tournament and then fighting to show each other up through March Madness, in quest of another National Championship. Each spring families stop speaking, spouses quit making love, cousins cuss each other out, friends unfriend each other. Mamas stop speaking to their own children. It's awesome! The simple fact, the sheer irony, that the day before my brother would depart this earth, I would have to leave his side and be at a graduation in of all places, the fabled Dean Dome on the campus of UNC-Chapel Hill is at best unbelievable, at the least surreal, if not downright cruel, even for a Blue Devil. Or it's just a hilarious coincidence. Finding myself amongst the TarHeels, I should have known things were going south.

We had been trying for forever, since we left Duke, to get Glenn into hospice. Week after week we were told "you're moving up the list." Death never cooperates. The week before my brother died, after arguing with the insurance company for nearly a month and a half about hospice care, being told we had "the next available bed" and seeing the fifth bed become available in three days, yet still no phone call, I ... was... livid. Livid! Suddenly, one beautiful December afternoon I get a phone call from an unrecognizable number, and I decide out of character to answer. The young lady explains to me, we're sort of like distant cousins and she had just heard what was going down. That she worked for a hospice place, and they had now offered five beds to the insurance company. This week alone. The deal was, insurance didn't want to pay for it since we were already doing home hospice and here's the part I loved, and I quote, "Gosh, he should be dead any day now anyway." Maybe it'll be in forty-eight to seventy hours.

Now read into "the deal" I made a quick call to our friendly insurance rep, Kathy, let's call her Kathy, 'cause that was her name, with the wonderful health insurance company known as... *(I'm not a dumb-ass as Carl the Cook says. I'm not getting sued just so I can tell the raw truth).* Here's how that conversation went.

Kathy answers and recognizes my voice immediately and tries to take complete control of the conversation, unfortunately for her I already had.

"Yep, it's me Kathy. So lemme tell you, how this is gonna go down..." and you could hear the wind suck out of her like that last shot Austin Rivers made at Carolina in 2010 with .06 left on the clock to give Duke the win at the Dean Dome. "This is how this is gonna go 'cause I just got off the phone with the hospice folks. You're gonna call them right now and inform them how happy, thrilled you will be for "Blankety Blank Insurance" to cover Glenn's stay, since he's almost dead anyway. I'm not a nurse. How many tens of thousands of dollars have my cousin and I saved you. I'm an unpaid, untrained, unofficial medical caregiving musician, saving your ass while busting mine. It's time for me to just be a brother." Jay and I were exhausted and running on nothing but ignored nerves by this point.

Long pause.

"Oh, absolutely Mr. Brown. We will have it taken care of asap."

Hospice beds fill up before they change the sheets. Somebody's always dying. Meanwhile my step-daughter was graduating from UNC and I wanted to go, but I could not leave my brother's side and feel good about it.

Finally, after the tenth person in the family privately tells me "Ya know, he may be waiting for you to leave so he can leave. He doesn't want his baby brother to see him die," Oh, and now it's MY fault he ain't dead yet? I gave in. Of course I'm thinking, The man is about to meet the Mystery. He ain't worried about where his little brother is. Keep your guilt trip to yourself.

I waited till the last minute and with his condition unchanged, I decided to attend the graduation, torn to pieces inside. The ceremony goes through the names of the students who are graduating from UNC's many schools and, God as my witness, literally as they said, "Here is your 2007 graduation class of the University of North Carolina at Chapel Hill," and I'm going to stand up, my phone rings. All I saw was "Jay." And my first thought was, "I will be damned. How can the World's Greatest Duke fan, die during a UNC graduation... in the freaking Dean Dome?!?" And then, I died laughing.

Jay soon informed me that they had loaded Glenn in an ambulance and were transporting him to hospice. I entered the hospice center at exactly 8:30 pm that evening and passed the main nurses station as you go in. I stopped, introduced myself, and they wanted me to sign the legal responsibility papers immediately. I politely said, "I'm going to see my dying brother first. (He was in the next room.) I'll come back and sign your papers." And, once again, as Daddy would have said, "I shit you not," the woman looks at me and says, "Can I ask you something?"

"Sure."

"Why bring him here now?"

Stunned I replied, "Huh?"

"Why bring him here now, in the shape he's in?"

I gently lay my left hand on her shoulder, and in that sincere, loving, serious, southern drawl looked in her eyes and said, "Oh. I thought that's what y'all did here. Take care of dying people and their families. It's time for me to be a brother. We've earned that much."

People say the strangest things when death comes knocking. My final, exact words were, "Don't worry Shoog. We won't be here thirty six hours, tops, and we'll be out of your way."

When I entered the room, Glenn was wearing his Fillmore t-shirt I got him back in 1996 in San Fransisco, when we played there. I had called him from Jimmy Hendricks' former dressing room backstage on a payphone, and thanked him for teaching and motivating me, for giving me all the talents he had and for nurturing them. Of course, he was his usual sentimental self and said, "Just get me a fucking t-shirt." Which I did. I was good at following Brother Orders. And now, somehow, and I have never figured it out because of where it had been, my cousin had clothed him in that shirt, to go and die, wearing it. I knew when I saw it, this was it. That, was poetry.

Glenn was soaked in sweat, totally comatose, literally panting, gasping, breathing like he was running. All I could think was, "No matter how hard we run, our demons are always nipping at our heels." My cousin Teresa stayed with us until 3:30 that morning, helping me arrive at a place you can never reach on your own, opening the door to your own heart to allow Death to "pick up the check." She asked me if I was gonna speak at his funeral, and I told her I had written a small book of praise. She encouraged me to read it out loud so Brother could hear it, somewhere in that distant land, where the dying go to meet the Maker. I awkwardly and reluctantly did and eventually Teresa went to the family room to grab a few hours of sleep. It was just me, my Brother and my Mac-Pro with a four hour long playlist of his favorite tunes drifting softly through the pale air. The night came and went and mid-morning I looked up and my stepmom Linda is standing there, staring straight at me wearing a look of deafening emotional exhaustion. "Your Daddy's in the car, and he's in bad shape. You need to go talk with your Daddy. I can't do anything with him." Bless her heart, her nerves were as raw as weathered rope taut and rubbed back and forth on an anchor amidst the perfect storm of life. I shook my head and went to Daddy.

Arriving to the car, Daddy was sobbing so hard he was literally convulsing, and if he didn't calm down, he very well might kill himself grieving. All he could get out was "I can't go in there. I can't go in there and watch him die. That's my son." And I totally understood. All of it.

The weight of this self imposed silent shame he had put himself under by denying the beatings, now down to the final nails being driven in this coffin, the endless conversations he must have had in his own heart and mind all these years, that weight was crushing him. How he had meant to just "raise him right," but Daddy had done what we all ultimately do, pass the rich, delectable plate of the family disease down the Dining Table of Life, like it's Mama Ellen's deviled eggs. And who don't love good deviled eggs? So rich we can't help ourselves but to overeat and suffer the consequences of a greedy, sour belly. You could see the infinite deep love Daddy held for his firstborn and by God, Daddy did love Glenn. If anything, he loved him so much he destroyed their relationship trying to perfect and protect it in that sour-mash, southern suicidal way. I could see my father's heart as crystal-clear as if it was the grand opening of the south's finest eclectic antique parlor. It was all there. Chaos and conflict. Childhood trauma and building a life with his bare hands to see it fall apart by the same ones then building another good strong one.

I calmed Daddy down enough to where he could listen to my brief words. Honestly, it went over my head that he needed to know I wasn't going to judge him for not going inside. I held nothing but love in my heart in that moment, for all of us. We were all doing the crappy best we could. I returned inside and told Linda, "Take him to the emergency room or Dr. McLamb and let them give him something to calm him down." He was too weathered, weak, and old to carry this on his shoulders and in his heart. A short time later, she let me know Dr. McLamb handled it and they were okay and headed home. "Call me if you need me, Shoog." Some things, we must go through ourselves.

By lunch, nothing had changed as my Brother continued grasping for every breath, trying to make it to his finish line. It was getting uglier by the minute. At 2pm, in walks our cousin and pastor, Phyllis, thank God! I didn't have to say a word. We were both thinking the same thing. He is fighting the final spiritual battle of his life; his body was the screaming witness to that. Even in a toxic coma, Glenn was doing what he had always done best, what he had to do, excelled at, fight for his ever-loving life. Running. Refusing to let the darkness have his heart.

Phyllis pulled out her Bible and began reading select scriptures she instinctively knew were appropriate. And effective. The ones that are the highest caliber of God's ammunition--Now I cannot speak for her, but that was the closest thing to an exorcism I believe I ever want to witness. It was like the very words she uttered were pissing off the bowels of Hell itself, spitting spiritual Truth onto the sizzling, cracking lies and venom of the devil himself, as Glenn's body began to reflect the inner fight even more. It wasn't palpable, vengeful. It was ugly. Raw. Rage. There was a moment where I thought, he's about to open his eyes and start cussing the devil out, backwards and swinging fists. As long as his head doesn't turn around in a circle, I'm good. Phyllis's voice grew in intensity, she went up and down, back and forth, over his spiritual body, pouring these ancient scriptures on for the soul-saving salve they were, letting them seep and settle deep into the very bones of his soul, far beyond intellect, words or the communication of this world. What she was doing y'all, was kicking the very devil's own sorry, ever-loving ass. Never, ever, forget, the devil is the ultimate coward. He's a nuthin'!

My greatest fear since Glenn had revealed his drug problem to me when I was ten was my Brother dying and going to hell. I don't know what you believe. Not for me to say or ultimately, honestly concern myself with. I know a lot of Christians will disagree, but, hell, I mean, Heaven knows, I disagree with them. Lead by example, not opinion and your mouth I say. It doesn't matter what I believe except to me and God. God speaks and interacts with every solitary one of us in a unique way. I believe there is a place for the human soul that is referred to as hell. That is realer than real. And neither you nor me want to spend any time there. I believe ultimately our heart either chooses love over fear or it doesn't. I believe there is a Way, a Truth, a Light if you will, one Christ that will lead you on your journey, guide you through life and to home. I believe each of us has to actively choose that for ourselves or not. My nightmare was Glenn would refuse to love himself his whole existence. That his heart was so injured, the eyes of his soul couldn't stand the gleam of the glare of the Light from God's own eyes shining on him. I believe my brother had the truest heart of a child and that child was wounded. Hurt. Too tender for this world. And sometimes the wounded die out on the battlefield. Sometimes they bleed to death. Slowly, no matter how hard you fight it. So, yeah, you damn right, I was haunted with a fear I could not extinguish. A supernatural one.

Suddenly, believe me, I heard it, this intense wave of peace washed over my brother's shattered body and the entire room. Phyllis and I looked at each other, then Glenn, and simply smiled. Basked in the warmth of relief's sunlight. Instantly his breathing became normal; he was at peace. He even stopped sweating. My brother didn't have to run another step for the rest of his life. And I had church inside my heart. Deep inside of me, I ran up and down the aisles and sang and spoke loudly, freely, in many tongues.

Because, now, I knew we were ready to go down to the river. At some point I glanced down and saw the knee he had busted open weeks before falling on Jay's steps. His body lying there, riddled with this ugly, mean, destructive disease, melting away, and there was that wound, the most beautiful, healing pink you've ever seen. I thought, how grand and graceful God is, that even in the very act of our dying, He is healing us.

A few people came and went, but for the most part folks did what you do during a time like this, let the immediate family have their time. My Mama's associate pastor Scott came by for a visit. He did what I imagined Jesus would have done. No judgment, no crass questions or inquiring minds wanna know, playing-church crap. Filled with an authentic love for others, Scott simply came to let us know we were being prayed for, that Mama was being ministered to also, and that he knew how much my brother must love me because one could see how deeply I loved him. There's that "because he first loved me" thing again. Stay with me now.

Aunt Inez had come for us because she knew my Brother and I needed a Mama figure and it was simply too much for our parents. Supported by Phyllis, Lisa, my wife Whitney and several others, I sat facing Glenn and the outside window so I could see the coming setting December sun. His breathing became more and more relaxed, and around seven in the evening I felt we were getting close. I kept my right hand on his heart and my left hand holding his. The last few weeks, Phyllis and a number of others had shared their own stories of their Mamas and others passing away. How often it seems, our loved ones don't pass over until that unbroken circle of love is literally physically surrounding them. I began to notice we had a circle with a gap in it.

Suddenly at 7:15 Glenn's vital signs disappeared and he settled down into complete stillness. He let out a breath and didn't take another. I could feel his heart still beating, faintly, erratically, but still there. It seemed like forever, thirty to forty five seconds of utter silence and no breathing but I wouldn't look up at anyone. They thought he was gone. I could feel his energy. I looked up at Phyllis at the foot of the bed, and she looked back at me with the sweetest smile. I shook my head. No. I could tell everyone thought I was in denial. I knew he wasn't gone. Not yet.

Suddenly Glenn lifted up off the pillow gasping for air like a child dancing over the top of the water, leaping with innocent glee, sucking in life after holding their breath under water as long as they could. It felt as if he was smiling and jabbing us in the side-- "Surprise," for one last laugh. Aunt Inez cocked her sweet little head back and smiled at me and said, ""Sneaky little buzzard he is, ain't he?" We all smiled. Glenn was still with us. I sat up straight and felt led to say this.

"Glenn just told me to tell y'all he's about out of here. He loves you and thanks you for loving him. If you'd like to say something privately, feel free to do so. He told me to let go of his fucking hand. Said it was annoying at my age. I told him, I've been holding onto it all my life. I've also had to listen to you tell me what to do. You're the big brother, you let go first. I can't."

I kept watching my Brother and the clock on the wall. At exactly 8:29, I heard the front door chimes and footsteps coming towards our room. It was comically surreal. I thought, "Really? Is Death that freaking rude that he has to make a grand entrance?" Our cousin Mike and his wife Julia appeared, and I swear to God Almighty, at the exact moment they filled the hole in our circle, my Brother faintly smiled, like he did sucking in a tote of a joint, that "Man, that is good to me, face." He never released that breath and I felt his heart stop underneath my hand. We were all sitting there, in a circle, at the gates of Heaven.

Then, my brother died.

We were silent for about a minute or so and Phyllis softly said, "*Chris* would you like for us to say a prayer?" I nodded yes. And as we stood up,

Julia's phone went off, and I swear on my soul, her ring tone was "Hallelujah, Hallelujah, Ha---lle--lu jah!" from Handel's Messiah. We all held hands and laughed. Glenn was definitely in the House now. When Seymour Funeral Home came to get the body, I offered to help Brian. Why, I have no idea. Like it was my chore I was raised to do or I'd get an ass whipping. He smiled, said that's unnecessary, and prepared Glenn so we could all have one last visit. I let everyone else go in alone, and then they let let me be with him by myself. He looked so old. Ancient. Like he was from infinity. He looked like the Gospel Truth lying there. My Brother was hurting no longer. And inside I knew Glenn was at peace perhaps for the first time in his existence.

Standing outside in the hallway, within a few minutes, Brian strolled out with Glenn's body, and from the way Glenn was covered down to the pace he pushed the stretcher, doing what Seymour's always done, he handled death with dignity. Down south, whether you're going to Heaven or hell, there's no reason to leave this earth any other way than proper and respectful like.

It seemed like our entire lifetime as brothers washed over me as his lifeless body passed by me, until the back end was going past. Suddenly I lurched out and grabbed the stretcher, bringing it to an instant halt, and Brian knew why.

Pride pulls and tears you apart, piece by piece, whether it's your own heart or the very heart of your family. It doesn't care, as long as it can have its way. Pride will tell you whatever you want to hear. And now, here we were, in the defining moment. My Brother is dead and I'm about to release his body for good and I'm filled with a mixture of love and pride, just like Daddy.

BURNING 'EM UP

About two months before Glenn died, leaving for Atlanta one night I got a call from my cousin Jay. I had a feeling I knew what it was about. My Brother had made the decision to be the first person in our family to ever be cremated. That's a big deal where I'm from. Problem was Daddy and Gigi owned the funeral policy and Daddy had made no bones about the fact he was against it.

This had gone on for probably fifteen years which even for us was a tad too long. Mama hadn't liked it either but she did eventually come around. What had started as a southern son "messing with Daddy" thing, had now become quite soul-serious. And I mean, Ed Brown serious. It was so serious, my Brother asked me for the only promise of his lifetime. To make sure it happened. He had his own spiritual reasons. He was a diver and that was the only time he felt free, ever, in his entire life, diving. Plus, one day during our journey, discussing it while he was undressing, he said, "look at me. Don't you think I deserve a new body?"

So this night, as I heard my cousin's voice say, "Your Daddy just left here, and, I don't know how to say this, but, there's something I think you might need to know..." I cut him off to make it comfortable. Don't make people you love, carry your shit baskets, through this life. I said, "Does it have something to do with cremating my Brother?" I could hear Jay's relief before he said, "Yeah." I asked Jay if I could meet Daddy at his house. I called Daddy, and very unlike me with my father, super direct, bossy, when he answered I said, "Daddy, I've already left for Atlanta. I need you to meet me at Jay's in fifteen minutes. I have NO time to waste." And the way he said, "Alright," said it all. The showdown was here. Daddy had decided without discussing it with anyone that counted, "Nobody was gonna burn his boy up" and had been going around telling a few folks. I was well aware of the country-crisis.

He was sitting there when I walked in and we retired to Jay's office. I got right to the point. "Daddy, I'm late for work, eight hours away already. We don't have any more time to argue and...." he angrily busted in with "You or nobody else is gonna put him in a fire!" I deeply respected my Daddy and his feelings. And I deeply respected my Brother's. So I let Daddy do his thing and tried to diffuse him with love. I asked him why, and he said, "Cause that ain't the way our people do it!"

I mentioned "Well, what about ashes to ashes, dust to dust," and he pathetically threw out, "but it don't say nothin' bout burning 'em up!" I was out of time.

As I began my closing argument, I happened to see my Brother stretching, straining his neck from the bed down the hallway, trying to see me. "Daddy. I gotta go. I respect you. I love You. My only Brother has asked me to carry out his wishes. I promised him I would. It is the only thing he has ever asked of me. Ever." Then, the Ed Brown in ME came flying out. "So... when that man down that damn hallway dies, who is also your son, his body WILL be cremated and his ashes WILL be spread off the north end of Carolina Beach. I don't care who owns the funeral policy. And I no longer care how anyone besides him feels about it. No one's ever asked me how I felt about it!"

"How do you feel about it son?"

"I don't particularly like it. But it is NOT my decision." Then I did what all good southern men do, when they're in a hurry and a pinch, and need to "beat Daddy on this one." I lied my ever loving ass off. On this second part. "I'll pay for the funeral if I have too, the funeral home is already aware of this issue AND I have spoken with my lawyer and you can't stop it." Daddy countered with, "Well, we'll just see 'bout that. I can get a damn lawyer too!"

And then I stood up and did something I had never done. Had never even thought about doing. I looked down at my own Daddy, placed my hand on his left shoulder and said, "I love you. You know, that don't you?

And I love him. This is over and done with right now. And anybody, anybody, that tries to stop me on this, is in for a serious, life-changing, altering experience. I don't want to say this to my own Daddy, but if you insist on this, it will get ugly. Daddy, if you love both of us, leave this be. I've pulled time for something stupid before. I'll damn sure pull time over this."

I left a defeated man, the man who brought me in this world, whom I loved more than oxygen. I left my own Daddy, to fend for himself in his grief and cried till I was south of Lumberton. Brothers and Sisters, pride is ugly.

Pride pulls and tears you apart, piece by piece, whether it's your own heart or the very heart of your family. It doesn't care, as long as it can have its way. And now, here we were, in the defining moment. My Brother is dead and I'm about to release his body and filled with "love and pride."

FROM CHAPEL HILL TO HEAVEN (cont.)

"Chris, it's okay, I promise. I got this," Brian assured me. It was the only promise I had ever been asked of and committed to with my Brother. I replied, as if a soldier and said, "No, you do not understand. You don't know my Daddy. And I love him. But if I walk in that funeral home and see my brother laid out in a casket, I'm gonna make CNN by lunch. And I don't want that, for any of us. This won't be over till it's over."

The look on the faces in that dull hallway of death spoke back. And I let go of my Brother's body and his spirit for it was now nowhere to be found. As I walked out with family to the expected duties, the cold December wind bitterly whipped about my face, snapping and biting, looking for a fight. But I didn't have a single punch left in me. I had never felt that alone, ever. And I'd never felt closer to GOD.

As we pulled into Mama's subsidized housing, the dull glow of her lamp told me she was awake. Someone had gone and picked up Aunt Louise, to help with Mama and because Aunt Louise was now our Matriarch. Anytime family died, Aunt Louise always wanted to be there as quickly as possible. Ten or twelve of us drew that unbroken circle around Mama as I knelt down and took her hands. She looked like a lost, frightened little girl, who already knew the what but not the why or when.

Her first and only question, "Did he suffer a lot?"

"No Ma'am."

And Mama squalled out a declaration not a question, "What are we gonna do without Glenn!" breaking the serenity of Heaven. With the available angels now awake, we smothered Mama with love, and she grieved that hard grief every parent, regardless of age, exudes, when they lose their first child. It's an unnatural occurrence and violates the very treaty of the common sense of every natural law we all foolishly believe this life offers and intends to keep with us.

Lisa wisely pointed out a nearby picture for distraction, "Ah, this is so good of Glenn, Aunt Sallie, when was this taken?" And I wanted to kiss her on the mouth. Mama immediately flipped into a fake comfortable grief with a sweet moment of gratitude disguised as nostalgia.

"That was the family reunion, two years ago," like it was a Kennedy Center Honors night. And once again, heard it all my life, because it was true, "Ain't he a good looking thing?"

Mama was fine and I could tell she was more worried about me because she knew what was coming. We stayed a good forty-five minutes until I got the go ahead from her. "You gone to your Daddy's yet?" knowing full well I hadn't. "Well, you run-along and go be with him. He's gonna take this hard too."

And so, with the required "shoogha" exchanged, we headed to the farm. As always, I was the last one to leave so I could close the door and look in her eyes and her in mine, privately. Mama was good. It only took a few steps outside her closed door before I heard Mama let go with that Mother's Death Squall, but it was understood. Give me my space. I know you'll be back. The ten miles to the farm were the longest of my life. I knew I would get hit over the head with something and what that something was. I even knew why and held a deep perverted southern respect for it. And I knew deep down it wouldn't touch a hair on my emotional head. Over the course of Glenn's illness and now death, I had hardened in some of my softest places. And no one seemed to have noticed, yet. Staring out the black window of night, scattered clouds and a handful of blurry stars, here came the questions, "How are you gonna handle... you think Uncle Ed will be... ?" Uncle Ed's gonna flip, folks. From the inside out. I knew it, he knew it, all God's children knew. A man's firstborn son dying is a big deal in our neck of the woods. A fatal wound to every man's earthly pride and his rightful, southern, namesake. His Original Joy.

Strangely enough, as the crushed, granite gravel barked underneath the tires, I felt unusually comfortable, assured in my own skin. I had learned long ago, death, when it finally comes, offers a consciousness in real time that cuts like a proper barber's blade, for those of us left behind. It is absolute. Unforgiving. It has no manners. Our childhood, the sunny days and spring rains, the hurricanes and thunderstorms, both the joy and the pain of our family's story poured over me in a kaleidescope of wet paint. Brightly colored, wet as a whistle, warm and calming, I gathered every ounce of emotional strength this universe would offer.

The porch light popped on, that reassurance your folks are still here in this world, and Linda greeted me with the love of a mother, trying to lift the unliftable from a son's shoulders. I grabbed all I could, cause there was a man down the hall and I knew we had a bridge to cross one last time. "Why don't you go back there by yourself first." Damn. What a wise, loving thing to say. I can't say I would have thought of that. I wanted to get this shit over as quickly as I could. I was a walking bag of weary.

Daddy was lying there, almost in repose, as if he was impatiently await-ing his own death. Staring at the ceiling, he didn't hear my soft footsteps hidden by the carpet, as I dreaded him even seeing me, because he would know. When Daddy saw my face, he jerked away in this eruption of nearly half a century of love. Real love. Earthly love. Imperfect love. And that damn guilt and shame still trying to swim amongst the same currents. My brother and father held a bond that not only was I not invited to join, but one I always admired and held sacred in my own way. Always and for-ever, I had refused to come between my Daddy and Brother, and at neces-sary times, dared anyone else to try. I knew them. Both. Knew their souls and the Scripture of Life written into them, a holy mystery that was for them and them alone to understand. Daddy loved Glenn, and Glenn loved

Daddy in a strange way, an odd way, a deeply painful one, no other soul could understand and they didn't need to. They were each other incarnate and this had been both the fuel of the raging fire and and deep embers of affection that burned brightly, deeply inside them both, beyond mind and body, deep into soul and spirit, there to illuminate and forge the unbreakable bond they absolutely did have. Cold, able to withstand the very fires of hell, a solid steel anvil of love between father and son. The truth is, Glenn was the refusal of a lifetime of authority, the breaking the rules, the hippie that crossed his own fences in his time, that Daddy, sadly was never granted but always dreamed of being in his own way.

And for my Brother, Daddy was the sheer burden of the steep, angered, discipline of generations of southernness; pride and shame, a broken, violated child's innocence, the time-honored, "You will respect me or die" bullshit and iron pride of deep southern traditions and endless guilt trips that circled the very bloody cross of Jesus of Nazareth. Some folks do mere guilt trips; we had created interstates in our hearts, to romp and roam up and down, whenever the thoughtless mind and reactive heart chose. Only a true southerner can break and bond with your heart at the same time.

I touched Daddy's arm and told him he went very peacefully. With his nod of "I'm okay" I took the hardback chair over in the corner at the foot of the bed. My cousins soon filed in and began to pay their individual respects and love on old Uncle Ed. For whatever had happened forty years ago, Daddy was such a sweet, good man. Maybe, in fact, because of that. I heard the strength when it swelled back in Daddy's deep voice.

"You took my rights away from me!"

I had accepted many years ago, once I realized Glenn was serious about cremation, there would be hell to pay. And I knew who would foot that bill.

I never flinched. It hurt my feelings, deeply, but I understood and respected Daddy's feelings. I took a peaceful breath, for I knew I would never, ever have to deal with this again. Oh, it would come up, be thrown in my face, but me? I was done with it. Sometime day after tomorrow, my brother was gonna be cremated, if I had to guard his body with a fucking shotgun. On this subject, as you loved to say Daddy, "Of this, let there be no damn doubt."

In the softest, most loving, almost pathetic voice of complete exasperation I looked Daddy in the eye and said, "No Daddy. I just kept a promise to my Brother." With my unbroken circle of witnesses, even Daddy knew he couldn't argue with that. He nodded his head and slowly went back to the polite, fake, comfortable death talk we all do. And I sat quietly in that hard-back chair, doing what Little Boys that become men like me do. I melted into the wall, trying to disappear in the physical but diving deep down into my soul for a fresh, spiritual breath. I never said another word till I hugged Daddy and said, "I love you. See you tomorrow."

Daddy replied with a breaking voice, "Have they..."

"No Daddy. You can see him if you want to, tomorrow. It will be the next day. They are required to wait 24 hours and for a certified death certificate." Daddy sank back on his tired pillow relieved to know I hadn't "burned his body" up. Not yet. I stepped into that hallway of my childhood, our bedroom doors floating by me like ungentle reminders of our past we can never escape. I noticed for the first time, the angry voices of the ghosts, were barely audible. Just whispers of smoke coming from the heart. But you can bet your sweet southern or Yankee ass, I was still thinking, "I better keep an eye on Daddy." I learned a long time ago, it ain't a done deal, till it's done deal with Ed Brown. And like Daddy told me on the phone years ago, when I told him, all to pieces, I was headed for a divorce, he said, "Now you get your mess together. You hear me. You got some of me in you too." You got that much right.

I got home, and of course I couldn't, I didn't want to sleep. As I entered Brian's office at the funeral home at 8 am, I felt the comfort we had grown accustomed to at times like these. It's why we loved and always used Seymour. They make the uncomfortable, palatable. After assessing my emotional state as funeral directors do, he went to make a pot of coffee for me and I headed for the restroom. As I rounded the corner of the hall, someone who graduated from our high school, came flying around the corner, slamming into me. I threw my hands up and caught him.

"Swear to God." Or. " I shit you not." Whichever you can swallow. First words out of his mouth.

"Damn boy. You're gonna be right back down here with your Daddy. I saw him yesterday and he looks bad."

God as my witness, to keep from overreacting, I never stopped walking and said. "Yep. I sure will. Why don't you go ahead and pick him out a casket? And make it a nice one," you insensitive, small-town-simplified moron! Once again, people say the strangest things come death-time.

And then I returned and planned a funeral for my brother, in peace, with my friend Brian. Brother and I never made to the six pack and the lawn chair. But we did make it from Chapel Hill to Heaven. Turned out, that was far enough.

PART 3

COMMITTAL AND INTERNMENT

DOLPHINS NEVER SWIM ALONE

By the time we finished at the funeral home it was pushing ten in the morning. When Brian told me, for the umpteenth time, if I wanted to clothe my brother's body for cremation, then I needed to return the clothes by 1:30 pm, it finally hit me. I had a couple of hours. Now that may seem like a long time when you're all decked out and dazed with grief, but I was in a pure panic when I entered Belk Department Store, my only choice for finding something suitable and approvable by no other than Brother. And me. Oh, and Mama and Daddy.

I ran into the men's department and looked around like a parent searching a lost child. A short time later I emerged with a white Nautica linen short-sleeve shirt with a new pair of button-up, bell-bottom Polo jeans in white. It was cool as the spring breeze blowing over Heaven. Almost as cool as Brother. He would have loved it.

Again no one in our family had ever been cremated, so my brother had lovingly appointed me "proxy by prerogative" years ago. His cremation had been discussed, debated and deliberated for years. Brother had joked and jabbed Daddy with it at every opportunity and equally let it be known he was, "dead serious." Mama had finally come around a hard corner to turn for a Baptist. But Daddy, never. Cremating, "burning up" his son's body was simply unfathomable to the Old Man. Unforgivable. And the sea of division that had always flowed between them and ever bound them together, now heaved and howled in a cosmic emotional storm even Death itself wouldn't quell. The ultimate final "Yes Sir" would be said for Daddy. The "Screw You" from the grave was my Brother's anthem already echoing through eternity. The saddest part is, if Daddy could have ever given it reasonable thought, Glenn wouldn't have taken a serious, spiritual request and turned it into the ultimate, eternal smart-ass protest. He was gonna get the last word in and piss Daddy off, try and hurt him, one last time. And Daddy was gonna tell him what to do 'cause by-God, Daddy "said so." If you don't see the sadistic sad southern spiritual lost-cause truth in all this, then I surrender.

This love, anchored by a self-centered stubborn pride, was the very bridge to each other's heart. Regardless, though I was equally pissed at both of them for putting me in the middle yet again, I had made a promise to my Brother and I would carry it out without demeaning or disrespecting my Daddy or dead brother's memory. Though I was weary clean through my rattling bones, I had more than enough spirit to see this through. Trust me, I got my licks in with Brother before he left. I earned that much being his stand-in, the one who had to hang around and take this emotional ass-whipping.

The handling and treatment of the deceased's body is sacred with my folks. We plan on having it resurrected and improved upon. Think of it as an engine and bodywork overhaul for the soul from the inside out. When Brian had informed me earlier in the day, by the laws of the Great State of my beloved North Carolina, the body must be in a "container," I swear I thought, "A container? You shit me not. I gotta buy a container to burn up my Brother in!" Oh boy, is Daddy gonna LOVE this one.

My choices were an inexpensive, cardboard "box" or the purchase of a "cremation casket." A what? The Daddy in me kicked in thinking, "Lemme get this straight, you're telling me I can purchase one of those nice looking wood caskets over there, to put my brother in for only $1500... and then throw it in a really badass fire?" My internal mind muttered exactly what my Daddy would have said, in that authentic, three syllable, southern way, "Sh(ee)itt." Daddy ain't gonna go for that.

What I had failed to understand that morning, was we could embalm and casket Brother and have a regular visitation. I did not realize that until I walked in that afternoon for a very brief private viewing. There were times early on I wish I had done that, it might have made it easier for Daddy having a body to mourn over, but the way it turned out was so eloquently

Faulknerian. I dropped off the clothes and several hours later I returned to the funeral home, walking Mama in with a handful of cousins and aunts. When we broke through the doorway Mama saw it first and broke, "Awe, my sweet boy," and her brief meltdown happened.

Brian had lay my brother out, dressed in white, on a century-old ceramic mortician's table, and covered him with a one hundred and fifty year old quilt made by his own Grandmother. It was the most perfect, fitting viewing I have ever seen. Glenn lie there, not embalmed, looking cooler than dead ever looked on any body, his hands folded, in need of them no more. Mama made her way up, to attempt absorbing a new reality and then she grabbed the quilt and started pulling it off of him, slowly, reverently. I looked over my shoulder and knew the family thought she was losing it. She wasn't. Mama just wanted to see his "outfit" as she called it. Mama approved.

A short time later as we all sat down in chairs, I began to tell the Fat Albert-Heroin story. Like an out-of-body spiritual experience. I began to softly retell that story, out loud, from my childhood like I was talking with Glenn. And I was. I was thanking him for being there for me, for saving me from perhaps a similar road. Mama understood, as she placed her hand of approval firmly on my knee.

Out in the hallway, Brian offered to take a picture with one of those instant cameras. I was in disbelief they still existed and thought, "Why in the hell would I want a crappy washed-out picture of my dead brother? Oh. Daddy." See. This is where they earn their money folks. We can't remember this stuff in the heat of the moment. Trust me, funeral-folk earn their keep, one way or the other.

Daddy had refused to come. I don't think he understood what was going on, or maybe he was just to wrought with grief. Or maybe he thought I had already, "burned him up," as he had so eloquently said, and would have to stare at a smoldering box of bones. Regardless, Brian took two pictures, and I refused to look at them, until a few years later after Daddy died. I can't tell you how many times I walked in Daddy's house and caught him adrift in a nap, those pictures lying in his lap. I took the pictures and Mama by the arm and walked towards the safety of the Carolina afternoon sunlight streaming through the make-believe, stained-glassed, windowed back door. As the cold December wind rushed into my nostrils, I felt an alive and grateful fire warming my heart. I relaxed for the first time in several years and purposely soaked it. My promise would be kept. My sweet Brother's remains were cremated the following day. Ain't got time for grieving, we burying folks 'round here.

I spent all day Thursday in a rush. Around 6:30 I drudgingly opened the side door to the funeral home, and there she was. As she had been my entire life, whether in the flesh as a child or in my heart, there stood the rest of my family, Magalene with her daughters, my soul sisters, Debbie, Jeannie, and Tia, and her grandchildren. As a true mother, she knew I needed her there to "hold my hand" one more time. She stood within a Mama's arm's length or eye contact of me, throughout the visitation. About fifteen minutes before the service was to start, they wheeled Daddy inside in a wheelchair, and yes, he went all to pieces. He was truly pitiful. I loved on Daddy and then it was time.

Earlier in the afternoon I had walked in the chapel. Not knowing how I would feel seeing the remains of my brother, I wanted that moment, alone, between us. It was the most perfect, beautiful thing I have ever seen in a funeral home. A wooden urn sat in the middle of a sacrificial table, surrounded by flowers, with the centerpiece I had ordered... a huge see-through vase with a bouquet of natural weeds and flowers found at the beach, with three red daisies surrounding one lone, white, one in the mid-dle. It was bookended by two huge framed 16 x 20 pictures of my brother. One on the beach smiling, the wind of younger days blowing through his hair again, much quicker than the young always believe it will happen; and a lonesome black-and-white early winter picture of taking his beloved dog Bessie for one more walk before he had to put her down. The epicenter of my brother's outer hardness was a place so soft, very, very, few were ever invited or openly witnessed. Excepting himself, a softer heart for everyone, including the stray cat on the street, never lived.

It was time for the family. As Mama and I entered the chapel I heard the song "Old Friend" by Warren Haynes and Derek Trucks beginning to play, and I thought, "Shit. I told you to start the song before we come in;

it's over six minutes long." But when I sat back in the front pew, wondering how many older folks were confused or rolling their eyes, honestly, I didn't give two shits. A great song always makes the moment.

The only other significant thing I clearly remember about my Brother's funeral, was a while later when I took the podium to deliver his eulogy, I witnessed the chasm of my family's soul. I had instructed them to seat Mama's people and Daddy's people on opposite sides, because we needed to do so, and so they could experience it without any unnecessary tension or drama. I looked up and thought, "I have been pulled between y'all my entire damn life. I will be damned if you will do it here." Then I realized, I was the one who said seat them that way. I was still doing my job, running interference to keep the peace. It's amazing how much bullshit we create in our own head and heart. How sin multiplies exponentially and muddies everything in it's pathetic, pathological path.

I'm sure like everyone who loves someone deeply, and is connected at the soul level, we want the world to truly know them. Brother had his issues but he had lived a full life. I also firmly believe that anyone should aspire to touch as many people as my brother Glenn did, at the soul level. Because the Gospel truth is, most of us don't. Most of us spend our lives hiding who we really are and playing church, wearing the mask we assume our world has picked out for us. Or worse, living out a lie. If nothing else, my brother was nothing less grand than the raw Truth in the flesh. The good, bad and ugly that creates this amazingly beautiful, broken life. Among the twenty five hundred words I had written and shared about my Brother, these illustrate the heart of Glenn's life and very Soul.

"I could tell you my Brother's life was a joyful, easy experience. It would make me the worst kind of liar. It would diminish God's goodness and amazing graces. The tide of life brings us all to the shores of acceptance at some point. His life was a journey at sea. He was a Lone Dolphin, swimming in, out, & around our lives in his own current. And although it often didn't feel like it, he was still, always swimming along with us, at his own pace, his way. He was brought to his knees, until his earthly pride and essence dissolved before our very eyes, only to reveal the truth. Glenn taught me that we truly are souls. What we love about one another, what draws us together &

drives us mad, what connects us & separates us, is the spirit. And not recognizing, owning and being responsible for our very own soul's journey, is not an option. Glenn recognized the dolphin in all of us. Dolphins never swim alone... because they don't have to."

After I finished, his best friend Mike Cox rose and told the absolute beautiful RAW truth about Brother. Brother had requested Mike and I do his eulogy back at Duke,"because y'all are the only two who will tell it, Warts and all." It felt like Glenn was walking around the chapel, in his white outfit, unable, unwilling to harm himself anymore, a smile on his face at the honesty of the occasion as well as the haven of Heaven. Grateful so many loved him so deeply. A few more spoke, notably his ex-mother-in-law Mama Pat. A beautiful, gorgeous, fun evening it was, unlike any before or since in our family. A celebration perfect for him. Folks engulfed us all, with love and hugs. All I remember, is my looking up at cousin Jay, who had an oddly cool look on his face. When I was finally able to reach him, Jay grabbed my arms and said, "Wonderful! Man, I didn't know whether to stand up and clap or cry! Best funeral I have EVER been to!" Like we just saw the Allman Brothers at the Beacon Theater. My folks are cool. This journey was finished, over for me, Daddy or the devil, Mama and morons, I was "good" with my Brother. The strangest thing was, it never felt like he was gone. In fact, I felt his presence now, in some ways, more profoundly than ever. Death does clarify a lot of life. A lot of what Life actually is and isn't. Doesn't it?

A few days later the doorbell rang, and I accepted the urn from Brian. I sat down at the kitchen table, both hands holding on to the bones of my brother. About the time I realized I was freaking out, I thought, "Shit." There was still a promise to be kept. I could hear my Brother laughing his ass off at me. He always got in the last damn word.

The very last time my Brother brought up being cremated, he was joking about something to do with Daddy. I shut him down and said," Man, last time I'm having this conversation. You tell me right now, what you want."

He replied, "You damn right I'm serious. Cremate me and when the water warms up, take me off the north end of Carolina Beach and spread my ashes." And then you could see the defiant smart-ass fall across his face. "I tell you what, you can take one handful, I said, ONE handful, down to our family cemetery," and here came the searing sarcasm that bitterness breeds. "One handful, and throw them across the sacred graves of my ancestors, to satisfy Ed's ass!" I looked at him like, what an ass you can be sometimes.

After the funeral, Gigi and I discussed it. And Daddy kept calling me every so often, inquiring, "had I thrown his son's ashes away yet," the soot of guilt rubbed in my eyes a little more. And then the perfect answer came. I could get a second urn, bury it for Daddy, and then go back one day after Daddy was dead, and do like Brother asked. So we got a nice small, weighted brass urn. I took it home, and did as my Brother asked. Sitting in my office alone, I removed one handful, ONE handful and placed in the urn. Then I thought, my hands are really small compared to Daddy's, so I put another in there, just in case Daddy looked in it. I didn't want him to feel slighted on the ass end of the ashes.

Soon Daddy called and the tombstone he ordered on all's behalf for Brother was here and ready for ceremonial installation. When Daddy walked up with that urn, I could feel his softest, tenderest spot, and it was hurting. Dripping with grief. He loved my Brother like no one else, regardless of any past. Then Daddy handed me a piece of six inch wide, PVC pipe with a screw on lid and a capped end. I thought, what in the hell? And Daddy said, "Daddy just thought we could put it in this. You know, this here PVC pipe lasts forever, that's what they say, Son." *(Daddy often talked about himself in the third person. Like he was Michael Jordan or something.)* And as Daddy sat there and balled, "I shit you not," I put Brother's urn in a PVC PIPE vault, screwed the lid on it, marked X number of my feet, from someplace and something only I knew, when Daddy wasn't looking, and buried it. Up till that point I was still considering carrying out Brother's wishes.

As I remained knelt down by my Brother's official "grave" as far as Daddy was concerned, I came to the realization, that my Brother was being a real ass that day and I was not gonna throw two handfuls of our eighty year old father's firstborn's crushed bones on the ground, "just to spite his ass." Enough was enough. As they left, I looked across the field into eternity and said, "Brother. I'm done. Y'all can dig this up later and fight about it, if this ain't good enough."

The third weekend in April, with Glenn's urn, we all met down at Carolina Beach. I had researched doing this and discovered there were laws governing "ash spreading" and now knew our Carolina statutes by heart. Legally I had to be in a motorized craft and two miles off the shoreline. We all gathered on that beach and when I opened the lid on Brother's wooden urn, I struggled to remove the now lodged ashes and I just lost my entire self. I have never felt that kind of "weight" before. I don't know if it was the sheer relief of getting there without a dramatic turn, or seeing Mama sitting there, trying to understand and honor her son's wishes, with the lost look of a little girl twiddling her fingertips nervously together. Maybe it was guilt of knowing Daddy wouldn't, couldn't come watch me just "throw them away in the sea." Or maybe, it was feeling the full weight of losing my Brother. He had been everything to me. Brother, father, friend, a problem and a joy. Gene Banks put his arm around me and said, "You can do this. It's okay now, Brother. You can let him go the way he wanted."

Then, I looked up to see two of Carolina Beach's finest in Blue, riding up on one of those beach golf-carts. And God as my witness, I thought, "if my ass gets arrested for spreading your ashes, Brother, I'm gonna..." and I busted out laughing. So, Gene, cousin Jay, and best friend/brothers Bill, Pete, Mike, Curtis, and Richard and myself strode out into the Atlantic. I lifted his ashes up to the Heavens and when the right wave came, I let my Brother go. I swam around alone for a few minutes, looking across the waves for a lone dolphin, to suddenly jump and turn a perfect flip of joy. He never came but all my Brother's love washed over me and cleansed my tired heart. And when I came out of that sea, I imagined the water dripping off my back was all the unnecessary bullshit we had all put each other through. And I vowed to leave it there, endlessly swirling around in a watery grave, never to be seen again. High or low tide. If only our hearts and minds were as consistent as the ocean.

Brother had gotten a tattoo in his late thirties of a dolphin leaping through a rough sea, escaping the throes of an angry dragon. He had had it for a while and one day I noticed for the first time, there were two dolphins. I said, "when'd you get two dolphins?"

Brother looked at me and said, "I've always had two dolphins."

"Really? How come?"

And his eyes misted up as he replied, "cause dolphins, never swim alone, Brother."

Writing this even now, in my leather recliner in Nashville, realizing my Brother's funeral portrait hangs on the wall over my shoulder, I feel guarded and safe. I feel protected. I feel loved. Cause I know, I have a Brother swimming through this life, all the way through it, with me. Always that one step out in front. And when the day comes that the right thought of him, doesn't fill my eyes with the tears of gratitude, well, shame on me. My Brother was simply beautiful. He was a beautiful, perfected mess.

And so was our Brotherhood.

BLESSING HEARTS

We melted our sadness and relief together into that crappy casserole of shocked grief and got through Christmas Day. It had worked out most of the last month of his life for me not to be in Atlanta with the band. Now, I welcomed in New Year's Eve in downtown Atlanta with Zac and the boys. I felt completely disconnected from pretty much everyone including myself. Glenn had made me promise him one day at Duke, right as I busted in the door from Atlanta, that I would "Promise me you won't quit the band before I die! You never know who you're going to meet!"

After the funeral, while there was a huge sense of relief--that his suffering was over, I was tired. Never felt that tired in my entire life. I wasn't old, but I definitely wasn't a kid at forty three. The stress of the back-and-forth travel, the extreme worrying I wouldn't be by his side when the time came and that he might be lying there wondering why, had truly beaten me down. I had begun to have mounting and slowly growing health issues myself, though I believed in the whole of my heart that all I had to do was keep going and God would guide me and take care of the rest.

But on that New Year's Eve, the gig was hopping! Zac was the biggest act in the southeast. It was indeed one of those rare bands that you know you're a part of as well as witnessing something very special, it's merely a matter of time before it blows up and the whole world gets Chicken Fried. Being a lil older and having worked with major acts the previous fifteen years, I knew deep down what they were about to experience, at a minimum, in every way. What it would and could offer. What it would give and what it would take. The sole commitment that this is your life's purpose for now, twenty four/seven. That night--after once again driving eight hours, sound-checking and now in the middle of a show--I began to face some hard questions demanding an answer.

Can I give this what it will take, especially from the drummer's spot, much less be an active part of a high level, highly productive songwriting team? I already knew from a tried-by-fire veteran's standpoint, what any artist or musician will honestly tell you. The drummer is the foundation, the heart of a band. Can I find myself again quickly enough, rest up, get strong and bust into the sunlight of a warm horizon of a bright new future and era in my career? And be a committed caregiver 24/7? Be there for my parents and the family? Can I walk away from this and not despise myself for the rest of my very damn life? I had worked my entire career to find a group of guys I melded with, that I fit with musically, culturally and most of all, spiritually. Never crossed my mind I'd show up and be the older cat in a fresh, new band. But here I was, kicking it from the drum kit in a huge ballroom in downtown Atlanta, and by the encore, as tired as I was, I lied to myself, "I'll be fine. Give me a month or two of rest, and I'll be back to being the full blown "Hound Brown.""

Zac had begun the process of inking a major record and distribution deal back in the fall with Live Nation and Atlantic Records and they were nearly done. After New Year's Eve, we were off all of January and most of February as they planned our southern invasion. All we had left on the old books were the *Lynyrd Skynyrd and Rock Boat Cruises* out of Miami. Boarding the plane with my wife and oldest stepdaughter, I hoped the cruise would fill my lungs and spirit with a fresh new air.

We had a ball for the first four days of the cruise, and there were actually moments of life again. I laughed, hung out, enjoyed performing but something raw nagged at me, deep in my craw. Picking at me constantly, like a buzzard on a lonesome county highway. The final evening of the cruise, I went out on the top deck, waiting on the girls for dinner, to witness a brilliant Caribbean sunset and have a much needed talk with my Brother's spirit. Leaning over the rail, I let the huge waves cleanse my mind. Then as the sky darkened, I accepted the harsh reality that when I got off this boat, I had two eighty year old parents mired in deep grief that needed me. I happened to glance down at the deck below me. There at the very back of the boat two decks below sat the entire band and entourage, eating, drinking, laughing, living life to its fullest. I knew right then.

I spoke to and over those guys, thanking them, at the soul level, for the brief run I had enjoyed with them. I took long looks at each face, and imagined how drastically their lives were about to change, because in my heart, I knew this was a damn fact: the Zac Brown Band was about to be a legend. That, is the Gospel Truth. So I made my peace with a thankful and very heavy heart and turned to go to dinner. The stuff we keep to ourselves is often too tough to swallow, too heavy to carry long distance and too much to share. With anyone. Except God. When we landed on dry land, Zac and I talked, the guys all called and joked about kicking my ass for leaving, but every single one of them understood what I was doing, why, and respected me for doing it. They were a great group of hip dudes and I loved playing with them while I did. So strangely enough, a part of me has always felt a part of the band. I don't talk about it. Won't. Don't need to. The Spirit world does fine on its own. I trusted the Mystery and did what I needed to do as a man, not a musician. I made my decision. For me. And regardless of any "cost" I have never once looked back. For the cost of turning my back and not honoring my parents and family was never up for discussion. With anyone.

The very first joke I ever saw in a *Playboy* magazine as a child, was a wife walking into her bedroom and finding her husband with another woman. The caption read, "You can't have your Kate and Edith too!" You could say, "You can't have your Grannies and Grammies too." I was at a real peace with my decision. Not some bullshit feel-good emotion on Sunday morning enhanced by a convicting sermon, music and raw emotions. And there's a place for that. I'm speaking of a true peace that gives you the strength to do what you cannot do alone. Truth be told the choice was made for me with the integrity and character that had been deposited in my soul as a little fellow. Where I come from, you do the right thing, because damnit, it's the Right Thing to do. Besides, I was now mainly focused on writing and Lord, have Mercy, I knew I'd have plenty to write about. On we go, our funeral is dragging out as all good southern ones do.

I let go of the Zac Brown Band and returned to what was left of my highly functioning, dysfunctional, family. There ain't no such thing as "normal." Save yourself the heartache and quit searching, cease comparing and be grateful for what you do have instead of what you don't. All through the spring into the summer I kept waiting, knowing that my strength would return, any day, any week. It didn't. At first it was daily, then multi-day trips to care for Mama, adrift in a sea of something between a grand-grief and depressive-guilt. My Mama had been in chronic pain basically since I was eight years old. Her neck and spine ruined from three massive car wrecks and the failed early operations of the late 70's and 80's had taken their toll. Now I had an eighty year old mother who had been on heavy narcotic pain medications for at least twenty pushing twenty-five years. For years, Mama had done a pretty good to great job of medicine management, but by the time I was in my mid-thirties, Mama was in bad shape more often than not. Mostly emotionally.

I had moved her to Raleigh in the mid '80's, and she did really well for a while. But that bitterness still burned in her. It was a bad family portrait hung in the perfectly inappropriate spot, hanging in a slightly gaudy frame, facing a mirror across the room from you. It was always there, slipping sideways on the wall, staring me in the face. She could not forgive Daddy. Or herself. Now I was the go-to family expert at handling the toxic waste of Sallie Mae's bitterness whenever it did raise its ugly head. Which for many years had been at the mere mention of the word "daddy." In short, I was completely over it.

Her depression and medicine use had gotten completely out of control by the late 90's and culminated one night with another backstage message. Short version, Mama was seeing snakes on her wall, in January. No Ma'am. We don't have winter-wall snakes in eastern North Carolina. Before I could get home, my Brother, without discussing it with me, had admitted Mama to a psychiatric hospital where she was quickly detoxed and within days was the life of the party for all the young addicts as well as the staff. Sallie Mae could perform like the legend she was under just about any circumstance. Yet this, would be her two sons one unforgivable sin. After she died, I would find her admittance sheet neatly, purposely folded and placed in her Bible, there for me to be reminded once again, you don't turn your back on your family. Ever. At the very least, don't commit your Free-Willed Baptist Mama to a psychiatric hospital for prescription drug treatment without her permission. Ride down that Guilt Trip, why don't cha!

Mama was proud. Another valuable family trait, especially for those of us hell-bent on eventual self destruction. Usually by the time a crisis was noticeable with Sallie Mae, it was already an epic adventure. By 2001, I was at new place in my career and marriage life. We flew Mama to Nashville for another Christmas. The deal was, "Mama, you can move to Nashville and be close to us or go to Goldsboro. But you have to live close enough to someone that can and is willing to help you, on a regular basis." We looked at different places, talked about it as a young couple and mother in law. In the end, it wasn't going to work for everyone. So it was Goldsboro.

Oh, how Sallie Mae loved the sound of that name. Truth was Mama did love Goldsboro. Deeply. It was home in her heart. It had just been too painful for her to live there for many years. Painful, often even paralyzing emotionally, to merely go there for a reunion, much less a funeral. After several heart to heart, son and Mama conversations, the realizations that Mama and her siblings were all getting old and needed time together while they still had it, Mama "decided" on her own to move home to Goldsboro. So in the fall of 2001, we had kissed Mama goodbye and returned to Nashville once she was settled. In my heart of hearts, I began to see Mama had to return home to the scene of the crime, our Original Family Sin, so to speak, if her heart had any chance of healing in this world. If she had any chance of forgiving herself. And the Gospel Truth is, we all have that problem. That's why we blame one another for the things that break our own heart.

Now, six years later, I was divorced, remarried, my brother was dead after being sick at least ten years, and both Mama and Daddy grave shopping. My place was at home. And God Almighty, as my witness, I grabbed it, proudly, purposefully, with passion and dared someone to try and take it from me.

Maybe I never bought Mama her Graceland. But by God, I could give her something much more precious. My own time. Myself. There are no do-overs in this life. Death doesn't give a shit about how you "feel" about someone, how deeply you love them. Death is the self-centered selfish final requirement for the gift of this life and entrance to the next. I chose "Granny" over Grammy" and never looked back.

By this point a certain life wisdom had greatly changed my perspective of my family. I had escaped the grasp or entanglement of the bitter web for the most part, for fifteen or more years, while remaining the baby rock in our family's cracked foundation. I had grown through my own experiences, therapeutic and cathartic, to understand my brother and his deep wounds. I no longer saw my Daddy through the crying eyes of a child feeling abandoned. He was my southern Robe of Respect and Family Tradition. And Mama was my window to the Good News of Jesus Christ, proof positive that things like true peace of mind and hope, are not feel good quotes stuck on a refridgerator magnet. They are raw and experienced in their Gospel Truth, only in the midst of the great turmoils of our lives. Faith doesn't make you "feel good," it faithfully delivers you. My Mama was the Lincoln Memorial of Survival.

When I returned from the Skynyrd Cruise, Mama greeted me with a genuine smile but I knew in the coming months that she would fall apart. She would face all the hard questions she never would or could before, about her firstborn son, deep in her heart. And then she would begin asking all the new ones, we ask the Dead, searching for those answers that never come to the Living. Mama was a solid rock of faith. Real faith. She knew what it was like to desperately grab a hold of any limb or branch you could find in a flood and hold on for dear life. It might get bad, even ugly, she would never be the same, but "in the end" she would be alright. Eventually, I had to make the decision and break the news to Mama that I would be dolling out her meds a week at the time. My nerves were shot from the endless middle of the night trips to get her up out of the floor, or finding her in her bed nearly comatose. Sallie Mae bucked that head up, but finally agreed, because she had to do it. Mama would argue with you till she had no more argument left. But she knew that it was only fair to me and my life.

And Daddy and Linda. GiGi had been dealing with Daddy's illnesses and surgeries for many years now, along with shouldering the issues of an entire family. I returned to the farm to a broken old man but Daddy would make it also. He had Linda by his side, two stepchildren, a son Tim, a world class cabinet maker, who reminded Daddy of himself in his finer days, always hard at work, and his BEST and tightest buddy, a daughter Bonnie. Try and bother Papa. Bonnie would go on your ass like a Tasmanian Devil. There were grandchildren galore by his side, and even me, when I could escape Mama for a few hours. Each time I would leave, Linda would privately look in my eyes and say, "You go take care of your Mama, I got your Daddy." And she did. Bless her heart. She loved my Daddy. The next two years Daddy's health, somehow steadily declined without killing him. How, I have no earthly idea.

About six months before Daddy passed, one morning out at the farm, he couldn't get his breath. Daddy had heart problems for so long they eventually couldn't insert any more stents. To make matters worse, he had severe COPD from smoking all those years. Each time I saw him suffer through this, I could see and hear him decades ago, puffing away on one and someone would get irritated. Daddy said, "I grow 'em, sell 'em, smoke 'em! I'd eat 'em if I could!" Lord have mercy, please be mighty careful what you say, especially over and over again. The power of life and death is indeed in the tongue.

This morning the ambulance from nearby Fremont just happened to be miles away, returning to their station after a hospital run. When the address went out across the radio, they knew who it was. Literally within two to three minutes of placing the call, here came Daddy's crew, "his Gals" as he liked to call them. There is no way Daddy would have made it out of the yard that day if they had not been so close. When Linda rushed back in the house to get her keys, I stepped up in the doorway of the ambulance and Daddy looked deep into my eyes. He was scared bless his heart. 'Cause he was dying.

In the emergency room, as they rushed to insert needles, do cutdowns, capping him with a mask while a ventilator was prepared, the Daddy I knew wasn't there. He was in the flesh flopping around, but the enormous fight and long journey he knew was coming, if he survived, was becoming too much. The problem was, Daddy wouldn't sign a living will.

He wouldn't read a living will. He wouldn't let *you* read the damn thing to him. Therefore, by not making a decision, he had made his decision. The modern medical circus was redundantly ridiculous.

I found myself alone with Daddy for a few moments once he was stabilized, so I drew close to him. I held his hand and spoke to him about his spirit in the way we had grown accustomed to for him and me, privately, personally. He was ready. I said, "Daddy, we all know you are not simply tired. You have given more than all you have." Thick, smoky tears pooled in the corners of his eyes. "You don't need to stay here to prove anything to us or anyone else. If you are tired of...." And Daddy starting nodding his sweet, old, white head up and down and began sobbing.

Two long weeks later, as they transferred from ICU to the floor, it was just one of those days where everything goes wrong and is wrong, no matter how hard you try. Daddy had sweated so badly in the bed in ICU he had absolutely no skin, just the rawest flesh, all around and throughout, well, where a man does not want raw flesh. He was having a rough, rough go of it. Daddy had never gotten so weak that he couldn't even lift his hips, which was sign number two we were headed in the direction of lying flat of our back, for good. It was beyond pitiful and had crushed his manhood. Then, here comes "Nurse Ratchett and the bedpan." It was the only way Daddy could "go."

Daddy looked at me, stretched across that hard bedpan, so awkward and weak it appeared his back would break, and said son, "You go on home and get you a shower and a nap. Daddy'll be alright." There he was. Still being Daddy, the Good Shepherd, even now taking care of his flock. An hour and forty five minutes later I returned. The elevator doors opened, and all I saw and heard was at least six nurses, piled up around the front desk, talking about last night's prayer meeting and some girl who had finally fell in love so the older women pretend again like they remembered how it felt, remembering when, back before they realized who they'd actually married and didn't hate him and themselves for doing it. I opened the door to Daddy splayed out over that bedpan.

"Damn, Daddy. You still ain't able to..."

"Son. Please get me off this god-damn torture bucket before it kills me," tears rolling out his eyes. "I've been on it since you left and can't get nobody to come help get me off." If not for the pure pitifulness of it, it would have been funny. It wasn't. Lo and behold, just as the very fires of hellish anger erupted in me, the door opens with Nurse Ratchett. When she saw my face she started stuttering, blushing, and I yelled, "Get out. I said, get... the... hell out of here. Go back up there and finish your conversation. Find out who Barbie's gonna marry. I'll get him off! But if this ever happens again, so help me Almighty God, I'm gonna stretch your ass across it for a few hours and see how you fair!" God forgive me, I was killing mad. But I meant it, and she left. And then Son Number Two got his dying Daddy, off the deadly bedpan. Bless his heart.

Ole Ed Brown resurrected his tired old body and spirit one more time, to the amazement of everyone, including God. There would be a few other trips but you do what you do during these times. Take care of each other. And forget about yourself. During this time of Daddy back and forth to the hospital, there would be extended times of relatively stable health ever so often. Even some days where he would get out of the house and drive his truck. There were some high points, especially when Mama's health started failing, where I would look up and see Daddy driving up in the yard, coming to check on me, "How's your Mama, Son?" One thing my parents had done their entire adult lives, while tearing each other down, was inquire with great concern about the other's well-being.

One afternoon, my phone rang as I was leaving Mama's. As Daddy asked how Mama was doing I replied, "Daddy, she's one step away from falling and breaking her hip or something worse." Mama had fallen six times in less than three days. I had to get her off the floor five of those times alone, and, honestly, I still don't know how I did it but I knew I couldn't keep doing it. You can't just grab an eighty-year old woman anywhere or way you want, and feel good about it. Ask Granny next time you see her! I had used a doubled-over, king-size bed sheet underneath her like a draw-sheet and tied it to me as well, to lift her up. But the last one had pretty much done my back in.

Sure enough, my phone rang the next afternoon about 2:45, "Your mother has fallen and can't get up... but she's okay." The commercial isn't as funny in person. The paramedics were walking in the door when I pulled up. By the time I got in the door, I was immediately "informed" in an over-the-top manner that "I have inspected her and do not detect any abnormalities." That is a quote. I politely responded with a "Great. They can confirm it at the hospital." I was immediately again informed that my mother did not need to go to the hospital, even though my non-super-human, X-ray eyes could tell simply by looking at her sprawled on the floor in a broken, upside down, downward-dog yoga position my Mama had never assumed, that her hip is most likely, very broken.

"Oh she doesn't complain of any real pain, and SHE says she doesn't need to go." The absolute ludicrousness of it was now boiling inside me. Of course she doesn't feel any pain! Most folks on 120 grams of methadone a day don't feel any pain either! Shit! The bottle's right there in front of you, and it ain't anti-acids! I managed to get the other milder, more common-sense paramedic off to the side where it was confirmed, Mama with the full support of Paramedic of the Year with XRAY Vision #One, had already decided. Mama ain't going to the hospital. Simply because Mama said so. So I played dumbass for a few minutes, thinking Mama's hip is gonna start HURTING and everyone will come to their senses and TAKE THE 81 YEAR OLD LADY WHO IS LYING IN THE MIDDLE OF HER FLOOR to the damn hospital! I also wanted to see just how these two chicks thought they could get her dead weight up and off that floor. After the bossy one, whom I firmly believe was already using men's public bathrooms in the great State of North Carolina, YEARS before state law HB2, finally admitted this was far beyond even her super human capabilities, I said, "Lemme show you how, Hoss." With my proven method of Mama-Lift and all three of us, we barely, and I mean barely, rose Sallie Mae up from the dead, so to speak. The fact that she could not only, not straighten her now deformed leg out, much less put any weight on it, seemed to only concern myself and the-shall we say, Reasonable Paramedic #Two.

Still, Sallie Mae was NOT gonna go to the hospital, and Baby Son was PISSED the F-OFF. I walked the paramedics to the door and out on the sidewalk, and politely informed them how super stupid and irresponsible this was, regardless what the old woman wants. I could even hear the two arguing on the way to the ambulance. Suddenly the nicer one walks back and hands me a small piece of paper with her personal cell on it. "We're going right up the street to eat supper. Just in case. It will be quicker." I needed somebody to bless my heart.

I returned inside and asked Mama how she fell. Oh, Mama was on her way to the bathroom, Son. Mama had to do Number-Two badly. Mama reached over to grab her always handy bottle of "Dr. Feelgood" and dropped it on the floor, right in front of her. So, after trying everything else, she decides, if she can slide down in the recliner just far enough to reach her bottle, she can grab it. After ignoring my pleas for weeks, to remove the slick cushion cases from the chair because her pink nightgown on those is like grease on ice, Mama slides down and as she reaches out for the bottle, the chair dumps her out. All her body weight came down on top of her left hip and I quote, I SWEAR this is a quote, Mama said, "I heard it snap like a twig." Come on, come on Congregation, say it with me. I shit you not.

Snapped like a twig, huh Mama, but it ain't broken? To quote the Warden at Shawshank Prison, "Looord, it's a miracle!" Miss Fuzzy-Britches didn't even need to dookie, not now. Imagine that. I said, "Okay Mama, I'll concede. Since your hip, isn't broken, you get to rest for thirty minutes, but then I have to see you get up and go to the bathroom on your own or I can't leave. Sallie Mae could play some cards. She did one of them "Trumped-Up" bridge deals, and countered with, "Let's make it 45."

One thing you accepted if you hung out with Sallie Mae Brown, much, was, 'It's Sallie's Way or the Highway." Sometimes both. I had grown tired of arguing long ago. So, we both sat there, her pretending like she was watching TV, occasionally trying to distract me, while she kept ever so slightly squirming around to check out that hip. I had seen her wince the first time. Realization Number-One. The hip is broken. I knew EXACTLY what was coming next. And I mean, literally, what would pop up, or out, soon enough.

One priceless thing you learn, quickly, among countless others, about old people on narcotics is, that they don't Number-Two very often or very easily. The old gray, digestive tract ain't what she used to be. *(Nowadays they have a name for it, OIC. Opiod Induced Constipation. And yet another new pill)*. Mama had been impacted so many times I quit counting, and I had a pouting suspicion she was now. If you don't know what impacted is, we won't be describing it here. Google it. Or watch that new idiotic commercial about IOC. You can Google that too. Forty five minutes come and go. An hour. Hour and a half. I can see the sweat bullets popping up and off Mama's tired old forehead, those two whiskers in her mole twitching. Every now and then I ask "You alright, Mama?" to which I got that "No, you know I'm not SMARTASS" glare accompanied by a hateful, indignant, southern rebel "I'm just FINE. Thank you."

About the two hour and fifteen minute mark, the sports news went to a Duke story and I let my guard down, until I heard the Yelp heard 'round the world, and turned to see Mama having to, having to, well, crap, having to shit so bad she'd kill you to do it. Realization Number-Two, pardon the pun, for Mama was, "Uh-oh, Mama's impacted!" And finishing off this unholy trinity of new knowledge at Number-Three, making me smile a little vindictive grin was, that ole methadone is wearing off, ain't it, Shoog?

She had sat there long enough for the initial shock to wear off and the hip to swell tremendously and now, having seen my Mama in pain, I could tell, she was really hurting. After all, this late in the day, wonder how much methadone Sallie Mae already has pumping through her veins, counting the extra two hidden in her recliner, that I know she took when she thought I wasn't looking. If you're ever around a senior and are wondering if their hip is broken, let them be impacted and that hit them too. Then you'll know for sure. Yep. Bless their hearts.

Mama... had... to... "go." Her bright idea was for me to help her "walk" to the bathroom. Yep. Walk. WALK Y'ALL! With a walker! On an unbroken hip, that "snapped like a twig," that's had hours to swell. I refused. With the final sands running through the homegrown, honey-comb hourglass, I even handed Mama the walker to show her, you can't even attempt to walk. Sallie Mae chunked that walker back at me like a bad, mad hockey player and commenced to making movements in that recliner I seriously doubt she'd made in near sixty years, if ever. The woman was in PAIN. And impacted or not, she had to go, was going to go, even if, as Mama liked to say, " it hair-lipped the whole Stallings clan!"

Earlier I had been cleaning the kitchen and had found one rubber glove under the sink, which I had chunked in the trashcan. On the way to the kitchen, I grabbed my phone and called the EMT's personal cell she had given me earlier. All I said was, "Need you. Now!" Don't ask me why, let's call it Providence, Divine Guidance or maybe I'm like Moses--I just have a supernatural knack for knowing where to go and exactly when, but something told me to retrieve that glove. After all, how often was I regularly cleaning up things neither you nor I wish to discuss.

With Mama literally turned completely sideways in that chair, trying to well, shit, with all her might, a concrete turd, I returned from the kitchen with a yellow gloved left hand and a small trashcan. She was already basically on her left side, completely on the broken hip and exposing her bottom side to me like "Here's your destiny, Hound. Could have been the Zac Brown Band, huh? They just won a Grammy. Your PRIZE is behind door Number Two!" But this dead, Red sea would not be parting all on its own.

I unsheathed my belt knife that I almost always wear on my hip, reached down and grabbed Mama's underwear and Mama screams (*Sorry, I know I'm wearing you out*), I shit you not, (*5-yard penalty, Intentional Pun*), "WHAT are you doing? I'm your Mama! I got some pride you know!" Pride. NOW you got pride? As I carefully ran that shiny blade of treasured relief underneath her panties and cut them away, I replied, "Ain't enough room left in here for pride and that thing. You want help or not?" For the record, Mama did nod, vigorously up and down answering my rhetorical question. It was pitifully vindictive. Not very often the baby in the family has complete control over Mama. Don't you dare ask me why, or how. Not ever. Don't wanna discuss it. I've never even pondered it myself, though a numb-nut or two has asked me over the years, what compelled me to do what I did next. "How did you know to...?" To what? Reach up inside my own Mama's hind end and grab a turd big enough for a hog to choke on, for a nice bookend or brass mantlepiece, and snatch it out? Where I come from, we call this... Common Sense. The woman had to go. The woman's hip was broken. She needed help. Bless her heart.

This is the most epic part of all. Call it, oh I don't know, a "crappy" life moment. Literally as I stand back up, holding a newborn baby "hanky" weighing in, God as my witness, at a good two and half to three pounds, I look up to see those same two EMT's sheepishly knocking on the screen door. "Y'all come on in. My hands are full at the moment."

I purposely stood there, in that dark little living room of public housing, until the Gals, yeah, let's call them "Our Gals," were close enough to see my pupils popping off the whites of my eyes, close enough for the breeze my flaring nostrils created to blow some common sense into them. I looked the know-it-all military acting, washed up fast-pitch softball player one in the face, held Mama's prize up and dropped it from chest height into that trashcan and softly said, "Man, I think that hip just may be broken." My ass has never, ever been kissed so fluently, sweetly, and appropriately. I enjoyed every last pucker, I had earned, and no Ma'am, I did not feel like blessing their hearts. Getting my Mama to the hospital was blessing enough for me.

So on an otherwise peaceful fall evening, I did the unthinkable for my Mama. There are some moments in your life you wish the mind could erase. And not only was her hip broken, it was broken in an extremely odd way. A few days later I escorted Mama with a new hip and wheelchair into the mandatory rest home stay for physical therapy. Sallie Mae did her usual cheerful thing, acting grateful and happy, to try and cheer me up, but I knew the reality. The average senior dies within three to six months after a hip break. And knowing how much my Mama LOVED to exercise or be told what to do, I felt great about these odds panning out.

Born to be the never ending surprise anomaly, however, Mama actually did great, and a few months later was being scheduled to be released to return home. Daddy was on a fairly stable trend, Mama was in good hands, so I made a much needed trip down to Atlanta for some business. A few days later, I was feeling elated to actually have a life for a change. Then my phone rang at 8:05 in the morning. I'm a musician. NOBODY calls me that early with good news. When the first thing they ask you is where you are, that's not a good sign. Mama had been fine, and suddenly after breakfast she began throwing up. Blood. Her lungs aspirated, and she had stopped breathing. Mama was on the way to the ER, and that's all they could tell me.

I was on the road in minutes but two hours later, I was told Mama was on a ventilator in a now induced coma and to get home. Soon.

The trip to Atlanta had been a breath of fresh southern air. Now days later I was making the familiar trip home, breaking every speed limit law in three states, knowing I would never hear Mama's voice again. When I first lay eyes on her, her face flush with the rosy, pink color of fake, machine-induced life, every bodily function a strange number, I noticed the walls were already adorned with drawings and quaint artificial flowers the First Baptist Church children had made out of construction paper. Mama looked so innocent and fragile. Her entire life lay before me, a lingering weak breath of a candle, this light I loved, barely burning, that the slightest breeze walking by might blow out for good. Her numbers were bad, and everyone prepared me for the worst. The days flew by, each additional one lowering the odds of Mama waking up. But seeing those children's drawings, the pure hearts of loving children pinned to the wall, hour after hour, talking to her, I can't explain it, but I knew Mama would wake up. My Mama would rise up and go home. If life could only be as beautifully simple all the time, as it is inside our moments of high hopes. Several days in, standing beside my comatose Mama, I get the call they're on the way to the same hospital with Daddy. Jesus Christ. That's all I could think. Jesus Christ. There is something about that name, especially in moments of anguish and anger. Besides it is ingrained in me "the Lord won't put more on you than you can take." Every time I hear someone say that I think, "The Lord doesn't put most of these things on me. I did." Stop asking God to do His and your end of the bargain.

Honestly, it doesn't really matter who's to blame when you're in those moments. Not to me. Getting through them and to the next one consumes you. Hours later both of my parents were in ICU hanging on for dear life, one on each end. I was tired. Tired of going days without showers, of some people talking behind my back about what I should be doing instead of what I was. I was tired of well-meaning people, walking up and laying their hands on my shoulder, immediately invading my most personal space without even a proper hello. I was exhausted from hearing, "Bless your heart," like I'm some charity case, or, "I've been praying for you," cause it's biscuit time at Hardee's and they got an audience, when you know damn well, you haven't crossed their mind nor should you have. I wanted someone to walk up to me and say, "Come on boy, let's go grab a hot dog" or tell me how their fishing trip or duck hunt went. The last thing I wanted was another reminder, one more nail handed to me to drive in the family coffin. I was tired of feeling guilty for being tired. But I accepted it for what it was, honorable and holy. The light in our family funeral parlor was growing dimmer, and I was growing weary of replacing lightbulbs.

The next morning I awoke to learn Mama was miraculously turning around, and when I walked in to see her exhausted face trying to smile back at me, I felt as guilty as I did elated. I was now wondering, are you hanging on for me? And knowing either way that her days were numbered, I began to admit only to myself what a failure I felt like. It wasn't gnawing at me; it was devouring me every day, all day, in the middle of the night while I was peeing, because I knew now I could not do both caregiving and music, and I would most likely never be able to do all the things I had wanted to do for my parents. It was already too late with my Brother. There was a giant IV of raw reality stuck in my deepest vein, sucking the very life out of me too. Soon, my parents would be dead, and almost everything I once treasured, just didn't matter anymore. I had saved family pictures, stories, an entire oral history for what? There would be no one to hand it down to and even that was my fault. All of this became a giant mountain of self-centered pity, selfishness, and immaturity, which, of course, was all my fault. What the hell had I done with my life? Self-blame. The devil loves that one too. LOVES it!

Yet still, I felt deeper than that, least enough to keep it in check, that I was doing what I had to do. What was right. Honorable. What kind of a man would go off and finish chasing his dreams and leave his parents to fend for themselves. My Mama was my responsibility and solely mine. I owed it to my Daddy and GiGi to be there every moment I could, because our numbered moments were now on the discount aisle on rollout prices. The only thing I knew for absolute certainty about this life of mine was, I would either be there, by my parents' sides, or dead in the ground myself. And soon enough the days would come where honestly I didn't have the energy to give a damn either way. I was a ship taking on too much water, and I was quickly tiring of paddling.

Boiled Custard

October, 10, 2009
Journal Entry

I got a bellyache, I'm ill as hell and personally don't give a damn what anyone thinks. Not today. Just finished making another batch of Aunt Louise's boiled custard for Mama. As I separated the egg yolks from the whites, whipping in the cup or more of white sugar, I could see my brother's diseased eyes. With the whine of the blender, I recalled his lonesome moans of a pain only the dying express with conviction. Adding the flour, blending it all into one creamy mixture, I felt nothing but anger as I added it to the hot milk, and somehow in the front of my mind the stench of urine and feces reigned over any attention I might pay this sweet cocktail.

The old family recipe has been around for a long time because it works. Once chilled to the consistency of a half melted milkshake, the homemade concoction soothes the worst of bellies, which is usually those of the dying or at the very least the deathly ill. The sweet syrup is really all Mama has been living off of since she threw up what was left of her stomach lining, aspirating her lungs with fresh blood and winding up in ICU. There is the occasional bowl of chicken and rice, or the salty broth, which has been added to her daily routine. Two weeks on a ventilator at eighty one will suck the life out of anyone. Daddy just got off himself, much to the surprise of all. But today his belly and crotch are raw, swollen, and distended much like his arms and hands. Even his skin is bursting open; his arms are turned nearly black from broken blood vessels and botched IV attempts. Hard to celebrate the small *victories sometimes. I said hard, not impossible. Celebrate brothers and sisters, celebrate them.*

Brother is dead. Been dead two freaking years this December. The last twelve weeks of his toxic life were spent in a cheap rented hospital bed in Cousin Jay's front living room, sipping on a bathroom Dixie cup half-full of boiled custard. He's gone, Mama and Daddy are not long for this world, and boiled custard pisses me off. Of course, once it chills and I deliver a mason jar to each of them, some semblance of pride, love or familial duty will make me come around. Come around to the next batch that is. Dying wears out everybody. And living, it'll kill you. I promise, sooner or later, it's gonna kill you. It's supposed to. That's why the recipe is so sweet. One more thing. Nobody's going to love your family the way you do. Nobody. They're not suppose to. My advice? Love them hard while you can. And let them love on you.

BLESSING HEARTS cont.

Mama returned to the rest home so weak it was expected she would never really recover. Daddy had a short stay this time and headed back to the farm, "to die." My biggest concern now was living the lie of assuring Mama daily that I was "hanging on to her apartment" so she could "go home." She had six more months to recover and return home, and then that was out of my hands. But not ole Unsinkable Sallie Mae. No Ma'am!

What would be Daddy's next-to-last trip to the hospital, both Daddy and our family had had enough. I tried to prevent the doctor from putting him on another ventilator. He did not want it. But we had the issue of "Daddy, you won't sign anything" cause, "Son, all they're trying to do is kill me." When the PA, who knew us well, came in and they rolled Daddy off to ICU, I smiled at her. A really calm nice smile. The kind that unnerves medical folks. One that says, "I'm about to tell YOU, how THIS one's gonna roll." We are gonna be rolling straight out the front door soon as we get the phone call from Heaven.

She said something totally fake and forgettable but nice, and I said, "Honey, here's the deal. He's an old man from a bygone era. They don't think like we do, nor is he ever going to. He shouldn't be asked or expected to. He's eighty-two damn years old! He's earned that. My Daddy ain't gonna sign no paper. He won't even read it. But you all know he doesn't want extra measures. So, you can tell that smart-ass arrogant doctor, on the next trip, I'll be right here. And I promise you now, I will stomp his or anybody else's ass that attempts it." I didn't yell. I wasn't ugly. I said it calmly. But I damn sure meant it. As Daddy had always said, "Enough, is e-damn-nuff!"

We all could tell this trip was different. Darker, a bleak view of a never ending season of suffering that had worn a man's manhood down to a cracked fragile shell. Daddy looked more like the antique barn surrounded by trees and weeds, leaning to one side, waiting for the wind to purse her mouth, blow a kiss of a breeze and flatten it once and for all. Surprising us yet again, Daddy went from barely, still being in the room with us, to sitting up in the so called hospital "recliner." Another modern medical torture device. I had recently been given a new cutting-edge video camera and was a tad past addicted to it. The following day was Mother's Day, and my female cousins had picked out a card for Daddy to give to his GiGi. When I arrived I was stunned to see how much Daddy had "improved" until I realized he was high--as--a--kite on major pain and anxiety meds. I knew it was only a matter of time before Daddy peaked and came crashing down through the woods so to speak. But we all joined hearts and soaked in Uncle Ed feeling "good" one more time. I tried to film what I could; Daddy was in RARE form. He knew he had a stage, an audience and enough juice to perform one more time. And he was hilarious, telling a few old stories that changed just enough to warrant your undivided attention, to see if you would witness an outright white lie or another shot of southern bourbon born and bred brilliance. I had been "told" several times to "put that thing up" and stop filming. Before long you could see Daddy's "energy" running low as he began slumping in the chair, becoming unengaged and unable to stay focused.

The Girls, Nancy and Barney were loving all over Daddy and trying to help him write a heartfelt note to GiGi. Daddy didn't care because Daddy no longer could. Suddenly he glares over at me and spouts out with a fatherly voice that would make the Pope happy, "Son, would you put that damn thing up, now? I've told you for the last time." And I laughed from the soul as I hit the off button and proudly replied, "Yes Sir." Why? Because, by-God, my Daddy said so. I still have the video somewhere on my hard drive.

He then turned to answer the girl's last question, tried to put the pen to the card only to see it fly off the cart and Daddy collapsed into that chair and said, "Y'all write whatever you want to. Uncle Ed is give out,

Shoog." And I knew moments later as we nestled him back into another stiff, uncomfortable hospital bed, Daddy was done. He was too tired to even try and care about the things of this world. The place where all of this earthly life becomes overweight baggage not allowed on the coming trip. Daddy was so ready to go home he would have had us roll him out to the highway in a wheelchair so he could hitchhike a ride to Heaven. There was nothing left unsaid, and I stood watch with the family the next few days as the old man we had adored, argued with and admired began to slowly sail out to sea, where the warm watercolors live and the dying go to surrender their flesh, give up the ghost and the spirit settles its final balance. Where the soul's affairs are saved, privately, once and for all.

That afternoon, Linda got back from a quick trip home and they had as sweet a moment as was possible, but we all knew this was it. Our voices, the ones he loved the most, were mere echoes now, bouncing across holy waters towards his setting sun. Within an hour we were offered a bed at the wonderful hospice center right up the street. We jumped at it. It's peaceful, quiet. You can relax and witness what you don't want to witness, in "peace." Around 4:45pm, I decided to go to the restroom and then the chapel up the hall. I was a few feet away from the restroom and I promise you just as clear as me speaking to you, a voice inside me firmly said "Go, tell your Daddy goodbye." All of a sudden, I didn't need to pee.

As I entered the room, they were actually taking Linda's blood pressure because she didn't feel right. When the girl finished, I leaned into her and asked if she would check Daddy's. It was something like fifty eight over thirty two, some nearly imperceptible number. With Linda on the side of his heart, me kneeled down on the floor bedside on the other, I placed my left arm up behind Daddy and my right arm over his heart. Linda drew in on the other side, smothering him with kisses and the last rites everyone should be entitled to, words of unconditional love. I wanted Daddy to feel us hugging him, holding him steady, ready to let him go. What I whispered in his ear, is between me and my Daddy. And God. And at 5:32 pm EST on May 13th, 2010, I felt my Daddy's heart seize up and stop beating. He came up off the pillow a little and had a brief look of pain, and settled back down into eternal rest.

My Daddy died. And just like Granddaddy had died in Daddy's arms on the side off the road in 1967, I was there holding my Daddy in mine best I could. And I know, with all I am, my Daddy liked that. And so do I. If he was here, Daddy would "say so," bless his heart.

SWEET PLATES

The day of Daddy's funeral I was down at the funeral home, hanging in the room alone with Daddy's body, because it was the only place I could find any peace of mind and quiet. Any real life. Here it was a couple of hours from the 2pm service and I'm sitting there in khakis, plain white t-shirt, ruffled hair and flip flops, waiting for a good friend of mine to come by and rehearse the song I planned to sing at Daddy's funeral, New Grass Revival's, "Plant Your Fields." Plus, I needed to put one of Uncle Les' silver dollars in Daddy's coat pocket. He had now lost the $3 bet with Great-Granddaddy Patrick he would outlive him to ninety-three. I figured with inflation, it would leave some to spare for Daddy. Yes. I am that anal.

Now some folks, like me, don't feel any different sitting in a room with a dead body than they do sitting at home on the couch with live ones. Sometimes, some of us prefer it. Least there's no tension. No emotional or spiritual bullshit to wade through. Well, least till the visitation starts. My dear, precious, southern soul brother, Spook Joyner, however, is not one of those people. Perhaps his first name should have been my first clue. The door opened up as Brian let Spook in the door with his guitar. I barely even noticed till I glanced up, just as Spook glanced over at Daddy and mumbled, "Shit, Chris."

I'm greeting ole Spook as he sits down in the chair beside me, and first thing out of his mouth is, "How come we got to rehearse in here man? How come you gotta do ole Spook like that?"

"I promise, Daddy ain't gonna lay a hand on Spook," I replied.

Spook countered with, "Good, cause if he does, ole Spook's gonna lay him out. Again. Spook don't like dead people."

I couldn't resist, "Dead people don't like Spook either. They don't like anybody. They're dead. But if I was you, I wouldn't dream of laying a hand on Daddy, dead or alive. But that's your call." Those sweet thoughts of his own Daddy, another man's man from another bygone era, washed over Spook's face and he replied, "Yeah. You're right. You didn't fuck with that crowd, did you buddy?" And we both, died laughing.

Spook closed that sermon down with, "You ain't right boy. Dead folks should be left alone. C'mon, how's this song go? Let's pick it." And so ole Spook Joyner of Nash County and Hound Brown learned "Plant Your Fields" at the last minute and sang it at Daddy's funeral. I did the eulogy, but honestly, Daddy's funeral is a complete morning fog settled over the swamp my mind had now become. I remember singing, well trying to, and how ridiculous I felt doing it, for some reason. I was already completely over the death thing as well as another funeral by now. They were nothing more than a "cleaning up life's mess," necessity in my mind. An hour or so later on a beautiful May afternoon in North Carolina, the procession ambled by the farm, and for a brief moment I could feel the genuine depth of the love Daddy did have for that land. He loved that farm, not the way most men love what they own. No, Daddy loved that land because it was the last thread of connection he had, the sacred one he savored all his life, to his parents and siblings. Because out here, he didn't have to squint his eyes to see his Mama, hear her voice back in the spring of 1933 calling his name for supper, teaching him his nightly prayers or singing as she planted those daffodils that still come up around the base of her pecan trees. He didn't have to make up some sappy sentimental tale and smear it all over your ears. Daddy could sit in silence and simply look out the window. It was Daddy who had placed the immense reverence and sanctity I hold for family, in my own heart. Now that was an epic moment, slowly carrying my Daddy past our family farm, to lay him to rest. And knowing now, for sure, there were some things that would have to rest in shallow unmarked graves for me.

As the funeral ended, I headed for my car and disappeared as quickly as possible without being rude. I didn't want to be seen. Soon enough the last car drove off, and I walked back up to Daddy's grave. Burying my own people, whenever I could, had become a very personal duty to me years ago, at my Uncle Cap's funeral, due to a grave digging crew with no manners. I don't deal well with people smoking and cussing in front of my grieving family. It's the "Daddy" in me. I always stay around and make sure it's done respectfully. I had also discovered through the years how much more sacred and grateful a burial becomes when you do your own burying. I grabbed a shovel and started "throwing dirt" like Daddy had taught me years ago as the May sun fell across my skin and face. I soaked in every last sun drop, the warmth of life filling up my cells. I noticed my breath filling and leaving my lungs, the way we far too rarely do. With real gratitude. The images of a lifetime swarmed through my mind, memories enveloped my spirit, as some of my Brother's buried ashes, a southern secession of the heart to Daddy, lay resting a few feet behind me. And then it hit me. Out of nowhere, like it was sent by the gods to startle the soul and wake you up from napping in life. My damn back was killing me. Same spot. Left side, that damn old tumor I still didn't know was there and a screwed up, twice-broken hip.

The burial crew was run by an old high school friend, Robert. Tossing one last shovelful, I glanced up and said, "Damn, takes more dirt than I remember to cover up a vault these days Pal. They make 'em bigger or something?"

Eyes twinkling, Robert replied, "We got a bobcat ya know."

The Daddy in me flew out before I could even think it. "Well, hell, crank that puppy up. Screw this. It's the thought that counts, right." I could hear my Daddy, no pun intended, dying laughing.

The setting sun partially blinded the old dirt path from my earthly eyes, its light and warmth still cleansing my soul, freeing me of new unnecessary baggage. I looked for Daddy's favorite fox squirrel that usually made an appearance and guarded our cemetery, only to find him gone as well. I felt that familiar gray asphalt, the one that I know its every solitary crack, lift the truck onto its shoulders, and came home to the family farm, for the first time, without Daddy. But I swear, I could hear Daddy chuckling, the way only he did. When Daddy was truly what he called "tickled." Happy.

That feeling we used to feel after being in the field all day long swept over me. Like John Coffey on my own Green Mile, I was "tired, boss. Dog tired." I was tired of anything to do with the dying. And much of the living. I pulled back up to the house, to see more than enough people there. For the record, we don't feel like entertaining your ass right after burying someone. For the love of God, please go home. Let the grieving fill up on banana pudding or pimento cheese, and take a nap. Come back later. We love you too.

I don't think I'd ever felt the kind of internal tension I did as I leaned up against the counter in that kitchen. I felt high on it. Looking across the room, everyone talking over each other, people calling out my name, "Do you remember when Uncle Ed did so and so..," the only other thing I recall thinking was, "I think I'm screwed." Because I realized I had been stressed out 24/7 for so long, that it was an arthritis of the soul lying in my bones. Living in the Valley of the Shadow of Death so long, I no longer even really reacted to it or took notice of the spell it cast; it took too much energy, I expected it, expected every morning, the day would be a different version of shitty. Not in a pessimistic way. In a honest humility that reality brings. I am a farmer's son. We know what's real. I tried to approach it with deep integrity, respect and gratitude. Seriously, I'm not an idiot. Everyone doesn't get to watch their parents live to that age. I respected their illnesses and suffering. The good fight. I looked, as deeply as I believe a mortal man can-and more than he should-for the meaning of it all, for that God-spot-I began to call it- in my heart and head. Because, I had seen enough to know, that they are lying there, if you're willing to accept them as they are. I was, however, also aware enough to understand deep inside, this is not good. Honorable be damned, grateful or not, waking up knowing today is in all likelihood gonna suck and may include death is having a deep impact on my health; mentally, spiritually, and physically. The only other thought I was deeply aware of as I scanned the room, soaking the moment into my soul, was perhaps a line for a new song someday, "I never felt so alive... as the day my Daddy died." I felt fully alive in every respect. I had already learned the faces you think you will see around you, comforting you, when death comes knocking are never the ones you actually do. And I was deeply grateful for many people in those moments, for the chance at reconnecting with long lost cousins like Donna while silently admitting that others, whom I thought I could never live without, I was no longer close to really in any way. No one's fault. We just didn't recognize each other anymore. Life, again, has it's way with all of us.

I soon left for Mama's place. (Believe it or not, Mama had made it home, despite everyone else's opinion and pretty much all state laws regarding the elderly.) So I headed for Mama's because I knew, there would be some shit, metaphorically, perhaps even literally, to deal with there. If it was not already waiting on me, it was coming any hour of any day. I was pleasantly surprised to open the door to my Mama-all cleaned up and dressed in her best funeral clothes, the nice, dark navy-blue outfit my first wife had bought her, makeup and all, every hair sprayed in place, twice, her ragged brown Bible lying ever vigilant underneath her left hand in her lap. Unable to physically attend the funeral or perhaps not wanting to be both a distraction to others and burden to herself, afraid perhaps of reopening unmarked graves and disturbing deep, salty, wounds, Mama had held church for us right there in her trusty, cheap green recliner. At the Altar of Mama's Lap. All by her lonesome self. My Mama could be a lot of things, some not so good. But nobody loved quite like Sallie Mae Brown. She always loved, deeply, when it counted. And love always counts. That went for everyone. You ARE required by spiritual law, to love everyone. Ooooh, yes you are!

I could tell she had earlier shed tears but now wore a smile borne of faith's devotion and the assured excitement to see me. First thing she asked me was "How was the funeral and how is Linda?" Over the previous couple of years, beginning with Glenn's journey, I had been surprised and shocked enough by authentic exhibits of caring and genuine love between and for two women who had literally despised each other long ago, that it no longer biblically confused me, as in a "passeth all understanding" kind of way. I had not only learned but had witnessed that if you live long enough in this shitty, fallen, broken world you will come to compassion for everyone. For folks you don't understand 'cause you've never tried to. The ones you don't approve of, even your enemies. Or you will find none for yourself.

God will make sure of that. He uses a thing called, life. You will lose your pride, all of it, on the way out this door. How quickly, painlessly, is up to you. Death seems to chalk up the common humanity in us like dead outlaws laid out on ice boards in front of a saloon, for the good of the public's soul and consciousness, as well as the gunslinger's. For all to see and count.

I spent the evening being grateful with the only living soul left who could possibly genuinely understand how I felt and and actually gave a damn. Mama told a few funny and even heartwarming stories of her and Daddy's early good ole days, careful to stop soon enough before the divorce year's caution signs started annoying me or herself. One thing my Mama did not ever do was reconstruct the truth, whenever she was feeling all cheerful and snappy, or to ease bruised egos, aching attitudes or even broken hearts. Not purposely anyway. To us, that's just plain ole lying and not only unnecessary but annoying and, in some cases unforgivable. At the very least, it's "illegal" according to the Commandments we straddle, strive and fail to maintain.

GiGi had made Mama several plates of food, and per usual, like it was medically required, there was only one plate she was interested in hearing about. "Tell me again what's on that sweet plate, Shoog?" She could be so damn cute you wanted to pop her on her hind end sometimes. I did what all middle-aged caretakers do. Threw my towel in the ring and called out the night's choices!

"I'll take a little bit of that pecan pie and some coconut cake," Mama said.

When I lay her favorite rooster-adorned TV tray in her lap, Mama looked me dead in the eye, very seriously, and said, "I said a 'bit,' not just one bite." In case you don't know yet, senior citizens do not play when it comes to their pain and anxiety meds or sweets. EVER. Especially at funeral time. So Mama got the whole slice of pecan and had finished off the coconut cake too, in under the accepted time required to consume that second cup of black coffee.

I finished "burying" my Daddy, alone with my Mama, because by-God, I wanted to. And that was that. Daddy was buried, respectfully, in a beautiful solid pecan casket I was allowed to pick out for him. I had chosen the pecan because of those trees his Mama planted back in the '30's and to celebrate he was now reunited with her. And now, it was Mama time. All the time I had left was for Mama, Because I knew that she was not long for this world either. For another brief moment lifted by grace, life was a fully loaded sweet plate neatly wrapped in tin-foil.

MAMA AND 'DEM

It had only been about five months or so since Mama had defied all odds and bets and returned home from the rest home. I had made a ten-day trip to Nashville back in the fall, honestly at the request and nudging of Mama to "get back to my life." I had some written work being published in a southern folklore-cookbook with the Zac Brown Band and several co-writing appointments with some high profile hit songwriters. I had recently reconnected with a dear old friend, who had been my first roommate in Nashville and was now one of the most respected copyright-administrators in town. Jayme coaxed me into coming out to "Smashville" as we call it, *(everyone should come to Music City at least once and have their ass as well as their dreams handed to 'em on a silver platter)*, and I knew immediately our reconnection was a God-send. She had been through some very tough and uncannily similar times with her family. And being in the business, she knew what I was up against, how high the odds are already stacked against us creative-folk, much less one in my long distance family situation. She also knew Mama was right, I desperately needed not only an outlet but someone "on my side" so to speak. Someone who believed in me, understood me, what I was going through, and most importantly one who wasn't afraid to push me or piss me of. A true friend who could help me avoid my greatest talent of all. Being my own worst enemy.

So in October, as we were preparing to release the Zac Brown Band book, *Southern Ground*, Jayme set up my first full-blown "Hound is back" in Nashville trip. She had me loaded for bear every day, schedule-wise, and basically propped open the door to Music Row with a sign that said, "He's one of us, he's already paid his dues and he belongs here." I got in late on a

Sunday evening, with my first writing appointment with a major hit song-writer, who was currently on another hit-writing roll with Montgomery Gentry, the following morning. A southerner like me, Jayme paired me with someone who understood who I was and wasn't. The next morning as I drove into Music Row to write I wasn't as excited as much I was relieved. I knew the high prices I had paid already, exactly how many road and studio miles I had logged. I didn't need, nor was I seeking validation from anyone, as deeply as I was a good solid opportunity with what I call a "next of kin," a kindred creative spirit.

It was a beautiful, stunningly so, fall morning as I headed down into the bowels of Nashville and Music Row proper. I had forgotten how beautiful "Smashville" could be this time of year. It was still fairly early, a lil before 8:00am and I noticed I had missed a phone call or two. Suddenly my phone kept going off, and I soon discovered I'd missed nine calls. As I scrolled through the numbers, recognizing several numbers from the resthome and the rest from various North Carolina cell numbers I said it out loud, "You gotta be shitting me." Before I even listened to the numerous phone messages I knew exactly what was going down. At first pissed, I began laughing as I listened to the fourth frantic message left by the resthome administrator. Mama was going home to prove to me she could make it on her own so I could and would go do the annual Christmas tour with my friend John Berry for the fifteenth year. 'Cause she knew I would not leave her to fend for herself in a rest home.

It seemed Mama had asked to see the administrator Jeff, whom she adored, the afternoon before, once I had left of course and couldn't know anything at least until it was too late. She informed him that she would be leaving the following morning to return home. For the record, he tried to inform Sallie Mae she wasn't going anywhere to which Mama replied, "I'm going home tomorrow if I have to call a damn taxicab." His only other main failing, besides thinking he could tell Mama what to do, was thinking the old lady was bluffing.

That morning had come, and Mama had her best friend and co-conspirator, her niece Carolyn, the daughter she never had and thought she could boss around a little bit, show up. *(Carolyn always sweetly played along.)* According to state records and eye witness testimony, with her bags packed, flying the coup at a high rate of wheelchair speed, Mama got all the way to sidewalk a few feet from the cab before they "pulled her over." Caught her. Now being quite serious, Jeff informed Mama he could not legally let her leave as I was her signed legal guardian, I was out of state and he could lose his job. Mama counter-offered with, "He ain't my guardian. I'm his guardian! I'm Mama, and THIS Hot-Mama is going to her Hen-House! With or without you," and dared him to try and stop her.

By the time I got back in touch with them, Mama was sitting comfortably in her trusty recliner, had EVEN gotten the staff to go to the freaking grocery store, because, and I quote, "Well, I can't be here with nothing at all to eat," and even had her medicines headed over from the pharmacy. The poor fellow in charge was out of breath and had been trampled in this senior-citizen, crime-ring-of-fire, long before I knew what was going on. As long as Mama had several boxes of Lil' Debbie Oatmeal Cakes, (the big ones) a minimum of twelve, full size, Dark Milky Way candy bars, and plenty of meds, she could survive anything. Mama said "they say oatmeal and dark chocolate is good for you!" I've told you-all for this entire "funeral," you cannot make this stuff up!

By the next evening, I was changing my flight for an early return after speaking with Carolyn. When she told me Mama hadn't gotten out of the chair in twenty-four hours to go to the bathroom, I knew it wasn't good. It took two more days for me to return. When I walked in Mama's place that morning, knowing she had been stuck in that chair for nearly three days, lets just say it was beyond horrible. Mama was devastated, defeated with embarrassment and began weeping. I got her up and with Carolyn's help managed to get Mama to the bathroom where she began the enormous task of cleaning Mama up. I went straight to the recliner and lifted it, took it to the back of my truck and threw it in. There was no salvaging that chair. Mama was exhausted. When her body felt her bed underneath her legs and back she was practically snoring before her head hit the pillow. As I slumped down on the couch Carolyn lovingly asked, "What are you gonna do?"

I replied, truthfully, "The only thing you can do when it comes to Sallie Mae Brown. Deal with it. Get her a new chair."

Getting back in a rest home you've just pissed off is not as simple as one might think. It's not a hotel you can check in and out of, especially when you're on Medicare. Mama had grown so weak lying in the resthome bed with minimal rehabilitation she was doomed to fail. The woman could distract any physical, or any type of therapist, and God as my witness, would have them doing exercises, before she would ever lift a finger or foot to do one. The first time they gave her that wooden thing with the round, square and triangular plastic inserts to put in their correct holes, Mama played along like she was the Village Idiot. Now, *that* was funny. When they caught on, Mama said, "You don't get to my age being stupid. Get that thing out of my damn face!" The first few weeks back home she never left her bed, and I positioned a portable toilet right beside her while I attempted to get her back in the resthome and continued to try and work, which was absolutely impossible. I made as many daily trips to her house as it took to keep that toilet and Mama taken care of, whether it was two, five, or an all-night stay. I was already an expert at getting Mama wherever she needed to be, whatever it took. Gradually and to everyone's surprise, she regained some strength but that final look of acceptance slowly began to spread across her sweet old face and we both came to the sweetest agreement one evening, we would enjoy these last days, weeks or months at home. All the nails were in this coffin.

To my pleasant surprise, I started getting calls from employees of the rest home and everyone was wondering "how Miss Sallie is doing" and "we sure miss your Mama." Finally I talked with the administrator, who assured me two things; they all knew she would be coming back when she left and they welcomed having her again. Resthome Folks. Angels on earth, they are.

The next five months were and still are a blurry video played in slow motion of pure stress with the occasional life moment with Mama that made it all worthwhile. I lived in a torn state of proud to be taking care of my mother and pissed off at the same time. One day, as I went to set her rooster tray in her lap, with the Chicken Pastry and collards lunch, (of course with cornbread) I had just made her, she was tickled to death. I was in no mood for anything except silence and doing what needed to be done. As I straightened back up from leaning over her chair, Mama tugged on my arm and said, "Come here and give me some sugar," like I was nine again.

I said, "Mama, c'mon now."

When Mama wants "shoogha," back home, Mama gets sugar. So I leaned back over and she pecked me on the right cheek with that soft weathered face and the double-whiskered mole. As I stood up Mama declared, "It's a shame you had to be my son." Huh?

"It's a shame you had to be my sweet Chris, you would have made me a good husband," and YES Ma'am, my ever loving Dixie-Fried brain flew clean out of the Chicken-Coup Sky!

"WHAT did you just say?"

As Mama started back into it, I huffed and trying my best to mince my words, said, "Mama. I... I... ahh...THAT may the most F-ed UP thing you have EVER said to me MUCH LESS thought. That is wrong on SO many levels I don't EVEN know where...," and without missing a skippy-dadoo-dah-beat, Sallie Mae Brown bowed up and said in a sarcastic-seizure, "You been out there in Nashville, with them people that think TOO much, TOO LONG!"

God-a-Mighty was my Mama a character. What are gonna say back to that? I went and cleaned the bathroom or found something or somewhere appropriate to bury my punished pride. Over the following months Mama's health and ability to get around greatly deteriorated. With CKD, chronic kidney disease, her legs would literally bust open and weep for weeks at the time. Until one day, leaving the doctors office, where they wrapped them up in gauze, I thought, "I ain't no doctor but I ain't no dumb ass either. There is no way her legs can heal, staying sopping wet in fluid leaking through her skin, that oughta be going out her kidneys." I got her home, and in the bed, and my sweet, devoted cousin Carolyn and I kept Mama's legs elevated, clean, dry and wiped down with alcohol swaps and the like. You could see them healing within a day or two. Apparently her amazing world-class urologist, which he absolutely is, *(the rude one with the narcissistic smug ego, that I still to this very day, wanna slap his ass across the exam room, and would have if I hadn't already been a felon, because he DOES need it.),* didn't know everything. Trust me his whole staff and the entire county feel the same way.

One night I came over with our regular Tuesday night, Fried Oyster Plate, to split for a Duke-Carolina basketball game. From the odd look of, "I'm hiding something and I want to tell you but can't," Mama was wearing on her face, I knew this was gonna be a "good one."

After asking several times, I finally left it to her to decide when and if to tell me. The game went to a break to which Mama did her usual reply, "Thank God, maybe that man will shut up now," and she turned the volume down on the television. Nobody thought Dick Vitale's mouth trap could ruin a good basketball game more-so than Mama. She used to yell, "Oooooooowwwh, I DESPISE that Man! I wish he would SHUT UP so I can watch the game!" He was forever "that man." Mama never did catch his name.

I noticed her upper lip beginning to tremble but at first I thought it was simply old age. When the first huge crocodile tears began falling across her face like a repentant rain in a grove of live oak trees, I realized, this ain't gonna be good. Mama could barely find the inner strength to form words, so I did my best to create a safe, sound space for her to speak her heart.

"There's something I need to tell you Shoog... and I don't know how to say this. You've had enough on you to kill a lesser man and..."

"Just tell me Mama. It's alright."

"No, it's not."

"Well, it will be 'cause your my Mama and I said so."

Mama's voice broke into a trillion pieces, a mirror, perfectly reflecting her breaking heart, the way the open confession of an inner deep self disappointment and embarrassment can do. "It's killing me to tell you this, but I know you need to know..."

And THEN it hit me. I felt the stiff blushing a true surprise, that isn't a surprise, but an inner silent prophecy you've ignored too long, coming to pass, brings. When you know you're either about to be pissed the f- off or sent into the Land-of-No-Return-embarrassment" yourself. Inside my mind was rolling over "To be sure not. Don't tell me you haven't..."

Her sentence ended with the last bit of emotional strength she had dribbling out, "I don't have any final arrangements taken care of."

My only thought was so deeply buried, it pinned me to the couch like a concrete vault, six feet under ground. "You have got... to... be... f@#!... ing... kidding... me," was the headline running across my mind but I took a breath and did what a Mama's Boy is destined to do. I lied my loyal, royal, Christian ass off again. "Aaah shoot, That's alright Mama. Don't worry about it," as I came un-freaking-glued inside.

My parents, both of them, had sold BURIAL INSURANCE, decades ago for a number of years, for Christ's-sake! They both even had cheap fake gold mini statutes proclaiming how GOOD they were at it! Mama had always told me she had a policy and it was taken care of with a small fee withdrawn monthly. We had openly discussed many times her burial plot out with Granny, that Aunt Louise had purchased for whoever wanted one. I knew very well Mama would be buried with them. It had vaguely crossed my mind a few times the past year to ask, as I managed her bank account. I had even asked several times and was told "Oh, that? That's been taken care of." Once again, one of those "comfort cliches" you always know is a lie.

So, I just lied until I had assured my old, sweet, embarrassed Mama, it was okay, and turned back to watch Duke kick some more BlueBlood-basketball, Carolina Tarheel ass; as a video of all my family's bullshit flew across my face at digital speed. Finally a smile I knew I couldn't stop, not so slowly fell across my face. Some life is just plain funny. An uncomfortably short time eased by, when Mama, still a little gun shy from breaking that news said, "Your Daddy called me the other day."

In the south, I mean the real south, when you come from a "broken" family like mine, there's a couple of phrases that you know are about to bring something, shit on a shingle, GRAVY-GOOD, your way when you hear them. This is one of them. Hearing your elderly Mama say, sweet as sugar in Savannah on a Scottish scone, "Your Daddy called me the other day," like they're still dating since last year's prom.

I'm thinking, "My Daddy, the one you love to wear me out about?" I dryly replied with the excitement of divorce bliss that every adult child who's survived a good one bears like an awkward accent. "About, what."

As Mama began to tell me what a sweet and caring phone call she got from Daddy, I floated by in an WTF out-of-body experience when it hit me what she was about to tell me. Daddy had mentioned to me, in passing, a while back that Mama was welcome to a burial spot out in his family cemetery next to my Brother's. I had mentioned it to Mama to diffuse a situation one afternoon, when after another bitter exchange with her favorite sparring-partner sister, she had exclaimed, "You can throw me out there in the woods with the Boogeyman, but don't you DARE bury me out there with them! You hear me?" I ignored it for what it was. Within hours to minutes, or days, Mama would always be coo-ing over a family story of love and redemption. I had also forgotten, she had recently asked me out of the blue where I wanted to be buried, which had seemed odd to me. I had replied, "Mama, I don't care. I'll be dead. Like the rest of us."

Mama begins her well thought out, rehearsed presentation of how she had thought about it and with "Glenn being out there and all" and you know it "always has remained home to me," (which was the truth, despite her bitterness) now accompanied by "and it would save us a lot of money," and here's my favorite part, "of course, if it's alright with you and all."

Hmm. Ahh. Let's see. Do I want to bury my Mama, next to a tombstone put up for my Brother by an empty grave that holds an urn inside a piece of six inch PVC pipe, (with screw on lids, mind you, just in case) in the bowels of the family cemetery, in the eternal presence of the very man you spent ten years dragging my childhood ass through court after court with, arguing over shit y'all couldn't agree on in a twenty-seven year marriage?" Plus, "You know your Daddy said he had saved the spot for you right next to him" and that would "put us ALL out there together, Shoog," when the time comes. "Wouldn't that be nice?"

The mere thought of me lying all waxed up, pumped full of fermaldehyde and suit and tie, in an overpriced casket, in a grave between my mother and father, literally drove me immediately insane! All I could see was a cute little boy in leiderhausen/knicker-bockers and a tie, lying between two parents, with grape snow-cone stains on his lil' white shirt. I finally joked, "Yeah, you know Mama, it SURE would be! I could have them cut a hole out, on each side of my casket when I go, and they could stick one of my arms out each side."

"Why in the world would you do that?"

"I been torn between y'all my entire life. Why stop a good thing when it's working, rolling strong into eternity."

"That ain't funny and it's sacrilegious!"

"Naw, burying all of us out there together, to argue through eternity? No, Mama, that's sacrilegious!"

Truth was, sitting on Mama's couch with time and a proper place to ponder, I realized it was probably the sweetest thing I'd ever heard. Daddy was tender like that. I asked him later what made him offer it and he said, "Well, I don't know son, I just thought you'd like to know your Mama was taken care of after all you've been through. Thatta way, you'd always know where she is, safe and sound, in the ground, right up there with the rest of 'em. " Like it was farm equipment and the final harvest had ended. So, in the end it seemed fate was deciding, that when the "time was right," and we had all, "come home" I'd be "out there, with Mama and 'dem."

I did worry quite a bit at first what Daddy's folks might think, till I realized every single one of them always asked, always had, "How's your Mama? how's Aunt Sallie," when they saw me in person or on Facebook and you could tell they genuinely loved her. Finally the thought would cross my mind how "in the end," the devil never can screw up love. Plus, if anybody, between Heaven and Hell had something to say about it, I knew exactly what to say. What Mama always said about graves that won't do their job and hold the spooks of life in the ground. "Piss on it!"

BEAUTIFUL MESSES

I don't recall how or even why. No memory of the tipping-point medical crisis that sent Mama back to the rest home remains. I only know there was one and Mama was okay with it. Now, I was standing here in the floor of Mama's den, alone, once again cleaning up somebody else's freaking mess. It was time to let go of her place. I wasn't angry; I was too tired for that. I wasn't sad like many friends and family thought. I wasn't clinically depressed as diagnosed by inquiring minds and noses countywide. I wasn't lost, oblivious to God, as soundly judged, tried and convicted by world-class homegrown theologians. Again, I felt closer to God than I ever had. I knew I lived in the palm of His hand. That's what kept me going. I was simply freaking exhausted in every way. The grown-up type you can't explain and don't need to for those who have taken this less-traveled family road or anyone else with half a brain who happens to be paying attention and not judging you. You get to an age where, when you wake each morning, your first unconscious thought is emotional as well as physical energy management. There was practically nothing of Mama's that I really wanted. I had her most important thing. Mama's love. Her Bible, her pictures and maybe something personal were all that were left that held any real value to me. Sure, there was the solid sterling silver, box-set of silverware but I had a "good idea" where that would wind up being and that was not in the box where it belonged. My highest and noblest expectations were for it to be scattered from one end of Mama's kitchen to the other end of God only knows where, and at least one tarnished black-as-sin fork or knife lying underneath the bed amongst scattered pills of various sundries and milligrams. Maybe I'd get lucky and find a valium or two. I could have used one by now. I set aside her "rooster tray" as she called it. It had too many memories to throw away.

The day before, while tossing out a pair of elf-looking boots Mama had had since I was at least ten, and not worn once since I was nine, I noticed chunking the second shoe in the "gone forever-pile," it was a lot lighter than the first. A few minutes later the "You better check this out," lightbulb went off. Inside the first lil bootie I found a pair of socks, folded up inside a second pair. Neatly. Purposely. That's when I knew, Sallie Mae is hiding or protecting something. Down in the very center I recovered the tiniest cutest Tupperware container complete with lid you have ever seen and inside, lay my surprise. A Dixie-defying inheritance. All of Mama's gold teeth. Focus on the gold. I did. I was so broke I couldn't care less nor afford to, that a couple of them still had the rotten half of the tooth clinging to that shiny treasure for dear life. Days later, I collected the better part of twelve-hundred dollars for Mama's gold teeth and her one and only family heirloom, an entire box set of real silverware, complete with original plastic covers, missing only one fork which I found later and not underneath her bed. Even your own Mama is gonna surprise you sooner or later.

So this final day had come, giving up Mama's apartment. A soul-stirring aura of great significance suddenly stopped me in my tracks as dusk was flicking her lights for the final act. I found myself standing there in Mama's bare living room, about to leave for the last time, with one large pile of boxes headed for the dump, one small box to keep, as I stared out the kitchen window. The walls looked like the Grinch had stolen Christmas, 'cept the Creature wouldn't be bringing back squat this go 'round. I had never felt truly alone till Brother died. Yet I couldn't honestly say I knew for sure what true loneliness felt like. By this point though, I knew loneliness was clawing and crawling up my sleeves uninvited, trying to make itself at home and settle in for good. I had felt stranded, for too long, on a crappy island so far out into the Nowhere-of-Life sea, that no map could ever be created to notate my current whereabouts nor had I been reported missing. In the evening's solitude I was taken aback with this strange dark but comfortable feeling enveloping me. And then I realized, this wasn't loneliness. I was being still. Being... still. I recall actually thinking that I could feel the earth spinning as it revolved around the sun, a divine magical equation of all creation which somehow included me, my silhouette, the dark shadow of the past cast across the kitchen floor, my present and future, all riding this cosmic wave of living, breathing, moving, dying and resurrecting life together. Yet all of us, standing perfectly still. My soul was simply stone wall still. So still the body, mind, and spirit are required to join in. It was like God walked by in person for the very first time and the tiniest glimpse of His Holiness had stopped time as I knew it.

The grave dust of my Mama's life was hanging in the air, a dirty glittering Christmas snow, glistening, dancing in a set of sun rays shining down through her darkening windows, as this overwhelming roar of silence began ringing from my heart clean out through my ears. My eyes tried to catch a ride on the specks of dirt flying through the stale air. Slowly falling like the perfect curtain call, a speechless, final, setting sun streamed through dirty window panes, illuminating this small corner of my Mama's place. Lighting up my world. It could have been at Graceland. The White House. Or our Biltmore Mansion. But no other room would ever hold the place in my heart this one did, and I knew it. The very place I once used to beat myself up for having to put Mama in, I now quietly held sacred. So I stood there and I held it. And as I let go of that little apartment in subsidized housing; I let my heart become my Mama's newly furnished, high-end, classy living room.

At that point, I got it. When you start packing up and throwing away your Mama's life, you are faced with the inevitable truth that almost everything we all covet, collect and argue over in this life has not one solitary drop of pure meaning or value. Not the kind we think it does, wish it did, or that makes our living here any better. The only exceptions are the written word of God belonging to your Mama, maybe a few pictures, a cracked Christmas tree ornament, or what's left of your childhood stocking. Maybe a coffee mug or faded portrait hanging on a now silent wall. Only those cheap things that lead us to the handful of priceless authentic relationships, the ones that have made and even broken our lives, defined it and made it worth boldly living. The ones that lead us to the only part of us that Death can never touch. Our hearts. These are the Sacraments of Life.

There's your heirlooms, your true inheritance, what you care for tenderly and pass down purposely. What draws you into God's own presence. The Living Room of Love.

I began to be overwhelmed with a very visual truth in that silent room, a space opened up halfway between Heaven and Hell. I saw my dying Brother sitting there at the end of Mama's cherry dining room table, so full of toxins he didn't know his own ass from the nearest hole in the ground while displaying the divine gift of an intellect that astonished us one last time with Uncle Henry's ship and Yankee Stadium. Mama drifted in and about, smiling and chatting, the epicenter of attention throughout the kitchen and decades of mashed potatoes that clogged my arteries, eaten after faded prayers that saved my soul. The smell of frying fish and hot cornbread filled my senses, as Mama was pouring us another glass of sweet tea with her offering of the sweetest thing in this world, a mother's love.

The depth of this gratitude astounded even me, while I was staring off into a childhood that soon made me cry as it did as a child, for sheer joy, bliss and the breaking of a child's heart. Nehi grapes and Baby Ruth bars, bubble gum, Uncles and Aunts. I felt that favorite, familiar scar pulsing deep inside my very chest, I could feel the stitch marks bulging and for the first time in my whole life, I intentionally wrapped my arms around the little fellow there, hiding in the darkness of the safest corner he had found deep inside of me long ago. He no longer annoyed me but was now illuminated as the most sacred part of me. My buried treasure. My innocence. The part that knows only love and real love makes this shitty life worth suffering through, that it's the only thing that heals skin't knees and broken hearts and can save your soul. It's the magic ingredient in all our soul food. As I heard the shouting and screaming of my parents at one another, the fighting, bitching and moaning over "who was right," and the unintended guilt trip of "saving this farm for you two boys," that little boy could see his brother was high as a kite again and even at eight or nine years old understood why. When their eyes met, he felt safe once again, because his big brother was home and ain't nobody gonna beat his ass today. My belly and soul was warm, soothed with the pure holiness that Magalene had poured into her chocolate pies and my very soul, the kindness she smothered my little heart with, the protection of her skirt; a solid armor that would save you time and again from dragons, enemy soldiers, the constant teasing of your older brother, and maybe even one day, your worst enemy of all. Yourself.

Glancing up as the last glimmer of sunlight quietly excused itself, a finished prayer, I turned into the shadows to see my Brother draw his last breath in and exhale, out on the other side, his face gleaming with a holy child's surprise at a new body, a clear mind, and a saved soul. Daddy's booming voice bounced off the walls, surrounding me like fresh dirt falling over a grateful farmer's shiny plow, turning, churning into a low rumble of sanctifying safety and protection, into moments of support and a father's faith. My heart bowed its head to the sound of the word, "Son," one more time. His eyes glistened with the delight off another covey of quail fluttering up and away into a warm green pine plantation, right there in that living room floor. He was there yelling at me to "straighten up and fly right" and staring me down when he had to make me do it. I felt the weight of his upper body resting in my arms, his honor and pride, his heart suddenly seizing to a stop as he gladly shed this life for the next.

I remember my mind and spirit being blown away with what I had been fortunate enough to see in my life and now, there in this sacred silence, was witnessing as a story. A supernatural one. Lifetimes, the ones that framed and created me, were flashing before my very eyes. Folks who had left home for places like Germany and saved the world from Hitler and made Elvis, Andy Griffith, and Billy Graham into legends. Who had produced a living and sustained a family with nothing but their hands, a plowed field, some cheap seed, a backbone and hope. I read these Gospel Truths, now chiseled in the headstone of my spirit. That our worst moments, the ones that break our heart where it can never heal and be quite the same, are the best ones, because they make it bigger. That when our self-pride perishes and falls away like the empty cocoon of a lie that it is, it creates that sacred space where the divine deposit that has been placed on all our lives can be redeemed. I realized I never was lost but now I was indeed found, and discovering my own soul's self, in the presence of the Holy, of All Holies. I stood there in a field of awe, with nothing but my Heart and the Great, I

Am. The strangest thing was, I had never felt that "at home" before in my entire life. Even the silence was my sanctuary.

And then it evaporated as I muttered an acknowledgment of "Man," and leaned down, surprised to now pick up the last remaining box of treasures in Mama's house, the others somehow mysteriously already loaded. Hugging it like my own firstborn child, I hesitated for a split second before shutting off the light. Mama's world might be gone forever here, but I had a museum display of original masterpieces hanging on the walls of my heart. As I pulled out to go check on my Mama one more time before heading home... because I could and by God I wanted to..., I thought, this world could wait, talk about me behind my back, help me, or kiss my Christian country ass. But bless your heart, don't get in my way. I am Mama's boy. And he believes, right and wrong, down to his marrow that "honoring thy father & mother" is a non-negotiable Commandment. A matter of the soul.

The rest of the year was a blurry-eyed steady rain of a welcomed weariness life eventually brings to us all. If you live long enough. All the cliches were now like cuss words to me, delivered sweetly and soothing to the ear, to numb the heart and mind from thinking for itself. "It'll all work out in the end" and "the good Lord won't put on you more than you can take" were words I began to clearly see for what they actually were. Thoughtless mind memes, good honest, well-meaning, loving folks feel a definitive need to say to you, to ease your suffering because the truth is, it's bothering them. No one wants to be around a "Debbie-Downer" but guess what? Debbie freaking Downer never asked you to take it on, and she's usually fine working her way through the Valley of the Shadow of Death, with her God. Saying those things to someone in these positions not realizing how many times they've already heard it today, is the equivalent to saying, "Yep, one day soon, you'll be dead too and none of this will matter." Or, "You can weather all this. Smile, cause it makes God happy when you suffer well and wallow in misery in His Name" and "If it doesn't kill you, well then You must be good with the Lord." I personally believe in a Trinity much busier, building Their Kingdom, than acting as a sadistic, saving puppet-master for a unique free-will-sort-of monkey on strings.

Sometimes, more often than not, it pays to just love and listen. We don't need to have the answer for everyone else. The grieving and those soon to be, have a heart, and God is with them on their Journey as much as he is yours. They're--just, in a different place than you might be. If you can't open your heart to hear their feelings and compassionately listen, and share in their sorrow, without regurgitating your immediate infantile spiritual needs and agenda onto them, then hush! Smile and pretend like you're listening. Jesus almost always asked a question to the one hurting, to let them know HE came with an open humble mind and in the contrite Spirit of the Servant's Heart, already clothed in Forgiveness. Jesus never asked someone a question of the Soul, the hurting one, and ignored the answer by replying with a haughty attitude of theology or selfish, self-aggrandizing, self centered, spirituality. And HE, was the Son of Almighty God. He has the right, he earned it, the hardest way--by loving those who can't love themselves much less a Savior, least at the moment, Yet He continues to have faith in them that they will one day have faith in him. Even Jesus leaves room for grace. Who in the hell do we think we are sometimes?

If this all sounds too bitter for you, then I haven't been heard in the way I speak these truths of mine. I come from the heart. MY heart. And though it may be deeply loving, I stand, walking tall, admitting it is flawed. It loves imperfectly. For now. But I do have an "image" hardwired into my spiritual DNA. One bright morning I'll make it to my full-blown image potential that God created in me. This I know. I was made in His Image. For now, I'm my own brand of a beautiful mess, constantly declaring the power of love.

I continued dragging my beautiful messy self, in and out of that rest home every single day, one, two, four times a day, whatever it took to make sure Mama was cared for. And Sallie Mae was doing what the old, cranky dying folks do at these restful, peaceful places. Becoming more irritated every day she woke up still alive and not in the presence of her Savior. The girls at the rest home, Mama and me were long ago deeply attached, and by now our small group was a family. And like a good teacher, one called to teach and inspire young minds and lives, those truly called to serve in a setting that can be ultimately supremely depressing, they are caring as much if not more, for the family members as the patient. After all, at eighty-three years old lying in a bed, eating Dark Milky Ways every day, as long as they bring you your medicine, how much do you really want or need?

I don't "like" folks. Life's too short. That's lazy to me. I fall in love with people immediately. I either get you and you get me, out of the gate, or usually I can't stand your presence or perhaps don't trust you. So those of us that were Birds of our Feathers had created a protective, deeply caring nest for Mama and were flocking together. There were Mama's favorite nurses, Courtney and Jeannie and the administrator Jeff and his assistant Geanine. And we were tight. Able to communicate the way true family always does, without even speaking, using a cut or roll of the eyes, a stare down, the Riddle-me-This face or my favorite... the "I really love you" look.

Thus they had become increasingly more and more worried about me. I could see the look in their eyes before they ever started asking questions about "my work," which was becoming nonexistent other than a day here or there, a few hours stolen when I could manage. I knew, I owned it, that I was broadcasting on the outside that my life was spiraling out of my control. Yet my heart and soul never, ever felt stronger or more intact. I believe the most basic thing I learned was how to truly suffer with those I love. And to quote Aunt Helen from the television show Justified, "... we suffer well together."

There were some great days and high marks. Days putting headphones on Mama's ears and filming her listening to my music projects I was working on. Acts of simple kindness by folks like Chris Bellamy, coming by having never met my Mama and insisting on playing her a few songs on his guitar. And those last-minute, special deep, unexpected, soul-freeing conversations.

Finally even Mama started getting on my ass about "gettin' back to my life." You know you're riding a wave of success when your Mama is fussing at you from a rest home bed to go live your life. One afternoon I came in, worn down to a weary even I didn't recognize. As I sat down in the chair beside Mama's bed, drawing close for some much needed comfort, she let me have it.

"Lemme tell you something. You are NOT gonna sit here and hold my hand and watch me die like you did your Daddy & your Brother."

"I'm gonna take care of you Mama. Selfish or not, I have to do it my way."

"No. You're gonna do it MY way. You can't handle it."

"Handle what?"

"Watching your Mama die."

With the assurance that Moses surely had in front of Pharoah, declaring what his God's demands were, I replied, almost emotionless, "I can."

"No. You can't."

" How come?"

" Cause I'm your Mama."

Hmm. She might be right.

I finally started making trips back to Nashville and staying for a long week to ten days and then coming home, truth be told, as much for myself as Mama. I had found out in March of 2011, the bad back/hip problem I had dealt with my entire life, included a large tumor embedded in my femur making up about 80% of the bone structure, hence unremovable. The difference was, I was now in my mid-forties and all my joint problems were unusually advanced for my age. We wouldn't know until late 2013, if it was metastasizing or not, so I began accepting what I had known and tried to hide my entire working life but could never prove or validate. The left side of my back couldn't function normally. I never once worried if it was cancer or not.

Hell, by now, most days I felt closer and more connected to death with every step I took, than most funeral home directors. It was gonna be what it was gonna be. Maybe I'd die too and wouldn't have to worry about shit. Wouldn't that be funny? Writing a book called Funeral in the South and I take the last spot. By April of 2011 my second wife and I were separated, having been completely, thoroughly estranged through this free-for-all family expedition across the great Valley of Death. Everywhere I turned seemed to be another beautiful mess. Where else are you gonna find real grace?

SLOW TURNINGS

You can't fake it with real people. They already know. They love you whether you realize it, like it, or accept it. My wife and I had been separated since April 15. Yes, that was Good Friday. No, I did not find that amusing. That we separated the day love "died" on the Cross. The toll of all the stress of my family's illnesses, the stress of me--being me--torn between continuing my career full time and being there for my family, had simply been too much. For everybody. Including me. Trust me, I was much more worn out with myself than anyone else could have been. I have to live with me twenty-four-seven. Next time, before you start bitching or correcting somebody for being themselves, give that thought a whirl. But there's much more to this life than love. Life is hard. And if you're gonna love in this world, I promise you the more you do, the more times your heart will break and the more hearts you'll break. It's what we do "down here." Love and hurt. If you don't believe it get real still and have a little talk with Jesus. The older I get, the more my heart slowly turns searching for the grace sufficient for this day, the closer I feel to what I believe is the Heart of Christ. One day we will find out for sure. And I have a theory that all of us broken, flawed, screwed-up, redeemable, loved beings will be shown we were much closer to that Sacred Heart, all the time, than we ever thought possible. And that much of our suffering is optional.

I spoke with my dead Brother's ex-wife, Paige that day. She had called to see how I was and I did everything I could to hide my true emotions. Her voice is one that emanates the deep care and love Paige has for all those that hurt because trust me, she knows, so imagine talking to your dead brother's ex-wife-the recovery expert and rehab-facility CEO. Of course

I lied a little. Only about what didn't matter, my emotions. She asked me how I was and what my plans were as I sat in my truck in the parking lot of an Office Depot and refused every tear that sought space to fall, a mere two miles from what had been my home a few months ago. Where even my damn dog was I hadn't seen in well over a week. I told her I was heading back to Nashville within the coming week. I'd been staying out at the farm with GiGi. Daddy had been gone over a year and I'd moved Mama out of her apartment back in February for the final time. Now it was my time, my turn, that much we both agreed on. My time for a turning.

The best stories are the ones that you can't figure out how they will end. They just do. And the best endings, are when there is no end. It's the beginning. Sooner or later, whether you want to or not, you are gonna give it up. You will have a slow surrender to "the Truth." I never have liked the word or idea of surrender. I struggle with it. Me and my people associate that with quitting and folks around here don't quit. We may run ourselves in the ground, which I realize now more than ever before means "the grave," but I'll be damned if we quit. Ever. Something in me had been turning over and over, slowly trying to wiggle its way out but refusing to give up the ghost. As I hit Patetown Road that day and headed back in the direction of the farm, I began to hear one of my favorite *John Hiatt* tunes, *Slow Turning*, roll over and over in my head.

" A slow turning...from the inside out..." This is why great songwriters-are great songwriters. They know how to hurt AND tell the truth. It had been a slow turning and it always is. You ain't gonna live this life and give up the ghosts it requires, mostly your pride and its plans, all simple-like. You won't neatly and nicely fold them up one day, like Granny's fleece lap warmer she doesn't need anymore.

The late summer shower that rained dogs and cats earlier in that day had ceased as I decided to go to the graveyard. I had no earthly or supernatural reason why. Everything looked well worn but cleaned the way I like to imagine my heart is because of a man who died on a cross. The earth tones of the old tobacco barns and dying farm houses radiated in the afternoon sun as she peeped her head gently through the clouds. I'd ridden this road a thousand times and it always feels the same. It's like watching a river of life return home to the sea. I drove straight past the farm, through the crossroads, past the old store. I pulled into our graveyard and cut off the truck. I did not walk reverently as usual but tired and with purpose, this past decade was a now a day's work, done. Under the rusted black cemetery arch I went and looked up at Daddy's headstone. I sat down on cousin Sarah's concrete bench and stared at my Brother's grave and the final resting place of my ancestors. And I swear on my soul, I could feel them all standing there as they each walked into the living room of my heart. Granddaddy even took of his fedora as he and Grandma Eva walked up together holding hands. Healed. They all stood their with their heads bowed as if praying and faded away. I stopped analyzing, thinking, I admitted to myself, maybe I was admitting to God, "I don't know." I do not know, not anymore. And I didn't. I don't have anything figured out and I know I never will, not that I ever thought I would or did. I noticed the crows calling over the top of my ears ringing, the sounds of the nearby swamp gradually cranking and croaking up for the evening. I'd been accused of a lot of things. Living in the past. Worrying about things that most people don't give two squats about. Caring too much. I like that one a lot. How in the hell can you care too much. Holding on. Holding on to that which you cannot keep. Guilty as charged? No Ma'am. Because though we can't hold onto love we can hold on to what it does for us, to us, in and through us. If we don't then I humbly suggest we're letting go of life itself.

I was embarrassed as well as glad to see Uncle Henry Garland had mowed the graveyard. I had been trying to do it more often. It was my generations turn. I did notice the weeds could use cutting around the stones, the fake flowers were fading and the ones on Brother's plot were leaning over. I didn't pull a weed or fix one flower. I didn't care whether Death's sting was the winner or not anymore. Not in that moment. I cried like a man does, when he's just so damn tired he doesn't know what to do and wouldn't even if he did. Only because he can't. More like a a soul-sweat than anything else. I pulled my Durham Bulls cap off, wiped my face dry, stood up and walked back to my truck. And for the first time I let it be. I let it all lay there in that quiet graveyard. As I heard Death snickering behind my back I thought "You can have it for now." Because I knew one day soon me and Jesus would be coming back for the last laugh. So boast and brag Death, you are the greatest of all lies from the Great Liar himself. Screw both of you. The striated pink blooms of the mature tobacco plants caught my eye, as they always had, faded from the days heat but starting to rise from the shower for the fall of another day. I noticed the cotton bolls were fully green and and still growing. The ground was damp. I stared at the sandy loamy soil. I felt it as I stood there on this sacred ground my heart was standing firmly upon. I felt the Rock of Ages upon which all these lives had been built and to whom they were given up. I felt alive. As I drove around the back side of our family cemetery I looked up at those Carolina Pines and I thought, "Nothing declares the glory of God like a wet Pine."

Driving off I thought I'll be damned if I'm gonna sit here until Mama's funeral comes. I may very well lose it all but it won't be for a lack of loving or trying. I'm done compromising and keeping my mouth shut when it doesn't feel right. I'm done with pleasing people who've never once asked you to do that, which we may be one of the worst lies we all tell in this life. I realized being true to your self, really true to the Truth, that lives in your heart, and it does Brothers and Sisters, might possibly be the way of the Cross. I was hoping to be alone when I drove up in the yard but I noticed Gigi's car underneath the Live Oak Daddy planted when I was a child. I did my best to clear my sinuses and disguise my state of being by pulling my Maui Jim's and ball cap a little tighter. She was back from the grocery store with a trunk full. I walked into the back bedroom where I grew up as a child and dropped my computer bag to do what all sons and southern gentlemen everywhere should do through perpetuity, help your Mama bring in the groceries. As I walked out into the hall she started yelling at me about dog shit being on my shoes. In my current state of heightened Super-Duper Spiritual Status, I thought, "to be sure not, I'm wearing my brand new, cool Camo-Croc flip flops!"

Turned out, it was on hers.

THE WISDOM OF DOG-POOP

I had started attending the little church I grew up in with GiGi over the past year. In fact I had just found out I wasn't even a member of my own home church. That's a little like being told your family ain't your family. Turns out Mama had moved our membership years ago when she finally moved on with her life. Linda had recently been very coy and wise with her successful attempts at loving on me, giving me space. She knew me and how to love me. Some of us are so fragile that we are stronger than a lot of folks. If you can't break you can't grow and if you had told me decades ago I would find myself where I now was in life, that things would be the way they were, I might have not liked it at all. I was working off the wisdom of a ten year old.

Perhaps my intentions were too high, maybe I was filled with a pride I was unaware of and like all of us, I wanted things to be the way I wanted them to be. Because remember, my heart was in the right place and I "knew what Jesus wanted." I had never bought Mama, Graceland, and I wouldn't. Daddy wouldn't hear my song on the radio and Glenn wouldn't hang backstage or enjoy the fruits of his labor in me ever again, maybe winning a Grammy or doing something special. As I stepped into my childhood room, painted a peaceful coastal blue, I realized again how powerful our childhoods are. I mean Mama & Daddy built this house in 1967, they separated in '77 and Mama stayed here with me until 1985. Daddy and GiGi moved back out here after the settlement and the second generation since me now knew this as Papa's and Gigi's place. None of that had ever mattered to me. It was my home. MY home. And always would be. Life may very well try and force me to leave it behind one day but it would never leave me.

GiGi had two of the loudest damn, irritating dogs you will ever meet. Scooter and Roxie. Scooter is the male and totes the largest scrotum or as Daddy liked to say, "Pecker," of any dog, pound for pound, that ever existed in this world. Unbelievable. You can't help but notice. Roxie is well...Roxie. Their barks are high shrilled, earth shattering and you honestly want to kill both of them. Brother and I used to joke around at supper time like they were Handsel and Gretel pretending to coax them into the oven. It was weird though, they only barked when Gigi came close to you or you to her. My life seemed to unravel around 2002 like a mentally mad barking dog. And I couldn't stop it. It was killing me and yet something my soul had to do. If you're gonna listen to your heart and follow it through, remember you're gonna have to let it break. You may come to experience what true loneliness actually is. You might understand fear like you never have. Looking back, my first wife and I were two young kids probably expecting too much of ourselves and each other. We both came from broken families and all the pieces were stuck to us like dog shit on a flip flop when you got a bag full of groceries in your hand and it's raining. When Glenn and Paige separated for some reason it unnerved me, it shook something up deep inside of me that had nothing to do with them. I knew in my heart by 2002 he was dying of something and I refused to let go of guarding his soul until his final breath faded into silence in a boring hospice room. Until GOD himself took it away. Hell, for years I had worried every time I got a phone call from back home that Daddy was dead. You can't smoke for forty or fifty years and expect your lungs to hang in there. I'd always felt Mama would last a while although she had now been at the resthome for the second time a year and it was now home. She was here but really not able to participate in my life. I'd been by her side taking care of her since the day Daddy left home and I knew in my heart the time was shortly coming for me to let her go. But our folks like to rest a spell before they cross over into Beaulah Land. And now I didn't blame them 'cause I was damn-sure tired myself.

Linda seemed to honestly be better than she ever had been and quite frankly she more than deserved it. Her and Daddy were married 31 years.

I had joked with Daddy on their last anniversary, "Hell, you're gonna pull sixty years any way you look at it." Mama and him had been married twenty-seven. I had grown tired of hearing people say, "there's a reason for everything," a long, long time ago. It's irritating. I wanted to" know." I wanted to "fix things." But between you and me, I realized maybe I should start living again. There was a woman I had loved I did not understand. She for sure didn't get me either but once upon a time she had loved me. Gave it her best shot at least, I think. I had once called her my wife. I hadn't had sex since the day after Christmas. Way too long for a man like me. I began to wonder what the Girls' children would look like. The yard at the farm desperately needed weed-eating and if I got asked one more time if I'd sprayed "Round Up," I was gonna spit number 08s out of my mouth like I was Daddy's Remington twelve gauge shotgun. Yet in my inner turmoil I slowly turned into a silent peace, and I began to look around. The people around me loved me a whole lot, especially when I didn't deserve it or even want them to.

But My Sweet Jesus it just never ends, never fails, does it? I was all ready to weed it that evening when GiGi opened the front door like it was 1973 and started yelling, "get your butt in here and eat supper first. You come eat this while its hot!" Don't all that "yakking" and barking that life brings let you know you're alive? I walked in the house to a spread of tacos with the works GiGi had made. One of my favorites of hers. Come to find out later she had a homemade banana pudding hidden. There was even leftover-cornbread wrapped and lying on the table. I first thought some-body else had done gone and died. My sister Bonnie had been sick for several years now and she had become the sole caretaker of the farm before Daddy died. It was her way of loving and honoring him. Picking flowers, grabbing the mail, fussing about this and bitching over weeds. Weeds. Weeds, weeds, weeds! I despise a damn weed. If I ever meet Adam I'm gonna slap him just for being stupid. Don't blame all this on Eve. If you're gonna be the man, be a man and leave the "apples" alone. There was maybe ten minutes of daylight left, supper is ready and Bonnie is adamant about me weed-eating! What the hell, why not. I love weed eating! Love the smell of the fuel, getting dirty, the light gravel and small rounds ammunition catching me in the shin. Love the way things look after you weed eat. Cared for. So I "weed-eated." I mean I weed-eated like a weed-eating maniac. As the sun began to fall I headed towards the shop to "put her up" for the day, the most unbelievable, brilliant emerald-green city came to life. A picture perfect field of green cotton, the dew settling and collecting in pockets of fog across the back side, moving like they had some place to be. The way I imagine the Holy Spirit did with the Ark of the Covenant as the Hebrews journeyed on. The tree line in the far distance was already turning a green-ish black. My eyes drifted up to see a full moon already high in the sky, as I felt that little boy in me running around the shop, Daddy calling to head in for the night. I noticed a jagged line across the upper left quadrant of the moon that I had never seen before. She looked like the perfect broken heart. I stood there in the silence of a living farm holding a weed-eater, staring at Eternity, and watched the brokenness dissolve back into a healed moon. It may be the most beautiful, peaceful thing I've ever seen. And tired and ill as hell I realized something. I believe the whole time I'd just been worried about being in this world, alone.

I made it back to the house for banana pudding. In fact I made it clean down the hall to my childhood bedroom again, when I heard Gigi's voice yell out, "Somebody's got dog-shit on their shoes again. Dragging it in the house! Check your shoes!"

Crap. It was on mine this time.

AN UNBROKEN CIRCLE

August 5, 2011
Journal Entry

"Uncle Walter died today. At 9:45 am surrounded by family with an entire community sitting in a reverent silence waiting for the call that was not only inevitable but also a long awaited "I shall be released" prophecy now made true.

I pulled up a chair at our church fellowship hall and spoke with him just two Sundays ago, mere weeks away from his ninety-first birthday. He had not a clue who I was, but all I had to do was say, "Uncle Walter, I'm Ed Brown's boy." The sound of my Daddy's name registered something deep within his growing dementia and hearing loss, within his spirit. Uncle Walter did what he's done his entire life. Smile from ear to ear. I said, "You're looking good, and I love you. I said you're looking good and I love you!" One more smile and a simple, loud "Yeah, yeah." If I ever knew a Christian, and I did, he died today and his name was Walter Edmundson."

Uncle Walter and his adorable wife, Aunt Mazzie were short in stature, maybe 5'5 to 5'2" respectively, and I do mean maybe. They lived in the quintessential Carolina farmhouse underneath a canopy of huge oaks and pines. The summer fields could be burning up, but the coastal sand in their yard would always cool your bare feet, and their home was one that you could smell the pie sitting in the window sill every time you passed by, whether it was there or not. Often you would go visit, and Walter and Mazzie would be sitting side by side in one big recliner, their feet sticking straight out in the air. Cutest thing you've ever seen.

Aunt Mazzie, or Mazzie Gray, as Uncle Walter likely called her as his high school sweetheart, had been waiting in Heaven since September 1st, 2007, for her beloved Walter. They were the truest of sweethearts. sixty-seven years of marriage. As I eased down our family road, once again, everything about the day drew me in. The old tobacco barns and packhouse, falling into time and not so much because of neglect but work, the heat rising off the pavement, the pines swaying in the wind--it's all a visceral portrait, a living, breathing painting and history of my people. I soaked it in because it gives me Life.

I attended church this Sunday morning. The sermon was taken from Acts 23. As we pondered the plight of Paul, the conspiracy of forty Jews with a lame vow to kill him, and the Governor coming to his aid, a heaviness seem to lay on our preacher's heart. Having a son in the Army, the additional news of thirty-one dead Special Ops Seals shot down in a helicopter had Greg more shook up than usual. A nearby twenty-one year old Sheriff's Deputy was laid to rest the day before, and there was the usual serious illnesses, cancers, blood clots and various ways someone is always looking to ask for healing on Sunday morning but complain they are dying after lunch. Uncle Walter's looming funeral likely seemed more of a relief than a chore.

Even in 2011, we don't get a Saturday paper, so dying on Friday around here does present its problems. It was now Sunday, and as I sat on a church pew I realized Uncle Walter's funeral was today because I hadn't read Sunday's paper. I made it through church but noticed I was on the verge of tears, numerous times.The sermon ended and I needed to go pick up my black suit. It may be August in Carolina, but Ed Brown's son ain't wearing a short sleeve shirt and khakis to Uncle Walter's service. I called the Preacher after church and shared a few memories with him about Uncle Walter. Gave him a mental picture of him in his prime, here at Antioch, a Deacon, involved in everything within the community.

I pulled up in the churchyard for the funeral hours later, and saw the VFD-Fire Truck in the yard next to the hearse. Uncle Walter was a charter member. As we waited for the family to view the body, I began to unravel inside, a layer at the time. In the back of my mind, since Daddy died I kept thinking when Uncle Walter's gone, home is no more. I quietly entered the back door, and as I came through the "Amen Corner" I noticed the Fire Department Honor Guard standing watch over his casket. I removed my sunglasses, and as I squared up reverently in front of Uncle Walter's earthly vessel, fighting it back, hard, I saw that fake smile the mortician always creates. Uncle Walter would have been smiling anyway and the casket reminded me of Daddy's. In a matter of seconds, many lifetimes swirled through my head, and the gratitude overwhelmed me. In my spirit I told him I loved him, thanked him for his life, and proceeded to exit before it got to me in front of everyone.

I made my way into the fellowship hall to visit the family, and the aging familiar faces, my aching back and knees, as well as the occasion, worked on me like a Potter and his clay. Cousin Gary, Aunt Bertha, and my fifth grade teacher Mrs. Meadows stood directly in front of me in the line. I had always adored Mrs. Meadows, but I had never once thought about why, until this day. When I looked up and saw her face, I remembered her loving on me back in elementary school, and just as she pinched my arm, with a clever concerned grin, I thought, "It was you!" She had been my teacher when my parents split up. She was the first one outside our home in this small community to keep an extra silent Surveillance of Love, eye on me. No wonder the past few years when she had told me I could call her "Kay," I always replied, "No Ma'am. I cannot do that." I couldn't out of respect and love even though I knew she had thrown away her huge green paddle with the three air holes cut in it. The one she tore many an ass up with back in the day. If parents had any sense at all these days they'd be making and giving these paddles to teachers. All of these years and memories were having their way with me when I felt that lil' arm pinch she is famous for, and she asked, "And how are you, Mr. Brown?"

I did what all lil' boys do who are in trouble with their fifth grade teacher. I lied. "Oh I'm fine."

She lovingly looked me dead in the eyes, and with the sweetest smile and that look on her face like I had been caught talking in class again, she replied, "Uh-huh." Folks, don't lie to your fifth grade teacher. There's simply no need to do that. Trust me, she already knows much more about how you're doing than you do. With your fifth grade teacher it's always rhetorical and prophetic. Great educators never cease educating the soul.

In a hot, packed church, I watched the funeral directors remove the spray, fold in the blanket and gently close the lid on Uncle Walter's earthly vessel. Ain't no box made in this world that can hold the spirit of any man as precious as him. It was merely a formality. I remained shaken in my spirit, the feeling that the holiest of ghosts was moving through me, through all of us. After an opening prayer and scripture, Uncle Walter's nephew, a sixty-six year old rock-musician-artist turned music minister brought the Holy Spirit into that subdued Free-Will Baptist church, perhaps like it had never been. Then it hit me. I had not attended a funeral at Antioch, my childhood church, since my Uncle Harold's back when I was twelve. And Uncle Walter's could well be the final one. And for the first time I felt like I had come full circle. I had come back home where I belonged for this. For all of this. I found that little boy inside of me again, the sacred part of me, sitting there on that old oak pew. I had stood witness to the tide changing this shore for the last time. I realized that they all live on in each of us, regardless of title or connection, that they each have touched our hearts and molded us, and now it is not merely our turn but our responsibility and birthright to take up this Cross.

After the graveside service, I returned to eat at the church with the family and upon my step-mom's strict directions, made a plate, with the required "sweets" to take to Mama. There's that simple yet powerful grace thing again. As I headed towards the resthome with said sweet-plate, that Bible verse from First Timothy kept rolling through my head or trying to. But I couldn't remember the second part of it. "The righteous Man walks... the righteous man walks..." Shit. I couldn't remember the rest of that verse to literally save my life. I was far from a righteous man, but it was time to walk. I needed to keep walking. This day, that was God's message for me. Rise. Walk. Keep keeping on. So I did. I spent the evening, sitting in a cheap chair by my Mama's side, content in the quiet contemplation of the Mystery of Life and the Unbroken Circle. I felt whole again. Cracked maybe, but whole. And redeemable. Because I felt loved. And I loved.

Mrs. Meadows knew that day when she saw me out of the corner of her eye, before she uttered a word, I was coming apart at the soul-seams. She just wanted to remind me I was loved, and that it was okay I wasn't okay, so she didn't have to spank my butt to get her point across. Folks, don't ever lie to your fifth grade teacher. She already knows you've "been bad." And one more thing. More often than not in this life, the one spanking your lil' ass is the very one that loves you the most. Praise GOD Almighty for Unbroken Circles. And quality arm pinches.

I WILL BE DAMNED

By the fall of that year, my trips back to Nashville were more frequent and fruitful. And I was mostly feeling "better" inside. Mama was doing really well, and other than the occasional, scheduled "Sallie Mae is pissed again" episode, she was "happy" at the Brian Center, whatever that does and doesn't mean. At eighty-three, Mama was gonna fool me yet once again. My friend Jayme had literally opened up a red carpet to Music Row for me, one I kept tripping on a little, still I felt like I'd never left and was quickly getting back in the loop and swing of things. By the end of September, I knew I was moving back. I could make trips home, and when I told her, I saw Mama's eyes light up knowing I would get back to my life's passion.

After shaking hands on a house rental in Nashville, I returned home to North Carolina on Sunday, October 2nd and had a wonderful visit with Mama for several hours. Even went to the Dairy Queen and got us a banana-split sundae to split. The next day we had a shorter visit, and I dropped by twice that evening to find Mama on the "throne" having never gotten off the first time. Her famous line, "I'm just fine," was all I got from her, so I worried a little bit I suppose. At forty-seven the pipes don't run as well, surely eighty-three has its challenges. I went home to the farm and left it with the Lord.

Wednesday afternoon I pulled up at the intersection where I usually turned right to go see Mama. But the yellow light changed my mind and I headed to Verizon first, to pick up my "new" replacement phone, *(the lame-ass refurbished one they give you because you PAY FOR INSURANCE)* and headed to the rest home. Why they call it that I don't know. Maybe it's because it's the last stop before you get laid to rest. Think of it as a final water break in the fourth quarter of Life. Now walking underneath the covered walkway, about to enter the rest home, I almost didn't hear my phone ring. I pulled it out and not recognizing the prefix or number slid it back in my pocket. Five to ten seconds pass, and this time I recognized the second number and answered. Something was up. I smiled, wondering what in the HELL has Mama done now? Just as I grabbed the door handle and opened the door, Mama's charge nurse Jeannie said dramatically, "Chris, where are you?"

"I'm here."

"Well get down here quickly. I just found your Mama not breathing a couple of minutes ago. We're assembling the cardiac team now."

There are very few moments in our lives where time doesn't literally stop. It actually does. Only when we feel God enter the room, or say, someone telling you your mother is not breathing. All I remember running down that first hall is the tunnel the yellowed light made in my line of sight and a sudden awareness that I was in a rest home and probably making some old folks nervous by running. I stopped running, and as I rounded the corner, I could feel Mama's spirit, as strong as if I were standing in a room next to her. My Mama's Spirit was still here. It felt as if she had snuck out the back screen-door, and now standing on the back-porch, I could tell by that look in her eyes, the kind a woman has when she is leaving you and gives you a "pity-kiss goodbye," Mama was about to go Home.

I was reasonably okay as I tried to enter the room, but they would not let me inside. I tried twice to enter and then I realized that Courtney, my favorite nurse, who knew Mama and I the best, was afraid I would flip the F- Out as close as we were. Realizing she needed the assurance she thought I needed, I placed my hands on her arms and said "Courtney. I have to see my Mama. Now."

As I broke the doorway with people on both sides of the bed, all I could see was Mama's belly, her blouse pulled up, until someone moved past me opening a hole for a clearer view. It was then I looked down, and I swear or promise on everything Holy, my first thought was, "you have GOT to be shitting me." It was the sweetest, saddest, most ridiculous thing I hope to ever witness. Mama was wearing her wedding band and lil diamond ring from her marriage to Daddy. Mama had only done that before on very special occasions and mainly because it was the only diamond she had. But see, love endures all things. Even divorce. Even our family.

Now, lemme be crystal-Kentucky-clear, about what I'm about to say next. I don't give all the decent damns in the world if you believe me. I saw what I saw. Felt what I felt. As my eyes raised up from Mama's body lying on the bed, Jeannie began the first compressions, and then standing just to her side but behind her, with her right hand on Jeannie's shoulder, I saw my Mama. She was wearing the same outfit, dark blue blouse and white pants. She seemed to be comforting Jeannie and then as she lowered her hand, Mama looked directly at me with a huge wink in her eye and shit-eating grin. The kind you wear on a "I told you so" moment. She was right. I couldn't have taken it. And my Mama smiled and went home to Heaven.

All those times people had laid their hands on me with, "I've been praying for you", etc., I heard the following so much that I got to the point I actually was offended at folks telling me, "It's different when your Mama dies, it's different when your Mama dies." It offended me because I thought, "Love is not a competition." I don't love my Mama more than my Daddy or my Brother. Then I realized in the deep humility, only Death can bring, what they had meant.

Gather 'round, lemme tell all you children of God something right now. When you finally bend your knee to a tile floor and lay your head on that cheap, white hospital sheet, wafting gently of old urine and Clorox; right next to the very heart of the woman that gave birth to you, and first realize "Mama is dead," Well, let's just say when your Mama dies, it is "different."

I walked back into the hallway and sat down in a chair Courtney had brought for me. I kept thinking, in a finely tuned dramatic, Judeo-Christian, reverent way, "It is finished." Not that Mama was Jesus. But, you know, maybe it was, finished. My duties as a son were over.

I instantly experienced "It's just different" like I never had. Everybody gets lonely. But as I sat there, the warm feelings of family responsibility were nowhere to be found, I was overwhelmed with what I can only describe as loneliness. True loneliness, for the first time. A searing, frantic, tsunami screeching and screaming across the ocean floor of your heart, bringing and then leaving, only, one thought. One feeling. One, existence. And a boatload of broken seashells. I knew for sure, for the very the first time, I was, indeed, alone, in this world. Because no matter what this life did or didn't bring, you could always call Mama. You can cuss each other out, pray together, paralyze that bond, not speak for months or even years, but Mama is always gonna be there. Even Jesus needed "Mama."

Then for some very odd reason, I attribute to my debilitating ADHD, I began to stare at this crack in the caulk where the top of the wall met the ceiling. I couldn't stop staring at it. Soon the crack appeared like the Grand Canyon, as I tumbled through the decades of memories & emotions, grasping for every piece-meal bit of my Mama I could find to hold onto. And then, as crisp as an un-welcomed Monday morning, I came to my shattered senses sitting there with my left hand on my knee, literally holding my own self up, too tired now to even be "John Coffey-tired." And then, it hit me. And I said, out loud, "I will be damned."

How the hell, am I gonna bury her?

I walked out into the late afternoon fall warmth, a gorgeous Carolina day, leaves changing, falling. I immediately noticed everything looked different.

The leaves weren't as sharp, the grass and tree bark not as focused as usual.

The whole world seemed dulled down to only that which is necessary to preserve life. I texted my brother/best friend Carl, and all it said was, "Mama's gone."

A few minutes passed, and Carl's reply read, once again, let's ALL say it together, "I shit you not," his text read, "Gone where, Hoss?"

I wonder how many men have sat at the head of their Mama's deathbed and laughed there ass off. Mama would've loved it. I texted back, "Heaven, if she had her way about it."

In a short time my Aunt Inez and Louise, Lisa and Carl, arrived as well as one of my dearest, long time, high school friends, Angie. Shortly after, her husband Stan entered with their beautiful son Tanner who has Aspergers, a severe/subtype form of autism. I was aware all autistic children are given a deeply unique spiritual gift that we don't have and Tanner picks up on other's sadness better than any priest. We visited for a bit and as my Aunts arrived, Tanner headed out with his Dad. Over my shoulder I heard, "Well, why don't you go tell him Son. I bet he would really appreciate that."

I rose up and bent down to Tanner, gingerly walking up to me, wringing his hands in anxiety and Holiness, and that child looked into my soul and said, "Mr. Chris. Mr. Chris... I am, I am so.... I am so sad that you are so sad that your Mama has gone off somewhere." And my heart shattered, broke, melted and grew three times three times its size in a single moment. I didn't need for anybody else to EVER express their sorrow to me or take mine on. Because I know GOD who sits on High sent that precious child in that very moment to say those very words over me. I saw God's reflection in that youngun's eyes. It was precious. And I knew, I was not alone.

I finally called Bruce, the body-guy, with the funeral home, being digitally & well prepared for death in Wayne County by now. This was the whole conversation.

"Is it your Mama, Chris?"

"Well, yeah, the herd's thinned out Boss."

"Well bud, I'm on a call right now, it'll be at least an hour and a half..." and I just interrupted.

I said, with authority, "Bruce, I got $7.28 in the bank and my Mama is dead. Y'all have always buried my people. Don't even turn the key in the ignition and head this way if... "

And then Bruce lifted, least he attempted, to lift that burden or lighten it on me for the time being. "Don't you worry bout it Bud. We'll take care of you." And they did. They always had.

By the time Bruce arrived, it had been hours, now going on ten pm. I did, for some ridiculous but very psychologically fascinating reason, what I always did. I offered to go in the room and help Bruce, who was solo, lift Mama on to the gurney. Our Pastor, Greg Stancil, put his arm on mine and softly said, "You don't wanna do that. Lemme do it for you," and I reluctantly relented. I glance back now and am so glad one of my last memories of my Mama isn't feeling her dead weight on my arms. I am grateful someone stopped me from being the last one in the room, "cleaning up the shattered mess" I reverently, pathetically and ever so lovingly suggested I do.

As I watched my Mama's earthly vessel rolled down that long boring hallway, I stood firm in the knowledge and truth that my Mama had never, ever tried to hide that she was an all original beautiful mess. A more directly, honest soul, right and wrong, has never and will never walk this ball of clay. And "the Great Sadness" overwhelmed my soul yet again as she disappeared around the corner. Oddly enough, I felt comforted by that.

The next morning, accompanied by my double-first cousin Teresa, I walked into the funeral home. We sat down with Brian, and he worked with me to bury Mama. And I swallowed the remaining part of my southern pride. Well, I tried to but I wound up sitting there choking it down piece by piece. I was devastated, as a southern man, to not have the cash to bury my own Mama. My obsession with that self-imposed guilt began the evening before in that rest home hallway. Minute by minute, unable to really focus, Teresa led me through it, as I began chewing on my most recent worst fear, piece by piece. I'm talking 'bout that pride you can't even begin to soften up, not the inspiring kind, but the pride that kills the soul. I knew it well and I gnawed on off into spiritual oblivion, in and out of reality, the rest of the day. The girls took me shopping for that damn pink nightgown Mama spoke so fondly of for years. The one at the funeral home looked like it should be on a porcelain doll trapped in a glass case. Teresa was adamant about taking care of Aunt Sallie's final request. Why I ask you, be buried in a pink nightgown.

Is that how you wanna greet Him? Like you just climbed out of bed? Again, her call, so I stood off to the side as I watched Teresa's eyes fall across nightgown after pink nightgown, with this love that would melt fire. Aunt Sallie was gonna have the "right" pink nightgown, by God, and Mama is still wearing it.

At the florist, I stayed in the car with Teresa as I began finally having my brief meltdown, and called my doctor. The prescription nurse answered the phone and all I said is, "My Mama just dropped dead and I..." And like that, my own bottle of Xanax was called in. Funniest thing, I found I didn't need it because Mama had bit the biscuit her last time, but rather, occasionally, to handle the sudden, southern-smothering of unbearable, grief-attention others require of the grieving. I just wanted to dig a hole and get it over with. What I did need though, was two redder than red roses for my Mama. And I was too embarrassed to tell my own family I didn't even have enough to pay for that. I had always called them, "my florist." Because they were.

Pinewood Florist sits nestled in this aging grove of tall pines and oaks and there's just that "something" about it. That place where you bought the corsage for your high school prom queen, Easter Lily's for Granny and now, roses to bury your mother. Once I finally stepped inside, "relieved" by that fresh, fragrant reminder that we're all dying, the beautiful smell of screaming cut flowers, I recall thinking, being so over the whole experience of death and all that goes with it, she could have handed me a bouquet of fresh cut thorns and I wouldn't have blinked, or cared. But God's sunlight streaming down through a dirty pane window, another day, soon to cash out, is always a good tug of the gravity of reality. That, and the look a room full of honest women assembling dead flowers can give you in unison. By the precious look in their eyes, You would have thought they were all singing harmony on "Just as I Am," as I walked down to the Altar of Mama's Love. Seeing this unique mixture of reality and motherly love, me mirroring the first day's passing without my own Mama, and their eyes lovingly brushing back with a tinge of sheer dreadful horror, you could instantly tell which ones had children and which ones had a son. The ones who knew for sure they were not long for this world, because they're Social Security & Medicare statements arrived monthly to remind them. That and the sure, slow, steady, natural decline of the body. The worse kind of worry lay in their eyes. The one a mother has when she knows there is nothing she can do for her child and is looking them in the eye. They too, soon, would have one last chore. To one day, simply leave behind, without explanation, apology or permission, their own children.

We tend to forget the one leaving us is probably feeling about as bad as we are at a minimum, I would think infinitely more. 'Cause if I had to suddenly leave behind all those I loved to fend for themselves in this broken world, in exchange for my Heavenly Reward, knowing me, I'd feel guilty as hell. I mean, I'd have to wouldn't I, just for the sake of tradition? I wouldn't be a true southern son, if I failed to commit and complete that one last available guilt trip, the silliest one, one on yourself. Just for the spiritual gratuity or greediness of grabbing the check and heading for the door. Would I?

When I softly, and pathetically barely uttered, "I just need two roses. The two prettiest ones you got," she loved on me with her eyes and said, "Are you sure that's all you need? For your Mama? Bless your heart. Shoog, these are on me. Would you let me do that much for you?"

I answered her by dropping my head to my chest, with a gratefully unspoken, "Yes, Ma'am, I surely, absolutely damn well will let you. Cause I'm ready to fall out on this floor." The crushing weight, of how the hell I was gonna pay for this, was dragging me to one of the worst places any of us can go, that grave we feel required to dig for ourselves. No, that ridiculous southern guilt, created by your own hand, that requires you to do it all. Create the ultimate, unforgivable guilt, properly administer it at the soul-euthanasia level, take it on and then drag your own self-centered self to your own emotional grave. All this because my silly "manly" southern pride was just screaming inside my head, in my voice, over and over, "I will be damned. You are one sorry sack of southern shit, you know that? I will be damned. I will be damned!" And so, as my emotions were demanding, I was. Damned, that is. There it is again! I tell You the power of life and death lies in the tongue, whether you're yapping on the town square, in a pulpit or your own mind. Careful, always be careful what you "say." The devil is always looking to jump all up in your soul's shit and mind's affairs.

And over the course of the rest of that day, a rude, squeaky, heavy, coffin lid of practicality, slammed shut on my heart, against the inner sounds and sanctum of sorrow, and the soft clanging of forks on dessert plates and me hoping for corn pudding casserole in a day or two, I hoped in a silent lost cause, somebody could make. Like Mama's used to taste. We never wrote it down, so now that was gone too. Sucked into the Great Unknown Black Hole of Death, where neither the Light of Life nor peace lilies can grow. In the midst of a separation, and with the last member of my immediate family gone, Aunt Inez, was hosting a family night in Mama's remembrance for me, her remaining sisters and the next of kin close by. A family needs to get together, it is drawn back to it's womb so to speak, at a time like this. Usually, so we can "support" and wear one another's nerves "slap out." But thank God, for Aunt Inez. This was small and quiet, reserved and private. Like she was. Reverent. My nerves couldn't have taken a replay of some of the earlier funerals in my life. As I sat in a hard back kitchen chair in her living room, my back and knees killing me, soaking in the aging faces and little that was left of what was once a huge family, my mind raced through the years, across endless countertops and tables of yesterdays, overflowing with homemade food, homegrown love and hogwash. I flew across visitation rooms in small southern towns, through sanctuaries of salvation and family cemeteries. I soared through Heaven and Hell for a quick visit with Saints and Sinners. The many memories of these occasions created a living movie of epic proportions, within me, one that Mark Twain, Andy Griffith, the Apostle Paul AND Billy Bob Thornton would approve of.

While my family went from talking softly, so as not to disturb the dead, into swapping sweet stories of deaths and resurrections of long ago, I could hear the squeaking of styrofoam coffee cups. And the always, peaceful smell and many memories of Magalene's chocolate and Granny's coconut custard pie began to soften me, with my first bite of Aunt Inez's famous pecan, as I knew it would those first conversations and encounters needed of death. The ones that spread that sacred salve of family, across your southern heart. I felt safe, insulated and securely trapped, set apart from this world by my Aunts and cousins. Protected from everything, except myself and this psychotic funeral film now reeling in my head.

Funerals of yore, where great lies of the bonds of affection and achievement are recounted amongst crowded rooms with front row tickets to the stage and family furniture is hawked on back porches in exchange for family secrets. Before the deceased is even out the door much less cold. Where you discover the closest friends and hear about the deep intimate connections you know damn well never existed with this person and the dead. That awkward one you always enjoy, where they feel "terrible," after telling you for the third time, in a row; her cat, the one she got from her cousin Marian ,who now lives in Detroit, who married Tommy T. Too-Tall from

Tifton, Georgia, who could have retired a full Admiral in the Navy after World War II, if it hadn't been for the fact his Uncle Jim in Indiana killed a man over a 1961 Impala, in 1948, and got death row for it, so Tommy had to go home to the family farm... yeah, THAT cat; had bursitis and spinal problems, JUST like your Mama, and now it's killed him, too. Killed him "dead."

Deep paranoia runs amuck, amongst those conversation and the whispery ones you already hear in your mind and around every corner you turn.

"BLESS his heart." I don't know what he's gonna DO without his Mama. Oh, Lord!" Shit. Trust me. Neither does he.

But me, I did what we all, the bereaved, always do. Stare straight ahead. Look at the world, now out of focus and FAKE it. Remind your body language to squirm every now and then, just often enough to keep a low cut, weak boundary that nobody here in the South is ever gonna physically or emotionally acknowledge, much less honor. Not when they can hug you and run their hand up and down your back, to the point, over and over, of you having mid-level nausea from the cocktail of cheap perfume and menopausal sweat. Especially "Aunt What's-Her-Name, Shoogar Shit?" Let's call her Great-Aunt Shoogar Shit. Your "favorite" one, who before her smoking, diabetic, COPD butt has cleared the door frame, has to make enough "Grief-Joy-Noise" to gain the attention of the entire front of the house. And show off her new portable oxygen machine, "she cannot live without." Since she just put her cigarette out before she stepped up on the porch.

"Awwwweee, Bless your heart, Sugar-Free, Sugar-Pie, Honey-Bunch of Notes, not your precious Mama! Lord in Heaven, Jesus in Jerusalem, what will you DO without your Mama?!?"

And your first loud thought, "Mama hated your guts and you despised her, last time I checked, which was day before yesterday I believe," drowns out your actual reverent remark of, "Yes, Ma'am, gone be hard. Just trust in Jesus. What else can we do?" That conversation, one of seventeen you know you will be forced to have with this "woman" this very night, always ends, with scripture quoting...

"Yes Darling, Lamentations 114:237 says, " he who grieves his dead Mama in front of me and doth not give me ALL the attention in the room, is a SHADY Sinner, not WORTHY of my LOVE. And Romans 186:21 tells us, You just trust in Jesus, Darling. Trust in him. You hear me? You just keep trusting in the name of Jesus. Lemme set this carrot-cream cheese-opossum casserole I made, JUST for you, down, and you and me gonna crawl over in that corner where I WILL turn you inside-out, ragged as Raggedy Ann's righteous-rear-end, emotionally and psychologically, Shoog." Always start or end all funeral talk with the bereaved with…"Shoog."

But PRAISE THE LORD, just in the nick of time, *(21-GREEN, 21-GREEN, JOHN WAYNE—HUT-HUT HUT)*, you realize you're staring at the Panthers vs Saints game and lost in a daydream where if you were Cam Newton, you'd fly your super-human, SuperMan ass on out of there. "Oh, I'm trusting in Jesus, alright. Yes,"Ma'am. Trust---ing!" I'm trusting He will guard the sanctity of my sanity and send you somewhere safe, far from other innocent grievers like me, and deliver us from this unnecessary nagging! Oh Death, where is thy sting? Where is thy Victory? Standing right in front of you. Pontificating.

And so, we nod our heads up and down, "Yes Ma'am, No Sir," and every now and then look them straight in the eyes and make the serious, funeral-face, while you're thinking, "My Holy of Holies, His Holiness, Omnipotent, Omniscient, GOD in Heaven, I WISH you would HUSH her for three… damn… minutes. Just three. My Father, who art in Heaven. Please come down here and make her hush. In Jesus' name, she shall be HUSHED, A-men!!" You finally quote your own Bible verse, "Jesus wept," and make one up she can't possibly know, making a satiated believer in your saved soul, out of her. Seeing an opening for an exit, you "fill-er-up" on sweets and salvation and pretend. Until you don't have to because suddenly, it doesn't hurt as bad. A high enough sugar level & cracking, confused, Xanax-ed nerves, drizzled in unnecessary & awkward conver-sations, always soothes the soul. That and the valium Aunt Sadie slipped you, that she got from Uncle Billy-Boy-Blue in the hallway, when Aunt Shoogar-Shit wasn't looking. Don't you even lie about that. I saw the whole thing go down.

Meanwhile, your soul, the only one you got and ever will, sits sizzling in the center of your heart, all bowed up in the righteous indignation of the pride that kills. They don't understand. How could they understand. I am hurting deeper than anyone who ever lived LIFE can understand! Mama is dead. MY Mama is dead. Then you remember what "they" told you the last few years. That very "damn thing" that wore your butt out, now comforts your achy-breaky heart.

"When your Mama dies, it's "different.""

Y'all. I will be damned. It *sure* is.

HERE COMES TROUBLE

I couldn't tell you where I went, what I did, that next night if you put a gun to my head. All I remember between that first day on earth without my Mama and her visitation is, Mama was dead. And the most unexpected of all people slowly drew to my side and would stand by me, a real Rock for the ages.

I had been so damn tired, I honestly didn't care what happened next, not because I didn't care. I simply didn't have the energy for it. A miserable feeling. Thankfully Carl forced me to go to a doctor a month and a half earlier, where I was informed if they could get most engines to hold as much pressure as my blood was, they'd last a lot longer. 210 over 168 sitting still, completely "relaxed" was my best that day. I was also informed of several brand new issues that wouldn't be going away. Praise the Lord we had gotten at least some of my medical situation I was lying about, hiding from mainly Mama, temporarily controlled. I was now feeling strong enough to go through the motions with that occasional moment your spirit rises above sorrow long enough to remember the promise of Heaven, to be reminded "This too shall pass." I'm just passing through, too.

I suppose I could drag Mama's funeral book out of Granddaddy's old trunk to stir my memory, but why? Nobody ever remembers much about a funeral visitation except, they are so ridiculously awkward that they rock! I LOVE a good funeral visitation. I mean, let's think about it. The very ones dealing with the shock of death are asked to stand there and "greet" people for several hours, accept the lame "Bless your hearts, he looks so good" and of course, my favorite, "Darling, I've been right where you are right now, I know!" I arrived early with assorted family, (that always includes surviving sisters/aunts & a mandatory number of three first cousins or cousins in law) to "approve" of the body. I knew for sure, that wasn't going to happen here. I did not "approve" of my Mama being dead. She never asked or got my permission. I looked up to see my old friends whom I had traveled the world with playing music, John & Robin Berry, with manager Terry Oliver, walking in the door. In the middle of a most difficult time for themselves, they had driven the twelve-plus, hour round trip from Athens, Georgia to pay their respects to "Aunt Sallie."

Almost like a good verse slamming into a mid tempo chorus, here came the funeral director at the same time. All I can tell you about viewing my Mama is this. As I approached her casket, everything was laid out beautifully. Perfectly. When I looked down it freaked me out! Mama had teeth! Again! She looked like she was forty-nine years old, her hair and make up done perfectly, wearing that damn pink nightgown I had heard about for so long, looking like she was headed to bed after a good night of bridge. The only thing missing was the air hanging full of Salem Lights cigarette smoke and cigarette butts with lipstick smudges lying in an ashtray. In those twenty or so odd feet, lifetimes whizz in, out & by your soul. You count how many steps it is from the door frame to the coffin, vowing for some deep down, southernly perverted reason, to ALWAYS remember how far it was. Mainly because the devil is always right there to drag you down that black hole of a guilt trip if you let him, as he tells you you must remember it was sixteen steps.

But the very moment I came to a standstill in front of my Mama's earthly vessel, I felt so at peace. The kind of peace you wish on everyone as well as yourself in these odd moments life offers. I reached down and cupped Mama's hands, to feel the harsh coldness, the hardness of the finality of death, just to be sure. And as I looked to my left, Robin, Aunt Louise, Aunt Inez and all the girls were talking about how "good she looked," while I thought; "she looks dead as a doornail to me." Out of the corner of my eyes I saw John standing at the very end of our little line, by the head of the casket, gazing not at Mama but across the years, through the decades he had been without his own mother. I could see that pain born of the deepest longing, written beautifully and painfully across his face. No matter what age, a child reaches for it's Mother's Love. The nurturing and assurance we are loved and cared for. And not that I needed being told, but I was reminded, once again, how supremely blessed I was to have had my mother, loving me, pulling for me, believing in me and wearing my ass out for over forty years.

Visitation started early as folks began to pour in and pour love all over me, and I instantly began to withdraw inside to the nearest safest place I could find. My estranged wife stood steadfast beside me most of the night. GiGi sat in a chair directly behind me as I stood at the head of the line, so close in fact, at times I felt her legs brush up against mine, letting me know she was there. Mama may not have been "able to make it" but my "step-mom" was there, guarding like Mamas do. Coiled like a copperhead, there won't gonna be no drama tonight.

The people, the soft forced smiles, all the "Shoogs" & "Bless your hearts" just fell over and all around me, piling up like fresh funeral wreaths around a freshly dug grave. I had no more room for storing emotion so they did what good folks, the salt of the earth do, they lay up the harvest of the heart for you. They come and store it up, inside of you, for the coming winters of life. It will be there when you come back for it years later. And trust me, you most certainly will. Over and over.

I had been on edge about something though, a something I couldn't put my finger on the entire evening. Something was wrong. I mean, besides being surrounded by a dead Mama, dysfunctional family and soon to be ex-wife. And then as I let go of another handshake & hug I looked up and I felt saved by grace once again. Magalene & her daughters made a bee-line for me and I interrupted the line to find the proper and appropriate place to seat them. One that let everybody know what she meant to me and as uncomfortable as I am saying it even now, what I meant to her. As I headed back to my appointed post in the line, I suddenly felt her baby daughter Tia, walking behind me, reach out and grab my hand and softly but firmly, the way the holiest spirit speaks, say, "Come with me my brother. I have a song just for You."

I love it when holy folks get around you. They're operating on a spiritual plane that could care less what this world is doing. In a way we all dream, pray, fight, want & need, but fail to do every day of our lives, save the moments grace opens a window to let us temporarily break the bonds of this broken life and rise to the full potential of our soul. As I sat down beside Tia, her still holding onto my hand, most of the room wondering what in the world is Chris doing, here came the Spirit. And if I never have church again, I did sitting on that gold couch in that funeral parlor with Mama laid out before God and Wayne County. Amongst an increasingly louder room, Tia belted out...

> *"mmm... Oooohhh.... In times like these....*
> *whooooaaa, oooh, ooh.... you need a Savior....*
> *In times like these ... you need an Anchor...*
> *Be very sure, be very sure*
> *Your anchor holds and grips the Solid Rock!*
> *This Rock is Jesus, Yes He' the One;*
> *This Rock is Jesus, the only One!*
> *Be very sure, be very sure*
> *Your anchor holds and grips the Solid Rock!"*

People pulled up around that couch as close as they could get as that beautiful soul lay it on me, and I stared at Magalene and her at me, directly to the soul, saying I love you, I love you too, over and over with our eyes without ever uttering a word. By the time I returned I knew I was halfway home and I returned with a renewed spirit as I settled in to finish out the night's responsibilities. Just when I thought I had experienced the final big moment of the night I looked up to see the side of a man, in sport coat and tie, his head recently shaved and fresh staples running across his purple, swollen scalp, and oh my God!

It was my cousin Timmy. MY cousin Timmy Ballance. The very one, who I had sat beside, bawling my eyes out, at my first funeral back in 1969 at Uncle Les' service. Lemme tell you the kind of folks I come from. The kind that coach football, are married with five kids but still open up their home to you. The kind that stand with you and watch you arrested and while the rest of your world reacts with judgement or embarrassment, they open their hearts and their home to you, they put their mortgage up to set your bail, to set you straight. Like a cousin who opens his heart and living room, creating a sacred place with enough space for your Brother to cut his deal with Death. I come from those folks the Bible refers to as "the salt of the earth," and mine still have their savor. Holy folks.

I am of the stock of the like of a man named Timmy Ballance. Who, battling his own terminal cancer, left Houston, Texas that very afternoon headed for eastern North Carolina and Aunt Sallie's wake. I couldn't ever feel more honored than for a dying, doomed man, whom you've really seen only maybe twice since you were a child, pay that kind of respect. That, is love. Normally a wake or visitation ends at nine-pm give or take an hour or two based on community response, but by 9:30 your funeral director begins to find the most incredible ways to get rid of people without pissing them off. But not that night. Nope, the night of Mama's wake I sat there with Tim and Kay until the funeral home staff basically reminded us it was over for the seventh time, that they were people too and not dead yet themselves and politely, professionally "ran" us out of the joint. I love Seymour Funeral Home. I really do. When ya gotta go, it's just my people's go-to place. You should try them out sometime.

I rose the next morning to relax into a panic realizing it was almost 10 am and I had forgotten to check the shape of our family cemetery. My heart fell through the bottom of Hades as I turned in and I could literally see the grass was, no lie, at least eighteen pushing twenty inches tall, resembling a good, solid, cover crop more than sacred ground. But as I made my way up the old path I saw a head bobbing up and down on a green riding lawnmower. It was Ben Sauls. The kind of Christian that watches over you. Calls you to his house under the guise of "taking a look" at something, only to put tires on your truck because you can't, and are drowning in to much pride to ask for help. The kind that cuts the very grass of the ground you will lay your Mama to rest in, simply because, he loves you. Doesn't criticize or condemn you for where you are or aren't in your walk with Jesus, grants you the grace and your Savior, God and Ghost their rightful Divinity to let you have your own journey, create your own story with God. The kind I see Jesus in. When I stepped out of the car, Ben cut the mower down so he could talk over it and spoke to me like my Daddy would have. With that slight bit of authoritative irritation that lets you know this is taken care of and a faint smile on his face he said, "Ain't nothing for you to do out here. You run on now. I got this. It's all taken care of. You got enough to do. Run on now." And I looked back into a face that understood what I still was barely comprehending. One that without uttering another sound said, "when your Mama dies, it's different."

Mama's funeral was as relaxed as any funeral's ever been. I walked into the fellowship hall for a pre-service lunch in some sort of crystal clear haze that somehow made life clearer. All the family, well, what's left of it, was there. Her surviving sisters and many first cousins, in laws and those next two, if not now three generations. Death changes us. Matures us. Kills our pride and self serving sufficiency. Cleanses us. Death resurrects us. From ourselves. Things that once kept us up at night are revealed for the frailties, weaknesses of the soul, that they really are by death. There were old and new wounds, as my eyes scanned that room, taking it in with purpose. But, I just didn't care anymore. Maybe there's a better way of saying this. I felt loved by everyone, far past nit-picking, needy childish emotional window shopping. We all quit trying to fix each other long enough to eat some homemade macaroni & five-cheese and deviled eggs. Those damn, delicious, demeaning, soul saving, rich, deviled eggs, that make you, yeah, poot for days. Oh, goodness gracious, c'mon and laugh Y'all. We're almost Home.

There were conversations that could have, would have been started anywhere else. Not here. Not when you are feet & minutes away from publicly professing your thanks to the Living God for a Mama like I had. Again, of all the funerals I've ever been a part of, in charge of, responsible for, there was no panic here. No fear. Not a word left unsaid between my Mama, my God and me. And that's all that mattered to me from then on. Because it's all that should.

My double first cousins, and Mama's sister Aunt Inez, quietly took a moment in the sanctuary alone with Mama. I believe it was Heather who asked me if they could put flowers in her casket and I softly, silently replied with a wink, "She'd be mad if you didn't Shoog." Mama was like an extra Grandmother to her. Mama always saw a lot of herself in Heather as well as a lot of what she wished she could have seen in herself. I had a quick moment alone with her Daddy, Jimmy, over in the corner, sitting in a hard ass folding chair, much more focused on what time it was and my bad back absolutely killing me than getting wound up over a funeral service. It was a brief but strong glimpse of our life long brotherly bond and the fact that even that has a sliding scale in this life. That look we had both always counted on was still there in each of our eyes, but at our age, there are too many people who need loving and you need to be loving, than to get your britches' leg caught living in the past. We understood without it being said.

And finally it was time. We gathered as a family at the foot of those old oak stairs leading to the sanctuary, the organ rolling hymns from my childhood into the room like holy smoke. As our pastor said "It's time," I looked up to see one of my oldest, dearest, friends, a genuine soulmate unable to get through the locked glass doors. I parted the family like the Red Sea, opening it so at least, I would know, they were there, for me. And they would know the same. They would know it mattered and how much. That I was holding them in the coming moment as they were holding me. Cherishing them for what a real relationship of any kind is. Sacred.

We did what southern families do at a First Baptist Church, look as formal & together as the next screwed up lot, and took our place. We did the up and down thing, singing hymns, praying, sitting down for a few words then rising again for another song. When you have a bad back, the first thing you do is look at an order of service to figure out how many damn times you're gonna have to bite the bullet and stand and sit, get comfortable as a soul can on an oak pew, then rise and stand again. I glanced over at the young children, now young men suited up as Mama's pallbearers.

As I sat on that second pew, staring at Mama's solid oak casket, the spirit world pouring over me, feeling all this love being sent my way, yet never ever having felt so alone. I'm sorry, I couldn't help myself. I wanted to stand up and freaking scream, "Aaaaghh!!!" I'm sitting there, my professional & personal life scattered like ashes, in the church of my childhood, staring at about $11-Grand I'm getting ready to bury in a hole in the ground. Just as I'm about to absolutely lose it, (and let me be honest, I have no problem occasionally "losing it," I find it quite healthy), I glanced to my right and saw my younger cousin Sean, the good looking one. The really good-looking one. Yeah, the one even your wife and teenage daughters fawn over and would whisk up, and I no longer felt alone. Sean was already looking at me, a younger man who had already lost his Mama, and understood what I yet did not. Losing Mama is hard. Sometimes, we can momentarily save one another's soul, lift the spirit out of the mighty mire, with that one honest look.

For some reason, I couldn't stop staring at him out of the corner of my eye. Mama adored Sean and his girls, Kaitlyn & Caroline, and they absolutely adored Aunt Sallie. He nor I had no way of knowing, in barely more than a month, Sean would be leaving us on Thanksgiving Day, for good. That the last funeral he attended before his own, he was honored to be a pallbearer for his Aunt Sallie. It still breaks my damn heart every time I see his beautiful girls on Facebook. He is so proud of them. Pastor Glenn moved on with the solemnities, in the exact spirit of my mother. He spoke of his first days in Goldsboro, as a growing pastor and meeting Mama, and instantly liking her. Being drawn to her. He shared the story of his first visit and them discovering they were both die hard Duke fans, and as he left that night, telling her goodnight, and with a smile had said, "I don't know now, but I think, you're gonna be trouble."

And then Glenn preached the only kind of funeral you can for a woman like Mama when you're a fine preacher like Glenn. An honest one. He spoke of her known strengths and deeper weaknesses. Of the still bleeding wounds her heart had carried for decades. He spoke of regret and redemption. Of sin and salvation. He went the absolute, dangerous extra step, declaring that Mama was his kind of person, that spoke her mind, all the time. That if she thought the gospel truth had not been spilled on a given subject, Mama would do it for you, in spite of you, being that rare kind of soul that can create the greatest love and cause the greatest harm. He preached the kind of honest funeral that can get a lesser preacher reprimanded if not fired, unless he's as good as this one. Because he had no choice, his own heart and soul would allow nothing less. Anything but the beautiful, messy ugly truth would have been a lie.

Finally he shared how Mama, called upon him in her last years one afternoon, in deep desperation, sharing she could no longer openly pray to

God. Prayer was fundamental to Mama's life and now she found herself in a season of life that no matter how hard she tried, she actually couldn't pray. She felt, something, not conviction, but she was feeling a deep sense of worry that there was something she was doing wrong. She felt maybe, lost, and couldn't understand why. To quote Mama, "I just can't pray anymore." That is devastating for a woman of faith like her, at any age.

And Glenn had consoled Mama with the truth, saying something to the effect of, "Miss Sallie, as we grow older and deeper in our faith, we can come to find ourselves in a place where we really sit in the silence of God's Peace, we experience it, and we realize there's no longer a need for the things of this world. When I can finally know, I am embraced in His Love, authentically, Just as I am, my soul finds a peace I don't recognize. A home, where the soul knows it belongs. And honestly, I think that's where God has now brought you in your life. I really do. You have fought the good fight. And your Father knows your heart. And He likes what He sees. An Honest Faith. You can trust your faith is and has always been in his Hands."

We should all live to be as blessed, I say.

I recalled that time late in her life and the profound soothing effect it had on Mama's soul and mine. Finally Glenn read a few words from me, as I was not dumb enough to try and speak at my own Mama's funeral. My words had seemed pathetic, when I sat down to collect them the evening before, but again, there was nothing left to prove, nothing needed to be said or done, or forgiven, that we hadn't laid to rest. So I had Glenn share a few of these thoughts...

"*Mama was a beautifully flawed creation, overflowing with love and affection as well as anxiety and sadness. Trials, tragedy and triumphs. She was laughter and the Christmas Spirit, Easter sunrise services, and the candles on your birthday cake. A last second Duke win, up-to-date Yankee stats and a good game of bridge. Mama was the sweetest sound to your ears, the smell of hot homemade biscuits, the wonder of a hummingbird and the sound of rejoicing, humming her favorite hymn. This woman was family, friends and fall in the mountains. Mama was an enjoyable trouble and the most beautiful mess. She was every mother's eternal bond with her children created by unconditional love and the burden of worry. From the first time I heard her voice and felt her touch, to our final visit, one fact remains. Just as she first told me as a child about Jesus and His love, I love my Mama because she first loved me. My Mama was for real. My Mama was my Original Blessing."*

Glenn had pushed me to play a recording, of one of my songs, *Along the Way,* I had written for my dying Brother, four years earlier, to conclude Mama's funeral. George Strait may not have cut it but the First Baptist Church approved. That's more than good enough for me, although I imagine George pays better. As I heard words & music I had penned waft across that large sanctuary, I couldn't help but feel Granny was there with us, smiling, being holy like the elders do, that sweet smell of of peach snuff on her breath. I sighed a big relief as the final notes faded and then Glenn did his final prayer. Open completing it, having thanked God on behalf of us, one more time, for Mrs. Sallie Mae Stallings Brown, our cool pastor, Dr. Glenn Phillips said... "and I just know how happy Sallie is today, healed and healthy at home with her Lord and Savior. I also know, when Jesus looked up and saw her, his faithful servant coming, he said, "Look out boys, here comes trouble." That love-able, Enjoyable Trouble.

We exited with Mama and I tagged along at the foot of the casket, that damn deep southern thing still there, always gnawing at me, telling me, I had to do one more extra thing. I needed to feel the weight of my Mama's coffin in my own two hands before I could lay that trust in the arms of any open grave. Kaitlyn was growing up so very quickly, more beautiful by the day, as her and her dad, Sean, rode with us to the graveyard. That, was a beautiful ride I still, and forever will, hold close.

I arrived to a graveyard that reeked of death to me for some reason. Maybe it was my pride weighing on me. The paranoia rolling around in my head that I could not pay for this. Perhaps it was the awkwardness of a coming divorce. Naw. It was those damn, huge, big ass, flies from hell, that were all over everything because of the dense grass that had just been cut. Thankfully there comes a time even for me and my folks, when there's nothing left to say. Pastor Glenn made a quick ceremony of it, closed with a prayer and we half heartedly visited in our old family cemetery, for the public show of it. Then, at my request, and I knew this would go over either like a fart on the second row of St. Joseph's Methodist Church or a surprise

Christmas present, Glenn announced, "Chris asked me to announce that everyone is invited over to Linda's house just up the road, at the farm, to visit."

I LOVE it when the love of Christ speaks. And everyone around knows it. It fries people's very ever-loving minds. It is far beyond doctrine, denomination and theology, opinions and even lil ole Miss Lottie Moon. It rises above the pettiness of this life's problems. GiGi had offered it to me, lovingly saying, there had to be a lot of my cousins that hadn't been out there since the old days and they might enjoy it. You cannot imagine the amazing grace I felt in that moment. And so, moments later, I stood in the kitchen of my childhood, making eyes with my stepmom GiGi and only GiGi, after my Mama's funeral, while cousins spoke about chandeliers that use to hang here, ass-whoopings that happened over there by that live oak tree and corn that got shucked in the summer of Seventy-Something. It was so surreal, so southern, so significant, it may have been illegal without us even knowing it. At the very least it was soul-saving.

As folks began to drift out, I slipped out, alone, and drove down to the cemetery. All I wanted in this world was to be left alone. Quiet. Just for now. Once I'd had enough of staring at the quaint, quiet fresh dirt that wouldn't say anything back, the dying, cut-flowers smell and having no more room for self pride, pity or piety, I turned and walked over to my cousin Sandra's grave and sat down on that concrete bench placed there for moments like these, facing the most unusual Carolina sunset. A light, quick little rain had settled the dust in the graveyard earlier and for now made it hush. Death had nothing more to say today. It had spoken plenty. The past no longer whispered in my ear, pulled on my heart. So I quit listening for its deceptive deceiving tongue since it had nothing new to say.

It had been a nice day, yet there was a massive, deep dark collection of broken, black as death, storm clouds against a backdrop of the most brilliant Carolina blue, burnt-singed orange sky, the green of the nearby pine needles bristling and framing an early falling dew from this unusually brilliant, soon to be setting, sun. One of those skies that people used to say, "There's a cloud a coming up," a storm that unnerves living folks, except this cloud had finally passed. I wanted the heavens to announce, "He has survived the darkness of The Reckoning," but the living were not here, the dead were not listening. I was exactly halfway between Heaven and Hell. Half past Sinner, working on Saint. It was, perfect. I sat there, safe in the solitude of the dying day, among the tombs and bones, the graves and resurrections of my ancestors, alone with my God and my Mama. And all I could think of, as my Brother and Daddy's spirit came to join us, as my mind exploded with the life, death and now the burial of this family was, "It is finished." This time, it really is, finished. Because it was. That, and, "how in the hell, am I gonna pay for this damn funeral?"

And for the first time since I was a small child, rising from the wreckage buried deep down in my softest place, I felt all of us together, resurrected if you will, holding hands, in the Gospel Truth. And it turns out, that's all the little fellow hiding inside me ever wanted from this world. To love and be loved. And he had been. Boy, had he ever been. Unconditionally, dramatically, loyally. Imperfectly. Gracefully.

That dark cloud soon enough claimed the sunlight back into its arms, and that moment did what those moments of grace always do. Disappeared as suddenly as it came, leaving behind an Illumination of the heart, a Salvation of the spirit and enough Heavenly Light to make it to the next broken moment where you will need some sort of deliverance, stumbling to the Table of Life and Love, where your soul might find an open seat, be still and fed. Where you will wait, faithfully, for your next Heavenly directions, whether you want to or not. It's a Journey indeed, passing thru this mighty world we live in, on our way Home. We all need plenty of good Soul Food to get there. Along the way, eat well, my friends.

Maybe Magalene remembered her original recipe and made a chocolate pie. Perhaps Nancy brought some of Aunt Rachel's pound cake. Wonder if somebody got lucky and finally deciphered Mama's corn pudding casserole? Or maybe another mayonnaise-miracle of deviled eggs, with the right amount of sweet relish and smoked papriki, lies on the countertop, awaiting to enrich us all! For sure there would be Julia's Vegetable-Beef soup and Mike Hook's homemade Pimento Cheese. I felt filled, full of this life and overflowing with the next, all of it from cradle to grave and beyond. And no matter what I thought, what anyone else thought, I knew, beyond all my now well-tested doubts, once again, I knew, my soul was Saved. How could it not be with the Gift of this Life, so precious that we all know each morning it will eventually, perhaps today, kill us. And that in and of itself guides and leads us to rest in the Promise of some Bright Morning when this life is o'er of flying away. Going Home.

Through the very dead-end door of all of our deaths, there is an Eternal Life awaiting. An ancient story of the Truth of Love. A Home. A man was nailed, nailed I said, one brutal spike at the time to a Cross. He was delivered unto death in order to give us life. Busted Hell wide open, he did, and ripped the keys away, silencing the Sting of Death. Stop analyzing it, arguing over it. God doesn't need your theology for His Truth to reign over this life, the next one or your heart. Accept it. Participate in the story. Keep coming back for more. Let it define itself and reveal itself to you, one slow step at the time. That's grace. And that, is Amazing.

Grace is what I feel flowing through my soul's veins in this fallen, fragile world. It is the heartbeat of all broken hearts. Grace is what taught me the best way, the hard way, that "the Lord is close to the brokenhearted and saves those crushed in spirit." In every single, solitary one of those screwed-up, broken, bittersweet moments of fear, worry and doubt, of blueberries and broken hearts, cussing and cousins, the smell and wreak of death, taking its sweet ugly time not just coming in the door, but slowly filling the room, boasting and bragging as it claimed those I loved the most, something divine delivered me through them. Delivered me from myself every day. It was Grace. We all lived by it, died with it, and coveted it like our very lives depended on it because they do. These funerals are merely my mile markers Home. Grace is my Highway to Heaven. We loved each other with all we had, not despite but because of our flaws. Our differences. Our wounds. Wherever this power comes from it is the most familiar place to my soul. My Home. That's where I am headed. This is a story, not of where I've been, but where I'm going, and exactly how I plan on getting there. By Amazing Grace. And real Love is the greatest thing we can grace upon ourselves and our world. Because, if it's grace, and LOVE is, it's always Amazing.

So in the end, I know no more than I did as that sweet child walking down to that first altar call, lost and found through the kind of faith only a child's heart can hold. Innocent. Trusting. Knowing. Because I innately understand the Mystery I feel pulsing through my very spiritual heart. I always have. I know beyond all doubt, I am loved. And what's really amazing is I've never, ever needed more. None of us do.

I did however learn along the way: never lie to your fifth grade teacher, sooner or later you'll drag dog shit in the house, and there really is nothing like a funeral in the south. Whenever you look up and see, Trouble coming, and you will, enjoy the moment and leave the door open for grace. And one more thing. "When I die remember sob, scream, and shout, sing "Peace like a River," cook a pig and drag it out. And bury me beneath the Weeping Willow with a Funeral in the South."

Of all of the above, it shall be said, "I shit you not." Once upon a time there was the cutest little cotton-headed white boy and he loved his family "to death." And everybody said, "Amen."

"Would you please stand and sing hymn number 421, *At the Cross*, first and last stanzas only."

> *"At the Cross, at the Cross where I first saw the Light and*
> *the burden of my heart rolled away*
> *It was there by Faith I received my sight*
> *and now I am happy all the way.*
> *And NOW, I am happy, all the Way."*
>
> Words by Isaac Watts 1707

THE END.

PART 4

BENEDICTION AND DISMISSAL

OLD SOULS, UNMARKED GRAVES AND THE RIDE HOME

I no longer hold the same "cherry picking" sentimentality for my roots. Drawn to the dusty farms and emerald pine plantations of Carolina, I hold a profound reverence for my people. When I pass Uncle Walter's house in the late evening I find myself bowing my head, nodding to the unattended slave graves up in the woods, aware that I was lucky to grow up when I did. As I watched my family slowly die before my eyes, I realized the time had come to set some things straight and let go of others. And I knew I would have no peace of mind, not my own piece if you will, until I did.

Over the years our demons become oddly enough, almost strangely trusted "friends." They always show up when expected, they do their same song and dance and change very little. I know what to expect from them and I know there is only one power that will hush them up and leave them whining and moaning, crawling back to their respective closets, graves or dark chasms of the heart they come from. I've been told much of late that I am an Old Soul. Old Soul or not, I'm learning. There are those things, the bitter ones, better left in unmarked graves. Everything else, lay to rest in your heart.

They say people run home when they get lost in life. Hell, I wasn't lost, I was broken. An empty Coca-Cola bottle smashed to a hundred angry pieces on a hot as hell Dixie county road. A child is hurt, injured, maybe even damaged. A man doesn't hurt. He aches. The Bible says, "When I was a child, I spake as a child, understood as a child. When I became a man, I put away my childish things." Years before I had left the farm as a child. Now I was aching all over, from my head and heart clean down to my toes. So I came home, to pick up these broken pieces, these parts of me I desperately needed to be whole and watched the sun set across a tired cotton field. And sitting right there in a sanctifying solitude I found the ROCK of my Soul, where He's always been. Jesus was in my heart.

My sweet Brother was born the living, breathing, first-born southern pride of the marriage of the past to the promise of a future, every newly wed couple holds in their young hearts and eyes. I will never know the why of that first beating. Brother quickly learned to provoke Daddy and then take his wrath nearly every time they were in sight of each other. And yet they loved each other as deeply as any two souls I've ever known. Maybe because of that bond. It was on Glenn's very deathbed that I realized for the first time, he had somehow taken on the pain of our family. Of generations. Like a true hero, that is a courage born only of a visceral fear you cannot avoid and a love that is willing to lay down its very life for you. Yes Ma'am. I am absolutely saying, I saw Jesus, crystal-clear through my Brother's heart. I learned about sacrifice and suffering. I witnessed redemption.

My Daddy was a damn good man. A loving, faithful stone of integrity and respect tempered by the fires of life. He was also a precious little six year old boy who got shamed into feeling worthless after the sudden death of his Mama, losing a third sibling, and the pain his own Daddy passed down to him as a southern birthright, with a mule strap one lick at a time. And this original wound would be his burden and blessing the rest of his days. Daddy was not bound to the past, but forever clinging to his Mother's Love in that Spring of '33. I felt GOD the Father through my Daddy' eyes and Life. Protective and loving. I came to understand forgiveness. Experience faithfulness.

Mama was the spirited, character-filled middle child of her clan of ten. The first one to recognize what her Daddy's wrath and pain was doing to her own Mother. Till her quick exit at the back door of life, just as she had said her whole life at the mention of his name, she would boldly state, "If you take me to his grave, I'll squat and piss on it." It takes an enormous amount of love for the human heart to hold that much contempt for anyone. Especially your Daddy. It's a fine line for the flesh. That is the Holiest Spirt flowing through spiritual veins such as these. I learned of surrender. Of sanctification and mercy. I embraced healing.

And then there's me. The Baby. A bomb did go off in our home in 1977. And I was left to clean up the mess. To wash the dishes after the funeral, take out all the trash and foot the bill. The epic weight of a Family's Love is far too big for any man to carry on his own. He can carry the memory of it in his heart, and I do. I will. All the way to my grave. Now that they're gone, I realize for the first time the treasure that is that little boy inside of me. It must be my job to love him. And so I will. Make a dog cry, won't it?

It's been good seeing you, having this time of fellowship together, but I think they're all ready to go home now. I just wanted to tell You, I love You. Be good to yourself. And when I go, I hope you eat till you pass out on the couch. Fix you a Sweet Plate for Mama and 'dem, Shoog. *Wink.*

"It is finished."

It already was. Grace came knocking to remind me.
When the past has nothing new to say, stop listening.
Funerals are about recovery. They are for the living.
Trust me, the dead do not give one decent damn.

"LETTER TO HEAVEN"

I took the drive. I had to. It's been been waiting for me at the end of this long journey and I suppose I've been scared of it, afraid of what the world would feel like without You, of what might and might not be. I never knew. I just didn't. And today, this day, I am so grateful at the view. It is overwhelming.

The road was two lanes, the climb constant and steep enough to try and claim tension as a way of Life. I caught what I could from the get-go, but I was only focused on keeping it between the ditches and doing what a man raised like me is bred to do. Everything he can, with or without the means necessary, and more often than not, far more than is required.

You were always there, I never knew a day you weren't. The comfort of that feeling that was and had been my blanket of security, the one I've known for many years, I'd outgrown, and like every child, I needed to fold it up and gently lay it away for those quiet, sentimental conversations had on family heirlooms, with good coffee and maybe a piece of homemade strawberry cake, where we find the safest place to fall and take the time and the courage to do it. When a favorite Aunt's quiet ear becomes God's own Living Room.

And I drove, fearlessly, full of fear, with the purpose a man's man drives with because he knows he must and the best demons Hell have to offer make him laugh on any given day. He drives with one destination in mind, to get to exactly where he needs to be. There is no road map or GPS to the banks of Jordan, only the sound of Holy Water falling and tumbling, stumbling, finding its way across the ancient rocks and hidden crevices of the heart. Once you've been there the first time, you remember. You will *always feel the winds of Heaven, falling across your face in quiet moments, drifting across the backs of the leaves, calling your name like your mother at the end of another good day. Calling you Home.*

But this drive was different. It was just for me. I drove to find my Higher Place, I drove from my Truest Self. I drove from the Soul and my Heart knew it not only had to go, it was already gone. I climbed across and over into this new day, into a small town square where the road never ends, where it's just getting started in the Blue Sky. The last time I saw pavement, was out of the corner of my eye, and I barely saw it then because Heaven was right in front of me. And I knew I was finally going to make it.

I can see from here that you are all okay and the little boy you all loved will always live inside me. I will fiercely protect him, love him like my own, but I am a man. I am part of you and you a part of me, and this road is showing me I must move on. That the road less travelled may have been the long way, but it was my shortest route Home. I can taste the morning coffee once again, like it's the first time. I've never known life without You yet I must. I need the colors of Life exploding in my eyes, dogwoods blooming along the roadside, an afternoon in Asheville, I need music, playing loudly, a piece of good key lime pie in a quiet cafe, a soft, firm kiss, and then another, maybe a new pair of shoes, to get what I pay for. I need that "one and only" to love and cherish. I finally made it home.

If I could write you a letter I would. I would tell you just how very much I love You and thank You for loving me. Let you know, as my rear view mirror and windshield told me, I AM okay. But I can't. So I will drive, with passion and purpose, and I will live and love as you all did. Driving is for the living and I am alive. I found a mountain with my name on it and a soft, safe place to fall. A tender place all my own. I wish you could see the view. As they say in the movies, "She... is stunning."

April 16, 2012 somewhere in the mountains of North Carolina.

FUNERAL in THE SOUTH

words and music by John Brown
copyright 2007 swamp art/bmi

There's nothing like a Funeral in the South
We send 'em off to Jesus with fried chicken in our mouths
In Dixie this tradition is the grandest one no doubt
Oh there's nothing like a funeral in the south.

We got drive up windows & slick limousines
Caskets laced in camo, marching bands in New Orleans
honey hams, deviled eggs, chicken by the tub
We wallow in our grief like the Mississippi Mud
we drown our sorrow with Pabst Blue Ribbon beer
And a rock solid faith relieves all our fears

There's nothing like a Funeral in the South
We send 'em off to Jesus with fried chicken in our mouths
In Dixie this tradition is the grandest one no doubt
Oh there's nothing like a funeral in the south.

We lay 'em out, decked out, dressed to kill
mortgage out our mobile homes to pay the funeral bill
the florist makes a killing, the preacher makes his case
a blue haired granny plays amazing grace
It's tradition the departed gets a tall southern tale
with a Mason Dixon eulogy no-one goes to hell

(Repeat chorus)

BRIDGE:

gossip's not a problem it's a real necessity
without it there's a lack of southern integrity
broken hearts are brandished & worn upon our sleeves
lying is permitted to preserve the family peace
fainting spells, moans & yells, chill the soul & spine
streets of gold await us all on the other side
Roll Tide

Oh there's nothing like a Funeral in the South
We send 'em off to Jesus with scripture in our mouth
In Dixie this tradition is the grandest one no doubt
Oh there's nothing like a funeral in the south.
So when I die remember sob, scream & shout
Sing Peace like a river, Cook a pig & drag it out
& bury me beneath the weeping willow
With a... Funeral in The South

GIVING THANKS

GOFUNDME CAMPAIGN DONORS

March 2017

Without these gracious folks this project would not exist. "Thank You" will never be enough from me to them. But I hope each of You will come to truly know how deeply your generosity has touched me. I can never write another piece this uniquely personal and important to me. Thank You for making it happen and for helping me lay this to rest. My Highest Thoughts and Deepest Gratitude, john hound brown.

THE FAMILY – $1000

Andy and Jan Marshall, of Puckett's Grocery & Restaurants Inc.
www.puckettsgro.com
Eagle Station, City of Patterson, Georgia

SPECIAL MUSIC AND HONORARY PALLBEARER – $250

Stewart Baker, The Sport Family, Matt Garratt

THE AMEN CORNER -- $100

Curt Hinton, John L. Gurley, Lyndie Wenner, Jeanette Edmundson Trimble, Leckie Lancaster Scott, Nan Kearney Thompson, Crystal Stone Berger, Nan Montague, Eugene Mobley, Mike Delk, Billy Terry, Paul and Chanda Newsome, Howard Jones, Chris Coleman, Shonna Tompkins, Victor White, Beth Spivey, Brian Knost, Mama Pat and Family

THE CHOIR – $50

Tim and Bonnie Bloodworth, Tasha Suggs Moose, Tammie Bass Beasley, Kim Herring Langlois, Braden Copeland, Lisa Brown Musselman, Jimmy Hare, Debbie and Uly Russo, Bobbi Ann Crawford, Tracey Baker Auman, Dean Whitley, Teresa Brown Byrum,

THE CONGREGATION – $25

Pat Bass Alford, Amy Thames, Teresa Hardy
visit www.gofundme.com/houndbrown
and follow the journey of Funeral in the South.

EDITORS

Holley S. Todd,

I reached out to my friend Holley, who had literally just buried her daughter Evann, a few weeks before we began the journey of editing *Funeral*. I waited as long as I could.

I felt awkward, selfish at the mere thought of that. Until I recalled those first weeks and months of my life changing forever. And I knew in my heart Holley was the only one who could do it. And do it justice.

Holley, you told me it might be good for you and a distraction after the first few weeks of editing. I truly hope it was. I pray in some small miracle-of-a-way it will help you and the family's broken hearts slowly start to heal. I know it feels like they never will. Always remember Holley, "if it's grace, and it is, it's always Amazing." Grace be unto you. Thank You for gracing me and many others with your talents.

Andrew Fadyen Ketchum

Andrew, who is an award-winning freelance editor, author, writing coach and currently serving as Adjunct Professor of Creative Writing and English at the University of Colorado, Boulder, was kind enough to come on board. Andy, thank you and bless you for blessing me with your talents.

I desperately needed your authentic and honest opinions and advice. I promise. Next time I'll really make you proud and "trim her down a bit."

Next Of Kin

I've been in a panic over this as we edited this book. For I honestly had no idea how to even begin thanking all the family, friends, and even strangers that have come into my life and blessed me over the years. I have done my best to honor and pay homage to my family and home-folks through this writing. I will always fall far short there. Words can only do so much of the heart's work.

This past era and most especially these past few years, since my family passed, have been the hardest of my journey. From mounting health issues and obstacles, to life changes and everything else, including loneliness and fear. I hope everyone will forgive me, but I'm going to take this chance to attempt to thank the people whose genuine love, prayers and support, challenges and occasional "blessing me out," whose late night all-the-way hot dogs, (*seriously Sis, best hot-dogs I've ever had and what were those other things?*) have kept me keeping on. To those who have touched me deeply, with a simple act of kindness, respect or maybe a NCSHP hat and made me feel whole again, I thank you from my heart and soul. For without family and friends I would absolutely be another funeral in the south. These loving souls and many more have kept me hopefully somewhere near sane and given me the space, grace, and dignity to discover and heal a very broken heart.

HOME and FAMILY

Aunt Louise Sparks, GiGi /Linda Brown, Jay Vail, Phyliss Vail, Mama Pat Delaney, Pam Allen, Paige Bottom, Carter Monroe, Kay Meadows, my late Aunt Marie Lancaster, Magalene Exxum and my sisters, Debbie, Jeannie and Tia. Brother Spanky and Sister Kathy Fischell, Carl and Michelle Lewis, John-Boy Isley, Stewart "Snapper" Baker, Teresa Brown Byrum, Lisa and Andy Musselman, Sharon Godwin, Angie and the super-cool T-Man, Tanner Mozingo, Bobbi-Ann-Crawford, Dr. Cort McClaren, John L. Gurley, Kaitlyn Jones, Pastor Bill and Terry Stallings, Sherri-Lancaster-Ball, Mark Lancaster, Freddie Lancaster and family, Eula Gray, Joan Hinnant, my coffee buddy Dr. Glenn and Allison Phillips and the Goldsboro First Baptist Church, Pastor Scott Thrailkill, Marty Gurganus, Dee and Beth Johnson, Jeffrey and Christina Minnish, Robert and Robin Thaxton, Thigie Thigpen, Carolyn Sullivan, John Sullivan. Pastor Greg Stancil and Antioch Original Free-Will Baptist Church, my First Pentecostal Holiness Church of Goldsboro friends, Tim and Bonnie Bloodworth, The Jimmy Head Family, Nancy Kirby and Ben Sauls, Bunky Goff, Greg and Wendy Thomas. And all my Falcon Football Brothers. You boys know who you are; Nad, Nature Boy, Golden Boy, Gunner, Grizzly, Thunder, Lightning, Simple, Mad Dog. Randy Pate, Bobby West and all the rest... and so many, many more you know in your heart who you are, as does mine.

TIFTON, GA FAMILY

Mike and Cindy Delk, Jeff and Lynn Parsons, Dr. Jim and Holly Scott, Rhonda Marion, Denna Kennedy Thompson and all the staff at Georgia Sports Medicine, Seven Springs Sports Medicien, Nashville, TN. Jamie Richardson, Terry Oliver.

NASHVILLE and MY JOURNEY FAMILY

Bedford and Melissa Combs, my special "Spirit-Filled" group, (Jobi, Aidan, Lynette, Madera, Bobby) Howard, Debbie and Daniel Jones, Jayme and Aubrey Calhoun, Colonel Garry Littleton and the entire Littleton Inc. Family, Sarah Scott Howdyshell, John and Robin Berry and family, Jay and Kay Pugh, John Pugh and family, Kevin and Sandi Sport, Papa, Mama and Michael Sport. Terry and Beth Spivey.

SPECIAL THANKS

Bear Roberts, you ARE The Man. Frank Green, you were right. Sometimes it just takes that first step. I wish Chap was here but he's in our hearts. I think I just heard Mike say, "Bless his heart!"

BELIEVERS AND INSPIRATIONS

Those who saw the value in this work perhaps before I did, when I didn't and cared enough to push me, love me, piss me off, and do all it took to get it out of me: the late Mike Chapman of course, Braden Copeland, Billy Gray Terry, Spook Joyner and Michael C. Steele.

MY TWO ROCKS

The son/nephew/lil' brother I never had, Cameron McClaren.

SamBeau, you rescued me buddy. I love you too. I know our time is short but we've had a long Beautiful Ride. Lily-Belle will be anxiously waiting.

My ROCK of AGES

The TRINITY:

FATHER, SON AND HOLY GHOST.

visit www.heartstreamjourneys.com

If someone you love, including yourself, is at a Crossroads, in dire need of an inner healing, please consider contacting my amazing inspired friends, Bedford and Melissa. Be that change. Be a blessing. Heal the world.

Paige... I talk a lot about
Amazing Grace here.
And you are exactly that
in everyone's life you meet.

Amazing Grace

I love you
yohin'

J
2017

"SamBeau of Plowology.
July 4, 2003-- June 6, 2017
"The Sweetest Dog that ever did so live!"

photography by www.sarahmarie.biz

logo by www.thebearoberts.com